Roger Bullock at Warren House, Dartington, 4 November 2004
Source: Kate Mount

FORTY YEARS OF
RESEARCH, POLICY AND PRACTICE
IN CHILDREN'S SERVICES

A Festschrift for Roger Bullock

FORTY YEARS OF
RESEARCH, POLICY AND PRACTICE
IN CHILDREN'S SERVICES

A Festschrift for Roger Bullock

Edited by

Nick Axford
Vashti Berry
Michael Little
and
Louise Morpeth
Dartington Social Research Unit

John Wiley & Sons, Ltd

Other Wiley Editorial Offices

John Wiley & Sons Inc., 111 River Street, Hoboken, NJ 07030, USA

Jossey-Bass, 989 Market Street, San Francisco, CA 94103-1741, USA

Wiley-VCH Verlag GmbH, Boschstr. 12, D-69469 Weinheim, Germany

John Wiley & Sons Australia Ltd, 33 Park Road, Milton, Queensland 4064, Australia

John Wiley & Sons (Asia) Pte Ltd, 2 Clementi Loop #02-01, Jin Xing Distripark, Singapore 129809

John Wiley & Sons Canada Ltd, 22 Worcester Road, Etobicoke, Ontario, Canada M9W 1L1

Wiley also publishes its books in a variety of electronic formats. Some content that appears in print may not be
available in electronic books.

Library of Congress Cataloguing-in-Publication Data

Forty years of research, policy and practice in children's services : a festschrift for Roger Bullock /
    edited by Nick Axford, Vashti Berry, Michael Little and Louise Morpeth.
        p.   cm.
    Includes bibliographical references and index.
    ISBN 0-470-01219-6 (cloth : alk. paper)
        1. Children—Services for—Great Britain.   2. Children—Services for—Europe.   I. Title: 40 years
of research, policy and practice in children's services.   II. Bullock, Roger.   III. Axford, Nick.
HV751 .A6F64   2005
362.7'0941—dc22   2004026269

British Library Cataloguing in Publication Data

A catalogue record for this book is available from the British Library

ISBN 0-470-01219-6 (hbk)

Typeset in 10/12pt Times and Helvetica by TechBooks, New Delhi, India
Printed and bound in Great Britain by Antony Rowe Ltd, Chippenham, Wiltshire
This book is printed on acid-free paper responsibly manufactured from sustainable forestry
in which at least two trees are planted for each one used for paper production.

CONTENTS

LIST OF CONTRIBUTORS

Ewan Anderson   Ewan's main research interests include boarding and residential education and care, youth justice and the development of children, especially in the Middle East. He is Honorary Visiting Professor (Residential Child Welfare) at the University of York and also holds posts as Emeritus Professor (Geopolitics) at the University of Durham and Visiting Professor (Middle East Development) at the University of Exeter. His major publications include a study of applying the *Children Act 1989* in boarding and residential environments and an atlas of global geopolitical flashpoints. He is a Fellow of the Centre for Social Policy at Dartington.

Nick Axford   Nick has been at Dartington since 1997 after working for the Shaftesbury Society in a family centre in London. He was jointly responsible for a Department of Health study on patterns of need and service use among children living in the community, and currently works on an evaluation of an innovative programme for disaffected young people, using a random allocation design. He is joint author of a review for the Department for Education and Skills of the literature on refocusing children's services towards prevention, and has been closely involved in developing and implementing several practice tools with clinical and planning functions. In 2003 he completed a PhD on childhood social exclusion.

Sue Bailey   Sue is Professor of Child and Adolescent Forensic Mental Health at the University of Central Lancashire and Consultant Child and Adolescent Forensic Psychiatrist for the Bolton, Salford and Trafford Mental Health Trust in Manchester. She came to know Roger and colleagues at Dartington when giving clinical opinions on young people detained in the St Charles and Glenthorne Youth Treatment Centres. She has written extensively about various aspects of the mental health of young offenders, including those who murder, and with colleagues recently developed a mental health screening tool for the Youth Justice Board of England and Wales.

David Berridge   David is Professor of Child and Family Welfare and heads the Child and Family Welfare Research Unit at the University of Luton. Previously he was Research Director at the National Children's Bureau and Research Fellow at the Dartington Social Research Unit. He is author/joint author of 11 books and numerous other publications on issues such as foster care, peer violence in children's homes and the education of looked-after children. He is a founding member of *Making Research Count*, a national organisation which exists to build stronger links between researchers and social care professionals.

Vashti Berry   Vashti joined the Dartington Unit in 2001 after working on the Equal Opportunities Policy Team at Northamptonshire County Council. Prior to this she was an academic tutor at the University of Natal in Durban, South Africa. She is studying for a PhD on the differential effects of domestic violence and child abuse on children's development, and working on a random allocation evaluation of a programme for young people who display antisocial behaviour. She has completed a small-scale study of asylum-seeking and refugee children and families in Ireland and co-authored best practice papers on user involvement and pre-school family support facilities.

Roger Bullock   Roger joined what later became the Dartington Social Research Unit in 1965, when it was based at King's College, Cambridge. He is an internationally respected expert on residential child care, secure accommodation for difficult and disturbed young people and various aspects of family support and child protection. He has a longstanding interest in innovative methods of dissemination and connecting findings to policy and practice, and has been closely involved in successive central government research reviews. Roger is editor of the journal *Adoption and Fostering*, Chair of Trustees of the Warren House Group at Dartington and Professor Emeritus at the University of Bristol.

Roger Clough   Roger is Emeritus Professor of Social Care at the University of Lancaster and Director of Eskrigge Social Research. His early work was as a teacher and housemaster in senior boys' approved schools, before lecturing in social work in Bristol. He has written extensively on residential work, community care and social work with children and older people, and recently completed a review of residential child care research for the National Assembly of Wales (with Roger Bullock and Adrian Ward). He was previously Chief Inspector of Social Services for Cumbria County Council and has undertaken enquiries, policy development and consultancy as well as acting as an expert witness.

Henri Giller   Henri is Managing Director of Social Information Systems and Honorary Fellow of the University of Keele, having worked previously at both the Institute of Psychiatry in London and the Institute of Criminology at the University of Cambridge. He has acted as consultant to the Youth Justice Board for England and Wales on performance management issues and is the author of numerous books and articles on youth justice, child care and community care, including *Antisocial Behaviour by Young People* in 1998 (with Michael Rutter and Ann Hagell).

Douglas Hooper   Douglas is a clinical and counselling psychologist as well as an academic who has long been involved in practice and research concerning couple and family breakdown. He was formerly Senior Lecturer in Mental Health at the University of Bristol and is now Emeritus Professor of Social Work at the University of Hull as well as a Fellow of the Centre for Social Policy at Dartington. A long research relationship with Mervyn Murch led him to become involved with the issues arising from family breakdown in the family justice context. Having taught and practised in the fields of both mental health and social welfare, he has focused on research and professional education in cross-disciplinary work.

Michael Little   Building on an established research centre, Michael is co-founder with Roger Bullock of a collection of research, development and dissemination activities known as the Warren House Group at Dartington. At the University of Chicago's Chapin

Hall Center for Children he leads a study of child development in the context of residential education. An acknowledged expert on child protection, out of home care and youth justice Michael has also supported efforts to improve international networks of policy makers, managers, researchers and practitioners working with children in need. He holds appointments at the Universities of Bath and Chicago and is the author/joint author of 15 books and eight practice tools aimed at helping put research into practice.

Jill Madge   Jill is a Lecturer in Social Work at the University of Plymouth. She was seconded for the period 1996–2004 to the Dartington Social Research Unit from Devon Social Services, where she worked as a child care social work supervisor. While at Dartington she completed an inter-agency audit of children's needs for the NHS and evaluated four small-scale experimental services deriving from this research. She was closely involved in the development and implementation of the practice tool *Matching Needs and Services* and trained social workers to use *Paperwork*, Dartington's clinical assessment tool. She also undertook service development work with the local Primary Care Trust.

Louise Morpeth   Louise moved to Dartington in 1997 after working for four years as a community health development co-ordinator with North Staffordshire Health Authority. She was jointly responsible for a Department of Health study on patterns of need and service use among children living in the community and has been involved in designing, implementing and evaluating new interventions, using need data gathered using *Matching Needs and Services* in a rural district in England. She has co-authored several practice tools aimed at getting research into practice, and in 2004 completed a PhD on the effects of the organisation of children's services on outcomes for children in need.

Mervyn Murch   Mervyn has been Professor of Law at the Cardiff Law School since 1993. Prior to that he taught at the University of Bristol, where he established the Socio-Legal Centre for Family Studies. His 30-year research career has focused on the interdisciplinary work of the family justice system, and he has contributed to policy and practice developments and to law reform in divorce, adoption and child protection. He has published numerous books on family breakdown, adoption and care proceedings, and he is a member of the President of the Family Divisions' International Committee and Interdisciplinary Committee. He has also served on various Department of Health and Lord Chancellor's committees and is a Fellow of the Centre for Social Policy at Dartington.

Roy Parker   Roy studied at the London School of Economics (LSE), worked in child care and obtained his PhD through research on foster care. He then worked at the LSE and was a member of the Seebohm Committee from 1965 to 1968. He moved to Bristol University in 1969, becoming head of the joint department of social administration and social work, and has been Professor Emeritus since his retirement. Roy's research has covered issues in housing, social policy history, air pollution, social policy theory, the elderly and, more recently (again), child welfare. Roy authored the 1999 Department of Health research overview 'Adoption Now' and is a Fellow of the Centre for Social Policy at Dartington.

Ian Sinclair   Ian is a Research Professor at the University of York and Co-Director of the Social Work Research and Development Unit. Before joining the university he was

Director of Research at the National Institute for Social Work and prior to that he worked in the Home Office Research and Development Unit. He has written extensively on children in residential and foster care as well as on young offenders and family relationships. He and Ian Gibbs are joint academic co-ordinators of the Department of Health's research initiative 'The Costs and Effectiveness of Services to Children in Need' and he is a Fellow of the Centre for Social Policy at Dartington.

Ruth Sinclair   Ruth is Director of Research at the National Children's Bureau. Previously she was a Research Fellow at Loughborough University and Head of Research and Evaluation for Leicestershire Social Services. She has written extensively about children in public care or in receipt of social services, in particular the assessment of need and planning to meet need. She also has a longstanding interest in the involvement of children and young people in decision-making, recently co-authoring a review of this area for the Social Care Institute of Excellence (SCIE). In 2002 she and Roger Bullock completed a study for the Department Health on child deaths owing to abuse or neglect.

Monika Smit   Monika is a senior researcher at the Bureau of the Dutch National Rapporteur on Trafficking in Human Beings. Previously she was Assistant Professor at Leiden University, specialising in research on unaccompanied minor asylum seekers and residential care for juveniles, and from 1998 to 1999 she lived and worked at Dartington. She has a master's degree in Special Education (*Orthopedagogiek*) and completed her PhD on juveniles leaving residential care.

June Thoburn   June is Professor of Social Work, School of Social Work and Psychosocial Studies, and Director of the Centre for Research on the Child and Family, University of East Anglia. Having started out in practice, she has been teaching and researching in the field of child welfare since 1978. Her many publications cover child protection, foster care and adoption among other topics. She is involved in the training of the judiciary and is frequently asked to provide expert evidence and consultation in complex child care cases. She is a member of Lord Justice Thorpe's advisory committee on training and has advised the Department of Health on developing a new framework for assessment.

Peter van der Laan   Peter is a senior researcher at the Netherlands Institute for the Study of Crime and Law Enforcement (NSCR). Previously he worked at the Research and Documentation Centre (WODC) of the Dutch Ministry of Justice, and from 1998 to 1999 he was a Senior Research Fellow at the Dartington Social Research Unit. He has served as a consultant on juvenile justice to the United Nations and the Council of Europe, and was involved in drafting two Council of Europe recommendations – *Implementation of the European Rules on Community Sanctions and Measures* (2000) and *New Ways of Dealing with Juvenile Delinquency* (2003). He has also participated in numerous juvenile justice missions to central and eastern Europe and is a Fellow of the Centre for Social Policy at Dartington.

ABOUT THE COVER

The untitled portrait of a girl with her young mother is taken from a classic mid-1960s study of children in the Gorbals area of Glasgow by the photographer Joseph McKenzie.

None of the 130 pictures in the published collection has a title, and it was clearly important to Joseph McKenzie, who spent his own childhood in an East End slum, that the individual images of children in playground gangs, dolled up in sawn-off wedding dresses for first Communion or doing family chores should not be allowed to sentimentalise the bigger, truer picture of a neighbourhood in the flux of dispersal and redevelopment. The series says as much about the child's point of view as it does about the faces it puts before the camera.

But in this case the portrait has defied its maker, having come by the name *The Beatle Girl* on account of the cotton print of her mother's dress, which shows the faces of Ringo Starr, Paul McCartney and John Lennon at the moment they were becoming the emblem of the Harold Wilson years and visible in almost everything. Forty years on, the artificiality of their gaze and the timeless candour of the girl's smile still jostle for our attention.

So we have borrowed *The Beatle Girl* for Roger Bullock's 'festschrift' for the obvious reason that it marks the mood at the start of his career and because we recognise in it a resonance between Joseph McKenzie's irresistible passion to capture the ordinariness and exoticism of a place and the diligence apparent in Roger's research. We like it also for what it says about the consistent focus of Roger's work and its origins in the Socialist Utopianism of the 1960s. The girl seems to be about to step out into a brighter world, perhaps as far as one of the new town tower-blocks of Cumbernauld or Livingston. She is wearing a hand-me-down party frock; she is holding her grandfather's walking-stick for luck; she has cut her own hair specially in a Beatle fringe.

That much is surmise, of course. More certainly, she will have hit 50 by now. She will know how mixed the benefits of sanitary high-rise living had proved to be by the 1980s. She probably knows almost as much as Dartington social research can tell her about continuity and change, movement and transitoriness, vulnerability and resilience. If this book should ever fall into her hands, she will discover that in 2005 the research evidence is prompting academics to ask the same question Joseph McKenzie himself posed in 1990 when his retrospective monograph was published: 'Could it be that many modern-day children are more disadvantaged than their Gorbals kind?'.

ACKNOWLEDGEMENTS

A publisher colleague of ours warned us before we embarked on this venture that difficulties in compiling festschrifts often mean that they end up as memorials. Thankfully that has not been the case here. For that we are indebted to numerous people. We are especially grateful, of course, to the contributors to the book, who have given generously of their time and thought. All were quick-off-the-mark when approached at the outset of the project and have been responsive to our requests throughout the process of editing. We are also grateful to colleagues of Roger Bullock who attended the seminar at Dartington on 19–20 May 2003 when this book started to take shape. All contributed to the sessions in various ways and enriched both the discussion there and the chapters that emerged. Colleagues in the Warren House Group at Dartington have helped throughout, with special thanks due to Kay Turner, who arranged the seminar, and Roy Parker, who offered valuable advice and guidance on producing edited collections. Sarah Blower, Helen Harris and Carl Staunton all assisted with the final edits, as did Roger's friend, Mike Harvey, and sister-in-law, Brenda Bullock (both of whom offered additional stories about Roger which, for reasons of decorum, have not made the final version). At Wiley, Ruth Graham, Gillian Leslie and Claire Ruston have been particularly helpful and made the production process as smooth as possible. Finally, we would like to thank Roger himself, who, typically, has been selfless in helping us to finalise the book's content.

Part I

SETTING THE SCENE

1

INTRODUCTION

Nick Axford, Vashti Berry, Michael Little and Louise Morpeth

The word 'festschrift' is German and means, literally, 'festival script'. There is a time-honoured tradition in some disciplines of academics collaborating to produce an edited collection to celebrate the distinguished career of a close colleague. Sadly, there are few such efforts in the arena of social policy and, with important exceptions (Bernstein and Brannen 1996; Green and Yule 2001), fewer still in the area of applied research into child development and children's services. The reasons for this gap are not immediately apparent, aside from different academic traditions, although one factor must be the relative infancy of the field and thus the dearth of people whose careers have spanned sufficient time to warrant having something published in their honour.

Roger Bullock is unusual, then, and it seemed appropriate to mark his official retirement with a collection of essays reflecting on changes to research, policy and practice in children's services since he started out as a young researcher in 1965. The topic areas selected are suitably diverse, reflecting the breadth of Roger's research interests, from residential and foster care to family support and the mental health of young offenders. At some point during his career, most of the kinds of children whom we would nowadays regard as 'children in need', or children at risk of social exclusion, have come under his research gaze. So, on any given day in the late 1960s Roger would no doubt have been found in a boarding school or institution for young delinquents searching through files or applying his acute observation skills to proceedings; today he is probably doing similar work but perhaps in the office of a social services team focused on supporting similar children at home.

The 40 years selected also mark a period of considerable flux in the field, both in terms of the direction of services as they have sought to respond to various factors, notably scandals and financial crises, and the role of research evidence in steering this zigzag course. In 1963 in England the *Children and Young Persons Act* was published, setting out an agenda for the greater use of family support to help to maintain children in their homes, and it is fitting that in 2003, the year of Roger's retirement, the government produced *Every Child Matters*

Forty Years of Research, Policy and Practice in Children's Services.
Edited by N. Axford, V. Berry, M. Little and L. Morpeth.
© 2005 John Wiley & Sons, Ltd. ISBN 0-470-01219-6.

(DfES 2003) to herald the most far-reaching reforms to services in England and Wales since the 1960s. This is pure coincidence, of course, but it provides a useful frame of reference within which to mark and weigh developments.

The book is not intended as a eulogy to Roger, although in places it may appear so, such is the regard in which he is held by his colleagues. Rather it is to mark and celebrate Roger's research career by taking a step back and reflecting on the changing relationship over 40 years between research, policy and practice in the areas that make up the new children's services. It is the focus on this relationship that, hopefully, distinguishes the volume from other reviews of the child welfare field (e.g. Hill and Aldgate 1996; Stevenson 1999; Fawcett *et al.* 2004). Roger was a fervent proponent of evidence-based policy and practice long before the phrase was invented. In the course of showing how research has been harnessed (and sometimes abused or ignored) in the pursuit of progress in serving vulnerable children, the contributors demonstrate, collectively, both the direct and indirect influence of evidence – the policies that follow research recommendations to the letter and those that emerge from findings and perspectives that clarify and aid the understanding of complex issues.

In pursuing these aims, the book also provides to some extent an insight into the contribution of a specific research centre, namely the Dartington Social Research Unit. This is unavoidable to the extent that Roger is and always has been associated with Dartington: indeed, to many the two are synonymous. But Dartington, of course, has always been a collection of people and its role, along with that of similar centres, such as the Thomas Coram Research Unit in London, in shaping social policy in relation to children could be the subject of another book – one that Roger is gently being encouraged to research and write.

As editors of the volume we are acutely conscious that some people reading the book will not know Roger Bullock or be familiar with his work. Rather than go into this here, sections at the end of the book chart the main landmarks in his career (Appendix A) and his major publications (Appendix B). The remainder of this introductory chapter sets out how contributors and chapter themes were selected and the brief that authors were given, before summarising in turn the focus of each chapter.

As noted above, Roger has turned his attention over the years to children with various types of need and who are served by all of the main agencies that comprise children's services – social care, health, education, police, youth justice and voluntary organisations. Although his expertise is by no means uniform across these areas, the new world of children's services heralded by *Every Child Matters* means that it makes sense to cover in some way all of the aforementioned areas. Authors were selected for their own expertise in the area and also because of their personal connections with Roger, forged through working together closely in a variety of settings over the years. All were extremely keen to participate and have worked with us patiently in bringing the project to fruition. We are grateful to them all.

By virtue of being written by different people and covering different topic areas, the chapters are all unique in their emphases and style. However, as requested, all provide an overview of developments in research, policy and practice in their area over the past 40 years, and all reflect on the contribution of Roger (and Dartington) to these changes. There is also consideration of how the research community, together with policy-makers and practitioners, can further children's well-being in those areas, with some of the key messages brought together in the final chapter. It is hoped that a range of people will find this book useful – undergraduates and experienced researchers, frontline practitioners and central government policy-makers, those working in the UK and those based in other countries. Whether the contributions in themselves offer any new theories, evidence or understanding is for others to judge – it would be a tall order in the space provided and given the parameters of the brief – but individually each one offers a useful summary of progress, and it is envisaged that, collectively, they will stimulate both the debate and actions required to improve services and so achieve better outcomes for children in need.

The book is structured, loosely, in the chronological order of Roger's research interests. Inevitably this is somewhat artificial, given that he has often been involved in several projects at once and returns continually to territory covered earlier in an attempt to open up new paths. But it is logical and also, to some extent, reflects broader shifts in children's services research over the 40 years covered: from the focus on children in institutions or those cared for away from their home or natural parents, through a growing acknowledgement of the wider needs of such children, to research into children with complex needs who live in the community and are supported at home. The chapters on discrete topics are book-ended by more broad-sweeping contributions considering, respectively, changes in social research since the 1960s (Chapter 2), the implications for children's services of the growing international agenda in social policy research and policy (Chapter 12), connections between social research and the creative arts (Chapter 13) and how the Research Unit at Dartington is seeking to adapt to a changing context (Chapter 14).

PART I: SETTING THE SCENE

Following this introductory chapter, Roy Parker provides a commentary on changes in social research in the UK from the 1960s to today (Chapter 2). The first section starts at about the time that when Roger obtained his first appointment, asking why social research was on the threshold of a new era. It considers political factors, such as the promotion of more effective economic and social planning and changes to the funding and administration of higher education, as well as technological innovations. Parker assesses the significance of these developments against the backdrop of the state of social research before the mid-1960s. Here he focuses on the funding of studies, the availability of statistics and other secondary material and the existence of campaigning organisations committed to assembling and utilising research evidence. He notes that high quality work on child care was 'extremely thin on the ground' in 1965.

The second section of Roy Parker's chapter discusses the salient changes that influenced the climate of social research from the 1960s onwards. Those selected are: changes in the position of research in the universities; the reorientation of the Social Science Research Council; the enhanced role of central government in promoting studies; and the academic move away from a positivist approach to research. The third section considers the present state of social research in the child care sector and compares it with what has gone before.

Particular attention is paid to the quantity and scope of the research and to its nature – for example, the kinds of questions that are being asked and the degree of interdisciplinary collaboration. Strengths and weaknesses are identified. Parker also explores the extent to which research and dissemination activities have had an impact on policy and practice in children's services. The chapter ends by considering changes that are likely to affect the climate in which social and, in particular, child care research is conducted. It focuses on the administration and funding of research, changes in government *vis-à-vis* departmental responsibility for children's services and the role of conviction politics.

PART II: CHILDREN'S SERVICES FROM DIFFERENT PERSPECTIVES

As noted earlier, Roger's research career began with studies of residential education, specifically boarding and approved schools: *The Hothouse Society* (Lambert and Millham 1968) and *After Grace – Teeth* (Millham *et al.* 1975). With this in mind, Ewan Anderson reviews the fundamental and virtually continuous change in education in Britain over the past 40 years (Chapter 3). He describes the broadening and deepening of education until 1979, highlighting themes such as the promotion of greater access and the introduction of more progressive teaching practices. He then charts the reorientation since the early 1980s towards preparing children for the world of work. Anderson offers a critical perspective on reforms in the period, focusing on the curriculum, inclusion and the introduction to education of market- and business-driven ideas.

Anderson's chapter moves on to assess the contribution of Roger and the Dartington Unit to the area. It draws on those publications of Roger's that focus on residential settings and education, noting their influence on research methodology, conceptual thinking, and policy and practice. Anderson highlights in particular the holistic perspective adopted in the publications, with their acknowledgement of the value of expressive as well as instrumental goals, and the way in which they sought to relate outputs and outcomes to the intention of the intervention. The chapter closes by describing how the work has since been taken forward and notes the central place of education in the new children's services.

Roger is perhaps best known for his work on the residential care of children, notably books such as *The Chance of a Lifetime?* (Lambert *et al.* 1975) and *Structure, Culture and Outcome* (Brown *et al.* 1998). Roger Clough's contribution (Chapter 4) begins with some personal reflections on hallmarks of work by the Dartington Unit, and Roger Bullock in particular, including the often imaginative style of writing and presenting material, the drawing on sociology to interpret phenomena and the willingness to listen to children's accounts of their experiences. It then charts several seminal studies of residential homes since the 1960s and shows how Dartington's research fits into this context, noting in particular its attempt to describe how places are different from one another and also to explain what leads to different outcomes.

The next section identifies key themes emerging from residential child care research in the UK. It sets out some of what is known about the effectiveness of residential homes, the factors that are conducive to good outcomes for children and how patterns of caring for children away from home in the UK have changed in the last 40 years. Clough then summarises what he sees as the strengths and limitations of this research, considering themes such as the style of regime in children's homes, the level of institutional abuse, the evaluation of long-term outcomes and the effect on children of the size of homes. The chapter closes with some reflections on how the links between research, policy and practice as regards residential child care might be strengthened.

Of course, children live in various kinds of institutions, including secure accommodation, and Roger has been involved in several studies of antisocial behaviour by young people and attempts by society to deal with it, in particular *Locking Up Children* (Millham *et al.* 1978) and *Secure Treatment Outcomes* (Bullock *et al.* 1998). In Chapter 5, Henri Giller examines the extent to which developments in the youth (previously juvenile) justice field over a 40-year period have been influenced by three themes that are the hallmark of Roger's work, namely: the impact of research on policy and practice developments; the appreciation of the need for a 'whole system' approach to social interventions; and a practice context in which services are matched to needs.

Giller's chapter begins by summarising changes in youth justice in England and Wales since the 1960s, looking in particular at the extent to which reforms exhibit a punitive or welfare-orientated outlook and the relative influence on them of research, political debate and economic constraints. It then focuses on initiatives introduced by the Labour government since 1997, in particular the Youth Justice Board and Youth Offending Teams. Giller sets out evidence regarding their impact, demonstrating advances in terms of greater consistency in pre-court decisions, the reduced use of custody and the secure estate and, generally, practice becoming more evidence based. The chapter concludes that there have been significant gains but also notes ongoing challenges, including the prevention of youth crime and the problems associated with placing young people in secure settings (especially given the inauspicious political context for progressive reforms in this area).

It is easy in an area such as youth justice to become preoccupied with administrative categories, such as 'locked-up', or the primary reason for a young person entering the system, namely crime. Roger has consistently encouraged a more holistic perspective and a focus on the child's needs in all areas of his or her life. Sue Bailey's contribution (Chapter 6) is therefore about the mental health of young offenders, in particular those in secure care. It starts by noting recent developments in child and adolescent mental health services (CAMHS) in the UK, including the push towards multi-agency working and evidence-based provision. Next, it charts the changing pattern of custodial options for and attitudes towards young offenders since the early nineteenth century, identifying both a growing recognition in policy circles of those young people's mental health needs and also concerted attempts by health and youth justice agencies to work together to address them. The chapter then reviews briefly some of the research into links between the mental health, social well-being and delinquency of young people detained in locked institutions and discusses the impact of those regimes.

To help with understanding and improving the fit between needs and services, Bailey turns to theoretical and methodological approaches associated with Roger and his colleagues at Dartington. These include the concepts of 'career', 'life-route' and 'process' as well as attempts to develop taxonomies of need with predictive power that can help with fashioning more focused interventions. Bailey then identifies advances since the early 1990s in improving the mental health of young offenders and discusses how research is contributing to this process. She concludes that there is a sufficient body of evidence to inform policy-making and practice aimed at improving the mental health of previous and existing young offenders but also identifies challenges for the future, including the need for services to engage children and families more effectively and the requirement to strengthen training for professionals working in this area.

As policy and practice for children in need shifted to supporting children living in the community, so Roger and his contemporaries in social research adjusted their focus. Some of these children live away from their birth families, but with other families. In Chapter 7, June Thoburn concentrates on children adopted from care – not an area in which Roger has specialised but one in which his work nevertheless has relevance. The chapter begins by considering the types of children this involves and the different routes they take into adoption. Thoburn discusses the social work processes involved in placement, listing the main decisions that need to be taken (relating to the child, to the birth family and to the prospective and actual adopters). She explores the different ways in which the success of adoption can be measured and, using these criteria, indicates how successful the adoption is.

The chapter then summarises, under several headings, what is known about the factors associated with better or worse outcomes for different groups of children. It discusses not only the child, birth family and adoptive family variables, but also service-related variables and the importance of the 'matching' decision. Particular attention is given to two themes, namely 'the respective places of long-term/permanent foster care and adoption as routes to permanence' and 'the impact on stability and long-term well-being of continuing contact with birth family members'. Thoburn notes that in both areas there are debates between researchers on how to interpret findings. The chapter ends with some reflections on the implications of the England and Wales *Adoption and Children Act* 2002.

Foster care has become more important relative to residential care over the years and is a subject area that Roger has studied more intensively, for example, in *Lost in Care* (Millham *et al.* 1986). Ian Sinclair explores the complexities associated with decisions about long-term foster children returning home (Chapter 8). The first part of his chapter looks at Dartington's account of the relationship between the child looked after in the care system and his or her birth family. It discusses themes common to the Unit's work, including the high percentage of separated children who eventually return home, the importance of symbols of belonging and contact with the birth family, the need to consider the child's best interests and subsequent environment, and the importance of the child's views. Reference is made to some of the rhetorical and imaginative devices employed in the Unit's writing and their role in enlivening the topic and persuading the reader.

In the second part of the chapter, Sinclair considers the extent to which other research on longer-staying children in the care system bears out or modifies these conclusions. Noting differences in emphasis rather than direct contradictions, he focuses, first, on the tensions regarding the desirability of returning home and, second, on evidence on contact and the long-term effects of care. With regard to the former, Sinclair suggests that there is a need for imaginative adaptations that go beyond a 'family good, foster care bad' position. He draws from his own work on long-stay foster children, noting their wishes and the sometimes negative effects of a return home. The same evidence is used to put contact in a more equivocal light and the question is considered as to whether its potentially harmful effects could be mitigated by treatment or by more purposeful social work. Sinclair's conclusion that 'outcomes depend heavily on setting' is linked to research on resilience, residential care and therapeutic foster care as well as to Dartington's work. The section closes with a brief reflection on the importance of the meaning that children attach to themselves and to events and people in their lives. The third section of the chapter sets out some implications of the above for policy, practice and research. It focuses on the dilemma that although children want to go home and will inevitably do so, going home is very often a bad experience.

As little as 10 years ago, the reflex response to evidence of child abuse or neglect was often to remove children from their families. Although this attitude persists in some quarters, on balance the nature of child protection activity has since changed, to some degree as a result of work by Roger. David Berridge starts Chapter 9 by remarking on the increased attention to child protection in England and Wales over the past 40 years and its impact on social care policy generally. He then charts the development of services to protect children from abuse and neglect since before the Second World War, looking in particular at how the Cleveland Inquiry helped to shape the *Children Act* 1989 and the focus on risk management in the 1990s. Next, he considers what has been learned over this period. He notes trends and cross-national patterns in referrals to services of children thought to have been abused or neglected, and discusses how the system processes cases.

Berridge also sets out central themes from the research review of child protection with which Roger was closely involved, namely *Child Protection: messages from research* (DoH 1995) – also known as the 'Blue Book'. These include the problem of defining abuse, the significance of context when considering the effects of maltreatment and the value of engaging and supporting families. Criticisms of the review are also noted; for example, the lack of research on ethnicity or institutional abuse. Berridge expresses his amazement that the latter has not received more attention, and wonders how he and others failed to notice the problem until it blew up in various scandals. The penultimate section identifies other topics that might have been covered – for instance, the impact of wider family and community factors on child abuse, and the failure of social research to exert more influence on policy and practice. Finally, Berridge appraises the value and appeal of the work of Dartington and Roger in particular.

The notion that family support can be a means of protecting children may not seem novel today, but little more than a decade ago it transformed the thinking of many working in the field. In Chapter 10, Michael Little and Ruth Sinclair show how considerable advances have been made since the publication of the Blue Book in terms of refocusing services away from a longstanding preoccupation with investigative procedures and towards meeting children's needs. They suggest that a new incarnation of family support is emerging, characterised by a focus on child development outcomes, the involvement of various agencies and the integration of specialist interventions within universal provision.

The chapter then charts some of the key research from Europe, North America and Australasia that is relevant to the challenges facing policy-makers and practitioners concerned with supporting children in need and their families. First, patterns of how agencies typically process cases are presented, with pointers as to how these system dynamics might be altered in order to respond more logically to service-users. Second, the needs of children are considered from the perspectives of developmental psychology, sociology and the children and their families, enabling insights into the way in which different forms of family support might better meet those needs. Third, evidence is set out concerning rigorously evaluated family support programmes designed to break the chains of negative effects operating in children's lives. Little and Sinclair end by considering the future prospects of family support, arguing that developments in the field are gradually improving children's services.

Of course, the well-being of children and families is by no means affected solely by designated children's services agencies. Broader socio-economic and political trends are important, as are other systems within which children and families move, including that of family justice. In Chapter 11, Mervyn Murch and Douglas Hooper explore developments in family justice research over the last 40 years. They draw on their extensive research into adoption and fostering, divorce, domestic violence and the representation of children in court. Much of this work influenced legislation, including the *Children Act* 1989 and the *Adoption and Children Act* 2002. The chapter focuses on studies in areas that remain particularly relevant today. One is the welfare of children in divorce proceedings; another is the participation of children in family law proceedings. Recent decades have seen children considered increasingly as participant actors rather than passive victims, but how has this shift to rights-based thinking played out in terms of children's experience? Finally, the chapter examines the extent to which the family justice system meets the needs of children and families. It highlights deficiencies in the current set-up, and advocates ways of making services less stigmatising and more conciliatory as well as strategies for making practice in the area more evidence based.

In the course of sketching out these studies, Murch and Hooper reflect on broader social and cultural changes and their effect on policy and research. This provides insights into three questions. First, what was it about the climate of the 1960s and 1970s that was conducive to the strong role in policy-making of child care and family justice research? Second, is it realistic to expect the continuation of these factors and the assumptions that underpinned social and legal reform? And third, will the kind of research endeavours with which they and Roger Bullock have been associated have a place in the new era of post-modernity? The authors end with practical suggestions for ensuring that centres such as the Dartington Unit continue to thrive.

PART III: LOOKING FORWARDS

All of the chapters in Part II take a subject area and consider it from different angles. Peter van der Laan and Monika Smit's brief was different. In Chapter 12 they take a perspective of growing significance for the children's services field – cross-national comparative research and policy – and apply it to one subject area, namely youth justice. It is an approach with which Roger has long been interested (e.g. Bullock 1992). The chapter starts by describing current developments at a European level concerning ways of dealing with juvenile delinquency. It traces broad trends in juvenile delinquency in western and eastern/central

Europe, recognising the limitations of the data but nevertheless seeking to explain the patterns presented. Next, the authors set out the most common developments in juvenile justice in Europe over recent years. They note the growth of diversionary and community-based approaches, but argue that custodial sentences continue to form the backbone of responses to youth crime in many, if not all, European countries.

Van der Laan and Smit then seek tentatively to summarise the headline similarities and differences between countries and relate them to socio-economic, cultural and political factors as well as to the welfare, justice and restorative models of anti-crime measures. They identify groups among which, at least in some European countries, crime appears to be increasing, including minority ethnic groups, girls, younger children and those involved in gangs. What actually is happening here, and how can the changes be explained? The authors also consider custodial sentences and the growing popularity of pre-trial detention, particularly in western European countries, pointing out that, remarkably, given their widespread use, knowledge about the nature and effectiveness of such measures is patchy. The final part of the chapter considers why England and Wales and The Netherlands appear to be following a different track from other European states.

Other ways of looking at the world are also having their effect on social research. Frustration on the part of researchers at being limited to particular 'silos' has led to greater cross-disciplinary working, including some unlikely collaborations between those who previously regarded each other's work with mutual incomprehension and whose only contact was in the college canteen. Roger has always been something of a polymath. In Chapter 13 he is given licence to 'let his hair down' a little and reflect on the influence on his social research activities of a life-long interest in the performing and creative arts. In particular, he asks whether the portrayal of situations in art can improve social research.

Roger's chapter is divided into six sections, each discussing an area where there appears to be a mutually beneficial relationship between artistic and research creativity. First is the development of ideas, in particular where they come from and why they flourish in some settings but not in others. Second is the distinction between the temporal and the eternal, and why some art and ideas survive while others fall away. Third is the relationship between form and content, with a strong focus on how the arts might help researchers to communicate more clearly and memorably. Fourth is seeking wholeness; both the way that looking at phenomena from different perspectives can help with obtaining an objective picture, and the manner in which this is presented. Fifth is the role of the artist and researcher in society, notably the apparent dilemma of popularity meaning vulgarity and the often uneasy relationship between social science and politics. Finally, Roger considers how science and art seek to present the truth. He suggests that social researchers might need to develop different methods and to some extent shift their focus if they are to explain more clearly child development in the context of children's services, and that this will benefit policy and practice.

How are independent research centres to respond to the changing research and policy landscape in children's services identified by each of the contributors? In Chapter 14, Nick Axford and Louise Morpeth explore continuities and change at the Dartington Social Research Unit. Far from offering a blueprint for what *should* happen, the chapter provides a brief case study of one centre's development at the beginning of the twenty-first century. It starts by identifying a refocusing of research topics, with a greater stress on children's developmental trajectories and outcomes and the development of theory – not so much of the sociological kind but rather in the form of a 'common language' for children's services. It also highlights attempts to sharpen the Unit's traditional methods, notably the exploitation of secondary data and mixing of methods, and illustrates how the longitudinal approach is being adapted away from retrospective studies and towards prospective and experimental designs.

The chapter then considers strategies employed in response to the changing research context, including efforts to pursue a programme of linked studies and investment in training younger researchers. The authors show how the Dartington Unit has focused increasingly on local service development, both at clinical and planning levels, and they give examples of the Unit's attempts to improve the dissemination and take-up of research – primarily through 'practice tools'. The organisational change that has taken place to support these developments is described, as are new international ventures in the form of comparative studies. The chapter ends by noting that the dilemmas faced by a centre like Dartington are, in many ways, perennial, and that much is to be learned from those who have traversed similar landscapes in the past.

The final chapter (Chapter 15) seeks to pull together some of the main themes from the contributions, reflecting on how lessons from the last 40 years translate into challenges for research, policy and practice in children's services in the next decade or so. We hope that the book does Roger justice and that in some small way it will help those responsible in various ways for 'making' effective interventions for vulnerable children to build on his impressive legacy to the field.

REFERENCES

Bernstein, B. and Brannen, J. (eds) (1996) *Children, Research and Policy: essays for Barbara Tizard*, London, Taylor & Francis.
Brown, E., Bullock, R., Hobson, C. and Little, M. (1998) *Making Residential Care Work: structure and culture in children's homes*, Aldershot, Ashgate.
Bullock, R. (ed.) (1992) *Problem Adolescents: an international view*, London, Whiting & Birch.
Bullock, R., Little, M. and Millham, S. (1998) *Secure Treatment Outcomes: the care careers of very difficult adolescents*, Aldershot, Ashgate.
DfES (Department for Education and Skills) (2003) *Every Child Matters*, Cm. 5860, London, The Stationery Office.
DoH (Department of Health) (1995) *Child Protection: messages from research*, London, HMSO.
Fawcett, B., Featherstone, B. and Goddard, J. (2004) *Contemporary Child Care Policy and Practice*, Basingstoke, Palgrave.
Green, J. and Yule, W. (eds) (2001) *Research and Innovation on the Road to Modern Child Psychiatry: Volume 1 – Festschrift for Professor Sir Michael Rutter*, London, Gaskell.
Hill, M. and Aldgate, J. (1996) *Child Welfare Services: developments in law, policy, practice and research*, London, Jessica Kingsley.
Lambert, R. and Millham, S. (1968) *The Hothouse Society: an exploration of boarding-school life through the boys' and girls' own writings*, London, Weidenfeld & Nicolson.
Lambert, R., Millham, S. and Bullock, R. (1975) *The Chance of a Lifetime? A study of boarding education*, London, Weidenfeld & Nicolson.

Millham, S., Bullock, R. and Cherrett, P. (1975) *After Grace – Teeth: a comparative study of the residential experience of boys in approved schools*, Brighton, Human Context Books.

Millham, S., Bullock, R. and Hosie, K. (1978) *Locking Up Children*, Farnborough, Saxon House.

Millham, S., Bullock, R., Hosie, K. and Haak, M. (1986) *Lost in Care: the problems of maintaining links between children in care and their families*, Aldershot, Gower.

Stevenson, O. (1999) *Child Welfare in the United Kingdom: 1948–1998*, Oxford, Blackwell.

2

THEN AND NOW
40 YEARS OF SOCIAL RESEARCH IN THE UK

Roy Parker

A NEW PROFILE FOR SOCIAL RESEARCH

All our careers are shaped by the climate of the times. That becomes plain if one reviews the 40 years during which Roger has been involved in research. When he obtained his first appointment in 1965 the world of social research was on the threshold of a new era, in part resulting from the election of a Labour government in 1964, and for at least three reasons.

First, the new administration was anxious to promote more effective economic and social planning, epitomised by *The National Plan* (1965). However, such planning required the relevant data, much of which was lacking. This was partly why the select committee on the government statistical service called for extensive improvements (Estimates Committee 1966). In the same year, it should be noted, there was the first ever quinquennial sample census.

The second effect of the Labour government on the development of social research sprang from the profusion of committees of inquiry that were appointed, many of which commissioned research in order to inform their deliberations. The Royal Commission on Local Government was a prime example. The first volume of its *Research Studies* (Local Government in South Eastern England) contained nine accounts of different studies undertaken by the Greater London Group at the London School of Economics (LSE). That volume alone ran to 570 pages and contained, some will recall, Bleddyn Davies's research on the child care services (Royal Commission 1968). Of course, previous administrations had launched committees of inquiry, but there were fewer of them and fewer sought the help of research. The surge in the first years of the new government not only emphasised that research was considered to be important in the policy process but, incidentally, created a larger body of researchers in its wake.

Forty Years of Research, Policy and Practice in Children's Services.
Edited by N. Axford, V. Berry, M. Little and L. Morpeth.
© 2005 John Wiley & Sons, Ltd. ISBN 0-470-01219-6.

A third feature of the incoming Labour administration's influence on social research was its close links with sympathetic academics in the social sciences, the most notable of whom were clustered around Richard Titmuss at the LSE, people like David Donnison (housing) and Brian Abel-Smith (health). Politicians such as Richard Crossman at Housing and Kenneth Robinson at Health were in regular contact with numerous academics, testing out ideas, seeking advice and, not least, being exposed to convictions that policy should be informed by careful research. Some of the academics in question were formally appointed as government advisers; for example, Tony Lynes (one of 'Titmuss's young men' as Crossman put it). At the time we all felt that our work would now find a considered hearing in the corridors of power. Indeed, at Housing and Local Government Crossman had set up a research advisory group (Crossman 1975, p. 192).

Other changes were also afoot in 1965 that were to stimulate the growth of social research. In the early 1960s the Robbins Committee had proposed an unprecedented expansion of higher education (Robbins 1963). The plan was accepted by the Conservative government and, in the following year, endorsed by its Labour successor. Most of the targets were reached and in some cases surpassed. Eight new universities were created, the colleges of advanced technology became universities and special attention was paid to enhancing the status of the polytechnics. There was growth in all directions; but the social sciences (albeit from a low base) grew faster than almost all other areas. That progress slowed by the 1970s but, even so, more departments of sociology, social policy and social work were established, whose members, according to the contractual and funding requirements of the time, were expected to engage in research. Furthermore, more social science graduates were produced, enlarging the pool of potential future researchers.

An important parallel development was the establishment of the Social Science Research Council (now the Economic and Social Research Council) in 1966. It followed from the recommendations of the Heyworth Committee on social studies the previous year (DES 1965). This was significant for two reasons: first, because it created a publicly funded *system* for the provision of grants to researchers and, second, because it also made grants available for postgraduate study. Neither of these opportunities had existed before, and the second, in particular, again provided more trained research workers.

As well as these important changes (which might be seen as having originated in political initiatives) a far-reaching technological innovation was just visible on the horizon. In 1966 IBM introduced the first disc storage system, holding 5 MB of data on 50 two-foot-wide 'platters'; but microprocessors, computers and pocket calculators did not arrive on the scene until the early 1970s. Their availability to researchers, however, was slow to spread; they were costly, sluggish and of limited application. Many of us, perforce, continued to rely upon such devices as the Copeland–Chatterton punch cards and needles, mechanical sorters and calculators, or waited in long queues to have our 'job' processed by one of the few monster computers available. Nonetheless, a revolution in information technology was dawning, although it was not until 1983 that the Dartington Social Research Unit (DSRU) acquired a computer of its own.

The significance of all these developments can best be appreciated by considering the state of social research before the mid-1960s. Little had changed between the Clapham Committee's indictment in 1946, when it reported on the provision of social and economic research (Privy Council and Treasury 1946), and what the Heyworth Committee found 20 years later. Few studies that bore upon issues of social policy had been undertaken and those that did relied heavily upon the financial support of trusts and foundations. In 1965, for example, the Heyworth Committee found that 33 per cent of all externally funded research in the universities was supported by UK foundations and a further 28 per cent came from similar overseas sources. The proportion was higher in social policy – 70 per cent and 5 per cent respectively. Even so, the combined resources of the trusts and the universities that were devoted to social policy and social work research were minuscule compared with today's expenditures – which have been augmented by monies from the ESRC and, importantly, from central government.

This was the financial background against which the changes of the 1960s have to be seen. They also need to be viewed in the light of the *base* from which researchers had had to work. Few relevant social statistics (apart from those on crime and population) were to be found. There was no General Household Survey or convenient compendia such as *Social Trends*, both of which first appeared in 1970. Some statistics that were collected for economic purposes were of limited use in the social field; for example, the regular Family Expenditure Surveys, the first of which dated from 1952. Other longer running economic data, such as the national income and expenditure accounts or the balance of payments information, gave us little help. Not only were sources of secondary data thin, but few enabled long-term trends to be discerned. (One exception was the *Children in Care of Local Authorities* annual returns that first appeared (for England and Wales) in 1952.) Furthermore, there were few sampling bases upon which researchers could draw, apart from general demographic data.

The mid-1960s, however, witnessed a fresh interest in social forecasting, in the construction of social indicators and in a better co-ordination, standardisation and systematisation of social statistics. This was reflected in the creation of the Office for Population Censuses and Surveys (OPCS) in 1970, which was achieved through the amalgamation of the General Register Office and the Government Social Survey (see Moser 1970).

As well as the inadequacy of basic social statistics, researchers before the era heralded by Roger's first appointment faced a severe lack of other secondary material. For example, there were few relevant journals. Although the *British Journal of Sociology* had been established in 1950, most others arrived much later. *The British Journal of Delinquency* (now *Criminology*) dates from 1966; *The Journal of Social Policy* and *The British Journal of Social Work* both date from 1970. The plethora of journals that exists today is a comparatively recent development, even in the USA. Looking back on my first research, *Decision in Child Care* (Parker 1966), I note that I was only able to refer to a handful of journals that contained 'robust' studies of foster care: there was John Wakeford's (1963) article in the *British Journal of Sociology*; several pieces in the *American Journal of Orthopsychiatry* and others in the *Smith's College Journal of Social Work*. Other American journals, such as *Social Work* and *Child Welfare*, carried few such reports, although the important works of Wolins (1963) and Fanshel (1966) were beginning to be reported in the latter publication by the early 1960s.

Thus, the small number of studies that were completed in the fields of social policy and social work, and particularly in child care, had few journal outlets, especially in this country. Moreover, not until the founding of the Child Poverty Action Group in 1965 (see McCarthy 1986) was there a pressure group committed to assembling and using research results to promote the cause of children. Some, such as the Women's Group on Public Health, which had been active in the early post-war period, had, by then, fallen by the wayside.

Despite all these drawbacks, some excellent work had been produced before the impending changes that I have been describing. However, much of it addressed issues of poverty and social security. For example, there were *The Economic Circumstances of Old People* (Cole and Utting 1962) and *The Poor and the Poorest* (Abel-Smith and Townsend 1965), published the same year in which Peter Townsend and Dorothy Wedderburn (1965) gave us *The Aged and the Welfare State*. The disgraceful condition of the elderly in residential care had already been exposed in Townsend's (1962) *The Last Refuge*. Housing policy and housing conditions were other developing spheres of research. Most notable were the studies undertaken by the Rowntree Trust Housing Study under Donnison's direction (for an overview see Donnison 1967).

By comparison, comparable work in child care was extremely thin on the ground when Roger entered the fray in 1965. There had been Gray and Parr's (1957) study of *Children in Care and the Recruitment of Foster Parents* (work commissioned by the Home Office from the Government Social Survey but only published in mimeographed form) and Gordon Trasler's (1960) *In Place of Parents*, which had made its appearance a few years later. Other books did exist, but, with a few exceptions, they were practitioners' accounts, often sensitive and insightful, but lacking in methodological rigour. For me a beacon of such rigour was to be found in Mannheim and Wilkins's (1955) *Prediction Methods in Relation to Borstal Training*; but few followed in their footsteps in the wider child care field. Indeed, it seems strange now that the Home Office research unit, whose first publication this prediction study was, did not embrace more work in that area, given the Office's responsibility for child care until the early 1970s.

Thus, in 1965 social policy and social work research was starting from a low base but with the discernible prospect of considerable expansion. Perhaps one sign of these changes was captured by the establishment of the National Bureau for Co-operation in Child Care in 1963 (now the National Children's Bureau). Not only did it launch its important cohort study on national child development (the first report of the findings appearing in 1966 as *11,000 Seven-Year-Olds* (Kellmer-Pringle *et al.* 1966) but it also undertook a comprehensive review of existing research in several countries on adoption, foster care and residential care. These were published as *Facts and Fallacies* in 1967 and demonstrated the considerable lack of relevant and reliable studies about most aspects of children's services (Dinnage and Kellmer-Pringle 1967a, 1967b; Kellmer-Pringle 1967).

THE CLIMATE CHANGES

It is, of course, impossible to chart all the changes that influenced the climate in which social research developed in the years between Roger's appearance on the scene and now. It is possible, however, to pick out some of the salient features. My choice would be: changes in the position of research in the universities; the reorientation of the SSRC; the enhanced role of central government in promoting studies; and the academic move away from a positivist approach to research.

The expansion of the university system after Robbins carried with it the assumption that social research of all kinds would flourish. That proved to be an unduly optimistic assumption for two main reasons. First, until the late 1980s the general grants available to universities included unspecified amounts for the support of both teaching and research. It was up to each establishment to decide how that money should be divided and, furthermore, how it was to be allocated between the research activities of different departments. At first, after the expansion, the social sciences and their research prospered; but particularly after the student upheavals of 1968 and 1969 pressures grew for 'better' teaching. Many diligent academics began to spend more time on meeting these aspirations and therefore curtailed their research activities. Furthermore, subjects like social administration, sociology, social work or politics were always poorly placed in the competition for specific allocations for research from the general grants. Most of their projects were labour-intensive. In contrast, claims for the establishment, upgrading and staffing of 'well-founded laboratories' were much stronger. Indeed, as new technologies proliferated, the claims of disciplines which continued to rely heavily upon people rather than machinery and equipment were progressively weakened.

All this became painfully clear when expenditure on higher education was substantially reduced in 1981 under the Thatcher administration. A larger and larger proportion of the universities' combined teaching and research grants was diverted to cover the costs of teaching the rising number of students. As staffing ratios deteriorated, the time that academics could devote to research was reduced. This expedient diversion of funds enabled the government to sustain its economies without having to face the unpalatable consequences of imposing a significant reduction in the student population.

However, this strategy eventually reached the end of its useful life as powerful interests in science, engineering and medicine began to be seriously affected. Faced with increasingly hostile criticism of the way in which the country's economic performance was being undermined, a new way had to be found to manage the reduction of expenditure on higher education. The Green Paper *The Development of Higher Education into the 1990s* (1985) indicated how it was to be done.

One part of the new approach depended on discrediting the expensive assumption that teaching and research were closely (if not inseparably) related activities. 'There is no evidence', explained the Green Paper, 'that all academic staff must engage in research.' Moreover, it added, 'the thrust of research policy ... will be towards selectivity and concentration' (p. 20).

That was what followed and what has increasingly become the touchstone for successive governments. The research assessment exercises (RAEs) now determine how much, if any, research grant individual universities obtain. Furthermore, the assessments not only examine the research 'output' of members of staff but also take into account the size of grant won from 'outside' sources.

The uncoupling of teaching and research in the government funding of higher education also had another consequence. The assumption that part of the salary of an academic covered the pursuit of their personal research provided a considerable amount of freedom in the choice of what they did. It was, therefore, an individualistic system, sometimes idiosyncratic and virtually uncontrolled. The new arrangements placed a greater reliance on research grants and contracts. University research, and its social research especially, found itself firmly located in the competitive market place.

Changes were also occurring in the SSRC, which, significantly, was renamed the Economic and Social Research Council in 1984. Fierce attacks had been made upon it on the grounds that much of the research that it supported amounted to little more than 'intellectual pastimes', or was politically biased. In 1981 Keith Joseph, as Minister of Education, appointed Lord Rothschild (1982) to undertake an inquiry into the Council's record and performance. He returned a rather favourable verdict and exonerated it from the charge of political bias. Many considered that this saved the SSRC from being dismantled. Nevertheless, major reorganisation followed and, at Joseph's insistence, the name was changed: specifically to omit the word 'science'. The budget was cut and there was a strong political expectation that henceforth the research that the Council supported should be 'useful', especially in ways that reflected the government's primary policy concerns. In these processes some varieties of social policy research benefited. A number of research 'initiatives' were launched, one of which addressed the problems of children in care and led to several useful publications (e.g. Clough 1988). Yet the investigation of major, broad-sweeping and critical issues appeared not to find favour (see Parker 1987). It is notable, for example, that the 'Future of the Welfare State' initiative was rather quickly discontinued.

Thus, as the SSRC became the ESRC one saw a shift towards what were termed 'real life problems' and an emphasis upon supporting research that served the needs of policy-makers and practitioners. This created opportunities for social policy and social work research, but it also imposed certain constraints.

Perhaps the most far-reaching change in the climate within which social policy research, and especially child care research, operated between 'then' and 'now' was the emergence of central government as a major customer. The Rothschild (1971) report on 'The Organisation and Management of Government Research and Development' heralded a period of increased R&D expenditure by central government departments; but it did so within a framework of the customer–contractor principle. The presumption was that research paid for by central departments should be relevant to policy or, at least, to the needs of policy-influencing 'consumers' within the civil service. This explicit guidance had four important consequences.

First, the application of the customer–contractor principle narrowed the definition of who was considered to be the 'customer' or user of publicly funded research. The interests of central government now had a clear priority over those of local government, pressure groups, voluntary organisations, the academic community, or the general public.

Second, the Rothschild principle gave the customers an additional responsibility, and therefore an enhanced power over research. Whereas in the past many potential customers in government would not have troubled themselves about what research should be done, they were now expected to suggest or initiate new proposals. They were to be assisted by research advisory committees that included outside interests; but, apart from the Children's Research Liaison Group, these became used less and less and many finally ceased to exist (for example, the Social Security Research Advisory Group).

In some ways, therefore, Rothschild created customers where none had existed. Many of them were untutored in the possibilities of research and were unclear what kinds of questions were amenable to research. However, matters improved, especially in the children's field where perceptive and shrewd customers searched out and called for research. Research management improved and ensured better liaison between customers and contractors. In addition, the need for the dissemination of results began to be taken seriously.

A third line of development that grew from the customer–contractor principle became apparent in the 1980s. As the R&D budgets in central government were cut, competition between customers increased, priority areas were specified and more exacting criteria were applied in assessing 'value for money.' Beyond that, however, a transformation was occurring in the Thatcher years from the 'administrative customer' to the 'political customer'. For example, during 1985 the Department of Health reviewed the organisation of its research programme (the Nodder inquiry). The three main aims to emerge were: to shape a programme that underpinned ministers' priorities; to make sure that demands for research could be dealt with quickly (that is, 'short lead times between questions and answers'); and to ensure the more economical use of the research budget (see DHSS 1987). Instead of money being distributed mainly to reflect the interests of customer divisions it was to be allocated in line with more general priorities like AIDS, the effectiveness of the acute sector services, and questions of professional staffing.

The amount of flexibility in the kinds of work that the DHSS was able to support was further curtailed by the termination of the small grants scheme whereby an earmarked budget was available to fund proposals emanating from independent researchers.

A fourth development that was fuelled by the application of the customer–contractor formula was a shift in the balance of contractors. In the past most departmental research was undertaken by one of four bodies: by an in-house unit (of which that at the Home Office was the prime example); by the OPCS; by outside units (like the DSRU) supported by programme monies; or by the universities. The balance between these undertakings altered because many in-house units were reduced in size or closed down; because the services of the OPCS now had to be paid for; and because the overheads charged by universities mounted as they assessed the costs more carefully. Relatively speaking, the outside units prospered. Furthermore, contracts now began to be placed with management consultants, who usually promised to deliver quick results.

In this climate 'strategic' studies suffered from a foreshortening of the time perspective. Ministerial views of what (if any) research was 'useful' exerted a more dominant influence, their views not necessarily coinciding with those of their civil servants, the scientific advisers or their own research units. Some areas, such as child care, largely escaped ministerial attention, giving the Department of Health's research division and the units it funded a measure of freedom in choosing their agenda. However, political influence on the topics chosen for support, if not control over what finally emerged, has been present across the board. For instance, until towards the end of the 1980s all but the smallest research proposals reaching the Department of Education and Science had to be approved by ministers.

It was not only the economising measures of the Thatcher administration that affected the role of central government in supporting social research. Abrams (1985) put his finger on another key consideration; namely, that the research which central departments commission flourished best 'in the absence of principled argument about social purposes' – that is, when there is a certain 'suspension of politics'. His formulation seems to fit the years of the Thatcher government and, more recently, New Labour, inasmuch as they have been driven by a determined ideological conviction and thus, having neutralised many sources of opposition, see little need for research to illuminate areas of uncertainty or as extra political ammunition in dealing with opponents. There is the parallel reduction in the use of committees of inquiry. These tendencies are certainly fostered by large parliamentary majorities. To extend Abrams's proposition, some might conclude that government-sponsored social research is seen as unimportant where the need for, or the belief in, negotiation declines.

Furthermore, what one witnessed in the 1980s was a shift in the essential character of policies: in a nutshell there was a shift from a needs-based foundation to one of cash limitation. This has been particularly evident in the recent history of government support for research in social security. In 1974 the Finer Committee on one-parent families (DHSS 1974) generated a few new initiatives and, while Donnison was the chairman of the (then) Supplementary Benefits Commission, there was another modest upsurge. There were no external units addressing social security issues, no recognisable programme of research, and the small internal research unit, established in 1969, did not survive into the late 1970s. The lack of official research investment in social security reflected a distrust and scepticism about needs-based research in areas that could not easily be disciplined by the principle of cash limitation. Other areas, like child care, were more susceptible, not least because expenditures were not on the vast scale of pensions and other cash benefits.

One should not leave this brief excursion into the years between 1965 and now without noting one particular modification in what might be called 'fashion' in social research. Whereas in the 1950s and 1960s there was a widespread acceptance in the small research community that progress (and professional standing) depended upon the application of as much scientific rigour as possible (the 'positivist' approach), the late 1970s began to see a change. The 'impersonal' and 'mechanical' nature of scientific rigour was accused of ignoring the individual, of gross homogenisation and of being incapable of taking account of the experiences and views of the common man or woman. Certainly, these were important deficiencies that began to be illustrated by the growth of oral history. Phenomenology, for instance, became a popular approach to research and there was something of a return to case-by-case description that had certainly characterised much of the child care literature up to the 1960s.

Of course, the reaction against positivism was not a tidal wave, but it was sufficiently strong to set back (in my view) the quest for the kind of reliable evidence upon which *general* policies and practices could be built. That is not to say that the case studies did not expose issues or show the potential narrowness of the questions being asked of or by researchers. Many did. But those who proposed quantitative studies did so with something of an apology. They were, after all, usually expensive, and required some mathematical competence and the availability of basic data. However, during the 1980s there were major onslaughts on the government statistical service. At the outset of the decade, Rayner (1980) conducted a review and proposed that expenditure on the service should be cut by 20 per cent, a target that by 1986 had been surpassed by £5 million.

Rayner argued that the primary duty of the Central Statistical Office (CSO) was to serve central government requirements. He found that the CSO was too heavily committed to serving the public at large (for a critical assessment see Hoinville and Smith 1982). 'In general,' he concluded, 'there is no more reason for Government to act as universal provider in the statistical field than any other.' Despite biting criticisms from Moser, as head of the CSO, and from others, such as Peter Townsend, most of the Rayner proposals (including the full-cost pricing of government publications) were accepted. The quality of social statistics declined. Fewer were published, valuable trend data were discontinued and presentation became less clear. In this sense an important source of secondary quantitative information was depleted, adding to the difficulties that researchers faced.

Enough, then, of 'the period in between', such a long period that it has only been possible to touch upon a few of the influential changes in the climate in which Roger and others worked. What is the situation now?

CHILDREN'S SERVICES IN PARTICULAR

Although Roger's involvement in research has covered a number of fields it has dealt primarily with children's services (until recently referred to usually as 'child care'). It is fitting, therefore, to end by considering the state of this particular sector of social research and to make some comparisons with what has gone before.

It is obvious that both the quantity and the scope of the accumulated research in child care are very much greater now than they were in 1965, or even in the 1980s. Remember that Jane Rowe's ground-breaking study *Children Who Wait* was only published in the early 1970s (Rowe and Lambert 1973) and that her important review of the implications of research for social work decisions did not appear until the mid-1980s (DHSS 1985). Even then it covered only nine studies, one of which was the DSRU's *Lost in Care* (Millham *et al.* 1986).

Nowadays we possess a reasonably good picture of, for example, the profiles of children coming into and remaining in care, of the predominant trends and, in particular, of the principal shortcomings of the relevant services. Not only has this resulted from the increasing number of studies but also from improvements in government statistics and from the 50 or so published inquiries into child deaths and other tragedies. Nevertheless, despite the considerable growth in research since the 1960s questions remain about its present nature and about its impact upon policy and practice.

Several things strike me about the first of these issues. Clearly what has been done has been much influenced by the questions being posed. There is, for example, a tendency to repeat the same *kinds* of questions without then standing back and considering what the answers amount to in terms of advancing our practical or theoretical understanding. A few 'literature reviews' have done this, but others have amounted to little more than catalogues, albeit useful for reference.

Even though some child care issues have been much researched, few studies have been replicated (and hence tested). That may reflect researchers' desire to plough their own furrow, or the unwillingness of sponsors to spend money on what seems already to have been done. Doubtless questions of career advancement and financial accountability exercise some influence on these tendencies.

The case for replication accepted, however, there is *also* a case for different kinds of questions to be included in the research agenda, breaking away from what Galbraith (1958), in another context, termed 'the conventional wisdom'. Take, for example, the re-emergence of political interest in 'prevention'. If this is to be informed by research, then some of the questions, logically, would have to address matters of primary prevention and not solely those that arise much further down the line. It would be unlikely that such issues could be satisfactorily investigated without a greater investment in interdisciplinary research that involved, for example, sociologists, labour market economists, geneticists and the public health community. Hitherto, studies of children's services have tended towards compartmentalisation, notwithstanding excursions into law and the psychological sciences. The narrowness that has followed, I would argue, reflects the restricted nature of the questions being asked and the way in which they are framed. This is understandable given the urgent need for policy-makers and practitioners to grapple with essentially 'casualty' situations; that is, situations that are only susceptible to what the health services classify as 'tertiary' prevention. But there is a conundrum, spelt out in the Seebohm Committee's (1968) report:

> Only when the imperative demands made by the casualties are diminished can prevention [that is, primary prevention] become possible; but the number of casualties can only be reduced by preventative action. It is crucial, therefore, that this vicious circle be broken . . . (p. 141)

The casualty services alone cannot solve the problems surrounding the deprived and abused child, although they may be able to ameliorate them. It is the *origins* of these problems that have to be tackled; and that is the rationale for pursuing primary prevention. Yet such policies face a battery of uncertainties about what should be done and how. It is noteworthy that what the Seebohm Committee concluded in 1968 remains true today; namely, that in no field of social welfare is systematic research more needed. For such progress to be made, however, the questions posed have to be cast in a much wider compass. Even so, it is not immediately apparent how best these should be framed. A great deal of imaginative thinking is still required.

It is tempting to believe that the funds for such enterprises would be hard to obtain, not least because governments tend to shy away from the possibly radical and costly implications that might emerge. However, do we as researchers pose these sufficiently broad questions in the first place? Unless we do, we can hardly complain that support is unforthcoming.

Of course, it is rather easy to pick holes in the current state of research into children's services; but it does possess considerable strengths as well. For example, by comparison with the past it is less haphazard, partly, no doubt, because there is more of it, which increases the chance that there will be more studies of particular issues. This has meant that there are now more researchers and hence fewer who are working in isolation on isolated projects. Another welcome improvement is the renewed emphasis on the need for scientific rigour, one example of which is the plea for more randomised-controlled trials. Another is the growing concern that social work should be 'evidence-based'. That said, it has to be admitted that there are still studies that fall short of these and other canons of scientific propriety; and that is a matter which bears upon the question of 'dissemination'.

Working, as we do, in a largely applied field, it behoves us to ensure that the results of our researches find their way to those who are in a position to use them. It is encouraging that so many funders now insist that dissemination be an integral part of the projects they support. Even so, one has to ask what impact this and similar efforts have had upon policy and practice.

The hesitancy on the part of 'the field' to utilise research results springs, I believe, from at least three sources. First, the potential users are often unsure how much confidence they should place in this or that study. How are they to decide? Second, practitioners often find it difficult to integrate the notion of probability into their professional judgements (see Parker 2002), and many struggle also with the idea that high risk can still mean low probability. A third reason why research has not made the impact that might have been expected lies in the nature of social work where each 'case' appears to require a tailor-made response, while what is offered by researchers is frequently aggregated data (see Little *et al.* 2002). Although managers and policy-makers are accustomed to employing such information, they often find themselves constrained by those immediate and political pressures that cast research results into the category of 'problems' rather than solutions.

I began by referring to the 'climate' that influences the character of research. It is appropriate, therefore, to end by considering what changes are afoot that are likely to affect the political context in which much social research, and more particularly research concerned with children, will be conducted.

Given that many studies will continue to be funded by government, the proposals set out in the white paper *The Future of Higher Education* (DfES 2003) are of considerable importance. The good news is that 'science and research' are to benefit from a 38 per cent increase in expenditure by 2005–2006, made available either through the Department for Education and Skills or through the Office of Science and Technology (DfES 2003). These additional funds will go to certain universities and to the research councils. However, the emphasis is to be placed upon the support of science and technology.

The implications of other proposals are less clear. There is to be a renewed emphasis upon the separation of teaching and research and a concentration of resources upon the best-performing institutions. Larger research enterprises and multidisciplinary work are to be favoured. As the paper claims, 'large groups of researchers ... perform particularly well – at least in the natural and *social* sciences' (emphasis added).

A second development that is likely to affect research into children's services in particular is the amalgamation of the responsibilities for these services under a Minister for Children located in the Department for Education and Skills (see CYPU 2003). It appears that the research and development division of the Department of Health will be transferred across, together with the Children and Young Persons Unit. How the budget for child care R&D will then fare is unclear, particularly in competition with the claims of education research. That apart, there are different 'traditions' of research and management in the two departments and a different political profile. All these factors are likely to change the kinds of questions that the 'customers' ask of research.

Finally, there is the political context in which policies are evolving. That context seems to be an uneasy mixture of political ideology and short-term expediency, a combination that does not auger well for research being able to influence policy. By their very nature ideologies are resistant to modification, and expediency usually demands the quick responses that research is unlikely to be able to provide. By contrast it is likely to prosper where there is honest doubt and a concern to address or understand emergent problems, not only of today or tomorrow, but of the years ahead. That is more likely in some spheres – of which child care is perhaps one – than in others, especially where researchers are able to show both the extent of doubt and uncertainty and what the future may portend.

This poses a problem for researchers anxious to see their work influencing policy. Should they abandon such aspirations and choose instead to concentrate on matters of more direct concern to practitioners? That is obviously a proper and worthwhile endeavour; indeed, it seems to be the cause to which much child care research is devoted. Yet I would enter a plea that the more general policy questions should not be ignored, even though the relevance of the research is not immediately acknowledged. As Roger has seen, climates change: yesterday's unremarked evidence can become today's guiding star.

REFERENCES

Abel-Smith, B. and Townsend, P. (1965) *The Poor and the Poorest*, London, Bell.

Abrams, P. (1985) 'The use of British sociology, 1931–1981', in Bulmer, M. (ed.) *Essays in the History of British Sociological Research*, Cambridge, Cambridge University Press.

Clough, R. (1988) *Living Away from Home*, University of Bristol Occasional Papers.

Cole, D. and Utting, J. (1962) *The Economic Circumstances of Old People*, Welwyn, Codicote Press.

Crossman, R. (1975) *The Diaries of a Cabinet Minister*, vol. 1, *Minister of Housing, 1964–66*, London, Hamilton & Cape.

CYPU (Children and Young People's Unit) (2003) *CYPU – New Ministerial Arrangements,* Circular Letter, June.

DES (1965) *Report of the Committee on Social Studies*, Cmnd 2660.

DfES (2003) *The Future of Higher Education*, Cm. 5765.

DHSS (Department of Health and Social Security) (1974) *Report of the Committee on One-Parent Families,* vols 1 and 2, Cmnd 5629.

DHSS (1985) *Social Work Decisions in Child Care: recent research findings and their implications,* London, HMSO.

DHSS (1987) *The Role of the Chief Scientist and the Departmental Research Committee*, Memorandum to Research Unit Directors.

Dinnage, R. and Kellmer-Pringle, M.L. (1967a) *Residential Child Care: facts and fallacies*, London, Longman.

Dinnage, R. and Kellmer-Pringle, M.L. (1967b) *Foster Home Care: facts and fallacies*, London, Longman.

Donnison, D.V. (1967) *The Government of Housing*, Harmondsworth, Penguin.

Estimates Committee (1966) 'Fourth Report from the Estimates Committee, session 1966 7', *Government Statistical Services,* HC 246, HMSO.

Fanshel, D. (1966) *Foster Parenthood: a role analysis*, Minneapolis, University of Minnesota Press.

Galbraith, J.K. (1958) *The Affluent Society*, Boston, Houghton Mifflin Company.

Gray, P.G. and Parr, C.A. (1957) *Children in Care and the Recruitment of Foster Parents*, Social Survey, SS 249.

Hoinville, G. and Smith, T. (1982) 'The Rayner Review of government statistical services', *Journal of the Royal Statistical Society,* vol. 145, pt 2.

Kellmer-Pringle, M.L. (1967) *Adoption: facts and fallacies*, London, Longman.

Kellmer-Pringle, M.L., Butler, N.R. and Davie, R. (1966) *11,000 Seven-Year-Olds*, London, Longman.

Little, M., Axford, N. and Morpeth, L. (2002) *Aggregating Data: better management information and planning in children's services*, Dartington, Warren House Press.

Mannheim, H. and Wilkins, L.T. (1955) *Prediction Methods in Relation to Borstal Training*, London, Home Office, HMSO.

McCarthy, M. (1986) *Campaigning for the Poor: CPAG and the politics of welfare*, London, Croom Helm.

Millham, S., Bullock, R., Hosie, K. and Haak, M. (1986) *Lost in Care: the problems of maintaining links between children in care and their families*, Aldershot, Gower.

Moser, C. (1970) 'Some Developments in Social Statistics', *Social Trends*, no. 1, 1970, pp. 7–11, CSS, HMSO.

Parker, R.A. (1966) *Decision in Child Care*, London, Allen & Unwin.

Parker, R.A. (1987) *A Forward Look at Research on the Child in Care*, University of Bristol Occasional Papers.

Parker, R.A. (2002) 'Evidence, Judgement and Values', in Tunnard, J. (ed.) *Commissioning and Managing External Research,* Dartington, Research in Practice.

Privy Council and Treasury (1946) *Report of the Committee on the Provision for Social and Economic Research* (Clapham), Cmnd 6868.

Rayner, D. (1980) *Review of Government Statistical Services: report to the Prime Minister by Sir Derek Rayner.*

Robbins, Lord (1963) *The Report of the Committee on Higher Education*, Cmnd 2154.

Rothschild, Lord (1971) 'The organisation and management of government research and development', in *A Framework for Government Research and Development,* Cmnd 4814.

Rothschild, Lord (1982) *An Enquiry into the Social Science Research Council*, Cmnd. 8554.

Rowe, J. and Lambert, L. (1973) *Children Who Wait*, London, ABAA.

Royal Commission on Local Government in England (1968) 'Research Studies', vol. 1, *Local Government in South East England*, by the Greater London Group, LSE, HMSO.

Seebohm Committee (1968) *Report of the Committee on Local Authority and Allied Personal Social Services*, Cmnd 3703.

The Development of Higher Education into the 1990s (1985), Cmnd 9524.

The National Plan (1965), Cmnd 2764, HMSO.

Townsend, P. (1962) *The Last Refuge*, London, Routledge & Kegan Paul.

Townsend, P. and Wedderburn, D. (1965) *The Aged and the Welfare State*, London, Bell.

Trasler, G.B. (1960) *In Place of Parents*, London, Routledge & Kegan Paul.

Wakeford, J. (1963) 'Fostering – a sociological perspective', *British Journal of Sociology*, vol. XIV, no. 4.

Wolins, M. (1963) *Selecting Foster Parents: the ideal and the reality*, New York, Columbia University Press.

Part II

CHILDREN'S SERVICES FROM DIFFERENT PERSPECTIVES

3

FORTY YEARS OF EDUCATIONAL CHANGE

Ewan Anderson

INTRODUCTION

Since the early 1960s there has been fundamental and virtually continuous change in education in Britain. Furthermore, the pace has accelerated. Between 1944 and 1979 there were only three Education Acts, one of which was the infamous *Education (Milk) Act* 1971, when Margaret Thatcher – then Secretary of State for Education – abolished free school milk. Since 1979 there have been over 30 Education Acts and a plethora of related documents and reports.

The gathering momentum in legislation can be interpreted as an indication of the increasing political importance of education. It might also be seen as the enhanced manipulation of education for political ends. The *Education Act* 1944 was one of the three pillars of the Welfare State and, as such, of great political significance. It greatly widened opportunities for an academic education by opening up the grammar schools to entry on ability. For the next 20 years there were significant changes, such as the move from selection to comprehensive schools, but education was rarely central in the political debate. This changed, however, in an unexpected speech by the then Prime Minister, Jim Callaghan, in the late 1970s when he was attending a function for something quite different. He suddenly started talking about raising school standards and giving more central direction to what was taught and how.

From then on, education has rarely been out of the spotlight. In broad terms, 1979 also marked the end of a period when education was viewed with optimism. Ideally, it was seen as a communal activity by which the individual would develop for the benefit of all and social class would gradually disappear. For a variety of reasons, particularly economic, the 1980s heralded a period of anxiety and discontent over education. The focus moved from the community to the individual and the maximisation of competitive ability. Thus, rather than facilitate a fulfilled life and the realisation of potential, schools were directed to develop the knowledge, skills and attitudes that would benefit the national economy. Clearly these two aims are by no means totally contradictory but the change in emphasis was profound.

Forty Years of Research, Policy and Practice in Children's Services.
Edited by N. Axford, V. Berry, M. Little and L. Morpeth.
© 2005 John Wiley & Sons, Ltd. ISBN 0-470-01219-6.

Since 1997, under New Labour, the trend of the late 1980s has continued, with some minor amelioration. Indeed, the pace of reform has accelerated, the preliminary discussion preceding the implementation of initiatives has been reduced and pilot studies or any other supporting research has been virtually abandoned. In fact, policy itself is changing. Whereas education policy once represented carefully constructed ideas based on logic, experience and at least some research, increasingly it comprises thoughts, often ill-considered, that are floated before the public to test response.

Over the same period, from 1963 until the present, there has been an unbroken flow of research on several related areas of education from, initially, the Research Unit into Boarding Education at King's College, Cambridge, and then the Dartington Social Research Unit as it later became. Although the Unit's output has focused particularly on residential settings, from boarding schools to secure accommodation, it has always given prominence to the holistic nature of the educational experience. The quality and coverage of the research has earned for Dartington and its team a unique place in British academe. The one constant, from Cambridge to Dartington, has been the presence of Roger Bullock.

However, while there have been obvious overlaps with education, the work of Dartington is considered to lie primarily in the field of social care. Therefore, the direct influence of Dartington research on government legislation in education is difficult to assess but it is probably true to say that a greater part of the effort has gone into *responding* to government initiatives. The influence of Dartington has been most obviously felt in the field of special needs and children who are, for various reasons, vulnerable. For example, there was clearly a contribution, both directly and indirectly, to the Warnock (1978) report on the education of children with special needs. So, rather than attempting to trace such linkages, it seems more appropriate to provide a commentary on a chronology of the *major* reforms in education – space permits no more – before attempting to cover some of the main Dartington outputs concerning education and involving Roger Bullock in that period. The ways in which Dartington has produced precisely argued criticism, constructed elegant and relevant research programmes and so influenced the thinking of the time will become apparent.

THE BROADENING AND DEEPENING OF EDUCATION: 1944–1979

In her survey of education in Britain since the *Education Act* 1944, Tomlinson (2001) lists for the period 1961–2000 over 180 Acts, reports and associated events. The rate of 4.5 such occurrences per year illustrates the turbulence in the system and also precludes, for each, any detailed consideration. The main impetus of the 1960s was towards promoting greater access to education. For all its good intentions, the *Education Act* 1944 had resulted in entrenched elitism and high-class provision for approximately 25 per cent of all young people. The introduction in 1962 of the Certificate of Secondary Education (CSE) for children aged 16 years broadened the qualification base, until then limited to the more academic Ordinary Level (O Level), which could be achieved by only a minority of pupils. Most important was the reorganisation of secondary education into a comprehensive system in 1965. Comprehensive schools were intended to provide education for all children aged 11–16 years, regardless of ability, class, gender or ethnicity. The aim was not only to attain the standards of the former grammar schools for a majority of the pupils but also, undeniably, to address social justice.

This second aim was pursued further in the *Plowden Report* (DES 1967), which justified the designation of six Educational Priority Areas (EPAs) – deprived geographic communities that received specialist help to improve children's language development – as well as positive discrimination in terms of more resources for children in deprived areas and the introduction of progressive as opposed to traditional teaching methods, in which children were offered a more exciting curriculum, personal choices and opportunities to learn at a rate concomitant with their intellectual development. The Plowden Report developed from an examination of primary education but the resulting progressive ideas led to the introduction of mode 3 examinations, in which teachers were able to set their own papers for 15–16-year-olds. Instead of acting essentially as an instructor, the teacher became an expert guide to help each young person to achieve his or her maximum potential. While these changing approaches were being digested, another fundamental change occurred, namely the raising of the school leaving age (ROSLA) in 1972 from 14 to 16. Thus, by the early 1970s, all pupils had to sit examinations, the CSE was in place alongside the O Level and mixed-ability teaching together with other facets of progressive education were in vogue.

The 1970s finished with a flourish, as opportunities for education and educational involvement were further enhanced through the reports of three committees, the findings of which were accepted by the government. The Bullock Report (DES 1975) recommended that there should be a general school policy for the teaching of foreign languages across the curriculum in an attempt to see that children had a language for life. The Taylor Committee (DES 1977) set out proposals for a new partnership in which parents, members of the teaching staff and even pupils would be represented on the school governing body. And the Warnock Committee (Warnock 1978) specified that children with 'handicaps' (or special needs), formerly accommodated in special schools, should, as far as possible, be integrated into mainstream schools with other children. What had been a broadening of the concept of education in schools was further underpinned by the *Sex Discrimination Act* 1975 and the *Race Relations Act* 1976, both of which sought to ensure opportunities for all.

By the end of the 1970s, then, the idea and purpose of education had been both widened and deepened. Most of the key changes became rapidly and deeply incised into the educational landscape and were thus resistant to removal by subsequent governments. The elements that did not survive centred around the notion of progressive education and the associated autonomy of teachers. Despite valiant efforts in the classroom, few of these new approaches had been adequately researched or tested and their comparative failure was not therefore unexpected. Many aspects of, for example, family grouping, mixed-ability teaching and open plan teaching seem to fly in the face of common sense and their introduction obviously lacked any evidence from practice-based research. The thinking behind them was at best Utopian but mostly connected with budgetary constraints. Notwithstanding these problems, however, the 20 years from 1960 onwards represent a period when genuine attempts were made to enhance the scope of education and thereby widen the horizons of all children and young people.

Such a wholesale reorganisation of education was bound to generate criticism. However, the reorientation evident in policy from the early 1980s resulted more from economic and particularly political, even doctrinaire, concerns. This can be illustrated by the introduction of the Assisted Places Scheme in 1980, the underlying principle of which was that independent (fee-paying) schools could provide an education that was superior to that in any form of state-maintained school and so should be open to children for whom the state would subsidise the fees.

EDUCATION FOR THE WORLD OF WORK: 1980–2003

In effect, from the early 1980s, the purpose of the school was redefined. Rather than being a place that introduced young people in a stimulating way to learning, thereby furnishing them for all facets of life, the school was envisaged as offering a preparation for work and industry. It was seen as a production line and increasingly business terminology became the order of the day. In addition, services were gradually centralised, so that the government became the instigator and controller rather than the facilitator of all things educational, although, at the same time, schools were offered greater freedom in self-government, so that the losers were essentially the Local Education Authorities (LEAs), which had traditionally been responsible for how schools were staffed and run. The most obviously positive group of measures concerned the curriculum.

In the context of vocationalism, a number of measures were introduced, starting with the Technical and Vocational Educational Initiative (TVEI) in 1982, which encouraged the integration of a vocational approach within ordinary subjects. City Technology Colleges co-funded by industry and specialising in particular subjects were established by the *Education (Reform) Act* 1988 and in the same year a White Paper on education and training (DES 1986) introduced National Vocational Qualifications (NVQs) – qualifications for young people aged 16 and over in subjects such as hairdressing and child care. In 1991, their scope was enlarged with the development of General National Vocational Qualifications (GNVQs) intended to support education and training for the twenty-first century. To illustrate the pace of reform, in 1996 alone there were 11 relevant Acts or reports.

The overall tone of the changes was indicated by the *Education (Reform) Act* 1988. Apart from introducing City Technology Colleges and expanding the Assisted Places Scheme, it introduced the National Curriculum with testing at key stages in core subjects. The General Certificate of Secondary Education (GCSE) replaced the CSE and O Level. There were national tests known as Standard Attainment Tests (SATS) to be taken at the ages of 7, 11 and 14. These and other changes to the curriculum can be seen as positive or negative, depending on whether they are perceived to be concerned with broadening access or with central government exerting greater control.

As part of the *Education (Reform) Act*'s thrust to 'marketisation', results from the afore-mentioned SATS would be used to construct league tables indicating the performance of each school. Schools were also allowed to manage their budgets locally and, in certain circumstances, to opt out of LEA control altogether and become 'Grant-Maintained

Schools' (directly accountable to central government). The consumerist influence was further manifested in the Parents' Charter (DES 1991) and the much-derided White Paper *Choice and Diversity* (DfE 1991). In the event, parents' choice concerning their children's education was severely limited, particularly in the case of entry to the more successful schools: it was a political sound-bite that meant little in practice. Clearly all parents would prefer their children to attend schools that are generally perceived to be successful but only a few possess the resources to take advantage of the legislation by, for example, moving into a particular catchment area.

Thus, throughout the 1980s and the first half of the 1990s the accent was largely utilitarian, focusing on the preparation of young people for the world of work, the introduction of business techniques to schools and the centralisation of control over education, most obviously through the curriculum. This record stands in sharp contrast to that of the preceding 20 years. It is clear that education had a more central role in politics and was used to address a range of problems, few of which could be considered specifically educational.

Following the election of a Labour administration in 1997, the pace of education legislation quickened but the trend continued in much the same direction. For the period 1997–2000, Tomlinson (2001) records 44 Acts, reports and events – an average of 11 per year! The centrepiece was *Curriculum 2000*, which gave academic and vocational studies parity of esteem and altered the Advanced Level (A Level) system so that pupils could study more subjects, including vocational ones. Other significant developments were concerned with raising standards of numeracy and literacy (National Strategies were launched in 1997 and 1998), educating children about citizenship (Crick 1998) and providing pre-school children in socially deprived areas with extra support through *Sure Start*. The overall focus of these changes is best summarised in *Learning to Compete: education and training for 14–19 year olds* (DfEE 1996):

> Investment in learning in the 21st century is the equivalent of investment in the machinery and technical innovation that was essential to the first industrial revolution. Then it was capital, now it is human capital. (p. 2)

Since 1997 schools have increasingly been treated as businesses with standards, rigorous inspections and, at all levels from the total establishment to the individual, management by objectives. In parallel, just discernible through the cacophony of 'business speak', there have been moves towards social inclusion. The result has been a plethora of initiatives and the descent of numerous experts and consultants upon schools. Indeed, as parenting appears to have moved substantially from the home to the school, a bewildering array of expertise appears to be required by teachers. In one school in the northeast of England with 52 permanent members of staff, the Head reported to me that on one day he had no less than 40 visiting experts.

As a final twist, the Labour government has floated a number of policy statements, possibly for discussion but more likely to prepare the public for imminent change. First, and among the more interesting, is the idea that young people aged 14 years or so should have the option of spending two days a week in the world of the work, one day in college and two days in school. Questions of how this would be organised, given the difficulty of finding work experience placements, and who would be responsible for supervising the young people appear not to have been considered. Pre-apprenticeships with plumbers, electricians and other craftsmen may sound beguiling to disenchanted youth but is training available to convert the craftsmen identified into teachers, and do they want to teach? The potential ramifications for child protection hardly bear examination.

A second such 'policy' is targeted at head teachers, who would be expected to carry out random drug tests. Since each test apparently costs £9, some thought needs to be given to the funding. More important, what is the legal status of the Head in making a decision, given that a positive decision would appear to offer a quick and sure route to litigation?

Third, and slightly less advanced, is the thinking on a new form of academy, an independent school run for profit by an entrepreneur. Business has already been quick to point out that selection for such schools would be on academic ability, misbehaviour would be punished with exclusion and children with special educational needs, since they cost more to educate, would not be considered for entry.

It is not too fanciful to consider that, with these latest ideas, education in Britain has gone full circle and much of the current thinking is now effectively pre-1944. No doubt, as with the introduction of progressive education, time and common sense will provide a natural filter for these proposals until there remain only the essentials required to meet the educational needs of children.

EDUCATION FOCI OF THE REFORMS

Thus far the chapter has described various Acts, reports and events concerning education in their chronological and therefore, in a sense, their political sequence. It is a bewildering array and the motivation for much of it can be variously interpreted. However, it is their effects on children and young people, schools and the national educational system that are important. This can be appreciated if the political aspects are eliminated and the contribution as a whole to British education is identified.

An examination of all the developments indicates that there are three overlapping clusters of reforms. The first of these is curricular. Curriculum concerns have been dominated by the introduction of the National Curriculum and *Curriculum 2000*. There is now a uniformity and level of central control that did not exist previously. Parity has been sought between academic and vocational courses and concerted efforts have been made to address the curricular needs of specific groups of children – notably those at the extreme ends of the range of ability or from backgrounds in which education is given limited value. What appeared as major failings, particularly when compared with many other western developed countries, have been addressed by a strong emphasis on literacy and numeracy. As national social and economic conditions have changed, so personal, social and health education – covering topics such as relationships, sex education and multicultural values – has been developed alongside training for citizenship. As a result, the curriculum is now far broader and deals with aspects of life previously considered way beyond its rightful remit, although, paradoxically, it became narrower in some areas, such as art and music.

The evaluation of children's performance within the curriculum remains a problem. There are proposals to discard the Advanced Level examinations, perhaps replacing them with a new four-part diploma based largely on the baccalaureate-style qualifications popular in several European countries. Whether this will be able to cover the needs of all children for some recognition of their schooling and the requirements of universities to select the academic front-runners remains to be seen. The universities' response has been mixed and there must be a danger that change may result in a total separation of the state and independent school sectors. However, it is in the area of children's personal and social development that, if anything, more attention needs to be paid to assessment. At present, there are no established procedures and, as a result, a significant proportion of the curriculum can only be reported by subjective personal statements (Inman *et al.* 1998).

The second cluster of reforms concerns inclusion. Special educational needs, the require-ments of minority ethnic groups and the importance of non-discriminatory practice overlap both the curricular and social inclusion considerations (Mittler 2000). The centrepiece, how-ever, was the initiation of comprehensive schools followed by ROSLA. The introduction of the CSE and later the GCSE qualifications ensured that the vast majority of young people leave school with some record of achievement. It is now accepted that the benefits of the best quality education must be available to *all* young people, whatever their setting. Indeed, the government's agenda for children's services *Every Child Matters* (DfES 2003) focuses specifically on inclusion and the rights of all children to a good education.

The third aspect of educational change since the 1960s is the market-driven/utilitarian perspective. This is apparent in the trends of 'marketisation', 'vocationalism', increased central control and the enhanced local management of schools. Schools are now considered to be fully accountable and competitive in the same way as companies listed on the stock exchange. They are inspected regularly, teachers are monitored and checked and young people are examined at key stages through SATS and public examinations. For many in education, the idea of government by audit and the fact that the young person is viewed as a product – a unit of human capital – are unacceptable. Published standards, inspections and assessments can only address the proximate, the quantifiable and the obvious. Education, if it is to remain distinguishable from training, is concerned more with the ultimate and the qualitative, the substantial rather than the superficial and values that are difficult to measure directly. For the inspection of schools, the Office for Standards in Education (OFSTED) employs a self-evaluation report, form S4, in which the major sections cover the following questions:

- How effective is your school overall?
- How well is the school regarded by pupils and parents?
- How well are pupils' attitudes, values and personal qualities developed?
- How well are pupils cared for, guided and supported?

All of these are followed by the question: 'How do you know?' At a recent meeting of some 50 representatives from boarding schools, the only serious response was 'through feedback' (a somewhat nebulous term). It is clearly important that if objective measures are difficult to employ then reliable subjective and unobtrusive measures need to be developed. As things stand, the only relatively reliable measures for schools concern academic performance, but analysis of the league tables has already indicated weaknesses in that area.

THE CONTRIBUTION OF DARTINGTON RESEARCH

This array of achievements, failures and noble attempts constitutes the educational back-ground against which the Dartington Unit and its Cambridge predecessor have worked. Perhaps it is best described as a palimpsest in that Roger Bullock, with a changing team of colleagues, has made a unique mark upon it and, despite the political vicissitudes, has main-tained the core values of children's welfare. Furthermore, he and the team have developed and retained a quality of evidence-based research surpassed – in my view – by few in the field. It must be remembered, of course, that social services and health care backgrounds are predominant in their work but their concern has remained greater than just education, social care or health. As a result, they have addressed what are perhaps the major failings revealed in this brief survey of education.

Throughout their research, education has been envisaged and treated holistically, recog-nising that there are expressive as well as instrumental and purely utilitarian outputs. The expressive outputs are concerned with ultimates, including values, moral codes, faith, cul-tural appreciation and creativity. They are ends in themselves and not milestones along the road to some other aim. However, by their very nature they pose problems for assessment. What is the measurable behaviour associated with virtue or altruism? The instrumental outputs of education include an array of skills that are means to some further end and would include logical thinking, lucid writing and numerical skills. Education also produces utili-tarian outputs devoted to the continuing operation of 'the system'. These include order and discipline. The message is that the rather arid, market-driven approach of the 1980s must be complemented by concerns for children's personal, social, moral and spiritual development.

The other critical failing in the rapid introduction of an array of new educational measures is the lack of evidence-based research to support them. In their research programmes, the Dartington team have sought to identify the goals or aims of the intervention, be it a school or a youth justice programme, and relate these to the outputs and outcomes for children. The models and procedures suggested for practice as a result thus have a valid research basis. These key elements, together with other aspects of their work relevant to education, can be il-lustrated from a sample of the Dartington publications with which Roger has been associated.

The first book in which the assistance of Roger Bullock is acknowledged was *The Hothouse Society* (Lambert and Millham 1968). This was the first sociological product of the research into boarding schools that was initiated in 1964 and included five projects for the Public Schools Commission. It described the boarding experience through the writings of the boys and girls who experienced it. In it, a number of themes, from the boarding house to the outside world, the inner (children's) world and the underworld were pursued with liberal quotations from the boarders themselves. In a sense, this book laid the foundations for the type of investigation that Dartington has pursued ever since, not least the interest in soliciting and interpreting the views of children.

The book developed the ideas of different types of goals and brought out the cultural congruence between the elite schools and top echelons of society. It led not only to reforms, such as more privacy for pupils and less rigid regimes, but also to an awareness of how boarding schools would have to change to meet the expectations of new generations of children and parents.

The first Dartington book in which Roger Bullock is listed among the authors was *A Manual to the Sociology of the School* (Lambert *et al.* 1970). This established a structure, still valid, for the analysis of educational and related institutions. Each establishment was analysed on a variety of scales, from the classroom to the boarding house to the social setting, and the key components of the social structure such as goals, control, roles and authority were examined in detail. It remains a landmark as one of the earliest attempts to dissect the key components of the organisation and to examine how they interact. Schools had previously been viewed essentially as 'black boxes' in which the inputs – the younger children – were in some way converted into the outputs – the older and more educated children. In particular, in this structure, there was a focus on the aims or goals of the schools and on their effectiveness in achieving particular outcomes. This applied element has become a characteristic of the Dartington research.

Innovations of particular importance in the field were the use of new scales of measurement, the identification of key social variables and the discussion of the relationship between those variables. While in one respect the school can be viewed as a unit, it comprises a variety of subunits: some for residence, some for formal education and some for leisure activities. It is an organic structure and needs such a systems approach to interpret its operation. Furthermore, the school is linked to an external environment that comprises not only the local community but, through legislation, national interests. The formal structure, as set out in the school prospectus and as seen by a visitor, is, as it were, the face of the school. In many respects, at least as significant is the informal or 'street level' scene, rarely apparent to the casual observer. It is at this level that there is likely to be more meaningful research on the implications of tradition, deviance, initiation or bullying. Since such activities are not on public display, they demand a high level of sophistication from a researcher if they are to be charted accurately. However, they do yield a further range of sociological variables with the potential for interesting correlation. In this way, the Dartington team was not only able to see what everyone sees but also to understand what few others could comprehend.

A Manual offered a comprehensive framework for comparing boarding schools, bringing together several aspects of organisation theory. It was obviously open to criticism but the extensive emprical testing ensured that it proved immediately helpful to others researching in this field and, in the longer term, has influenced the way that managers and inspectors view residential settings.

The application of the theory on which *A Manual* was based was seen in the publication of *The Chance of a Lifetime?* (Lambert *et al.* 1975). This was a survey of boys' and co-educational boarding schools in England and Wales. Of particular and lasting importance were the holistic approach to education and the designation of goals and styles of operation as 'expressive', 'instrumental' and 'organisational'. Some elements of education, such as music and art, are an end in themselves, whereas others, such as mathematics and languages, are more obviously a means to an end. In some establishments there is a balance between the two while in others the latter (instrumental) or occasionally the former (expressive) predominates. In some schools, education itself may be subservient to organisational roles but these instances would be categorised as malfunctional. This discussion might have remained at the theoretical level but action research within the schools allowed it to be used to assess the effectiveness of schools in achieving different goals. Furthermore, a unique opportunity was taken to experiment with the various general conclusions from the research in the progressive Dartington Hall School in Devon.

The contribution of Dartington Hall School and other English progressive schools is set out by Skidelsky (1969). The link between the school and the research was nurtured by Royston Lambert, who was appointed Headmaster in 1968 while remaining Director of the Research Unit. His initial aim was 'to become non-head of the first anti-school in the country' but the constraints of current reality limited his scheme to a number of interesting experiments. He focused on three aspects (Kidel 1990):

- the need to open the school into the world;
- the need to break down the division between school and work or life; and
- the need to broaden the schools base across existing class boundaries

The most successful of the projects was a link with Northcliffe School, a secondary modern in the coal-mining community of Conisbrough, Yorkshire. An array of exchanges and schemes was developed, based upon the original thinking of the Dartington research team. There were some extremely interesting results, many of which supported Lambert's original concepts (see previous paragraph). However, the exigencies of the day-to-day running of what was a complex system militated against close monitoring. It was a noble experiment, in many ways unique, brought to a close by the national economic crisis in 1974.

The Chance of a Lifetime? was the first and only major study of boarding schools in Britain. It provided a methodology for comparative work and showed why some schools worked better than others. It indicated what needed to be done to improve boarding education and how it could be integrated into the emerging comprehensive state system. While the horror stories revealed by the research achieved publicity, the book also confirmed that many schools were effective and that pupils found their time there stimulating and enjoyable.

While the Unit's work in boarding schools was progressing, the problems of approved schools – reform schools for young offenders – were being addressed using similar techniques. In *After Grace – Teeth* (Millham *et al.* 1975) the attempt to convert 'black boxes' to 'grey boxes' continued. This was a comparative study of the residential experience of boys in approved schools. It identified the goals and styles of the schools and, through in-house observational research, examined their effects on staff and children. Of particular interest was the work on styles of setting, reflecting much of the research undertaken earlier in boarding schools. Based on the relationship between expressive, instrumental and organisational goals, different styles of setting were identified. These were then classified in a variety of other ways so that, for example, family-group schools were distinguished from therapeutic communities or campus schools. Of particular relevance was the balance between the mechanisms for control and those for care. In the case of approved schools, it was also possible to follow the possible effects of the establishments on the young people after their release. Finally, the internal elements were brought together to produce a model that set approved schools in the context of the entire field of residential care.

These four books illustrate the thrust of the Dartington Unit's research programme in the early years. Theory was used to provide a foundation for evidence-based, applied or action research. Concepts and procedures were developed to allow transfer between the various settings. An holistic approach to education was adopted and the effectiveness of each institution, in the light of its own goals, was established. Carefully constructed and valid research informed practice.

Building on these foundations, the work of Dartington as spearheaded by Roger Bullock obviously developed. By the late 1990s, the wide experience of the Unit had allowed it to produce a series of highly focused books. One that is particularly relevant to understanding the educational needs of children in their wider family and social context is *Matching Needs and Services* (Bullock *et al.* 1995; Little *et al.* 2001). This provided a methodology for assessing the needs of children and using this information (following all the research on outcomes) to design effective services. Thus, the principles established by the evidence-based research of Dartington have been brought together to produce a model set of procedures. Research has been used not only to produce ideas and concepts but also to inform professional practice.

The work can be further illuminated by subsequent studies in the field of residential care. In *Making Residential Care Work* (Brown *et al.* 1998) the relationships between structure, culture and outcome were examined in nine homes for children. It can be seen that the grey box envisaged in theoretical work was evolving closer to a white box. Of particular interest in this work, bearing in mind earlier research, was the division of goals into societal, formal and belief and the establishment of a linear model in which the relationship between these goals determines the staff culture, which in turn shapes the child culture. Thus, the tautology that 'A home is good because the children do well. Why do they do well? Because they are in a good home' is broken and the vital conditions for effective practice are revealed. The research and development link was further developed in *Structure, Culture and Outcome* (Bullock *et al.* 1999), one of a series of practice tools that provide a summary of evaluated evidence-based work to help practitioners and managers to make difficult decisions – in this case how to run effective residential services.

CONCLUSION

This chapter has charted the key reforms in British education over a 40-year period and identified the major developmental themes. It has demonstrated how the Dartington unit has been relevant both to the improvement of research and to reforms in policy and practice. These developments continue in current work with which the Unit is involved, including a randomised-controlled trial to assess the effects of residential education, the use of 'theories of change' to assist with understanding *how* interventions work and new ways of gathering children's views, notably using audio-computer-assisted techniques. These developments are highly relevant to the field of education given the emphasis in government policy on the role of education agencies in meeting the needs of every child.

The research at Dartington has shown a continuity of purpose, a breadth of vision and an understanding of the vital link between research and practice that has provided one of the few reliable and valid constants in the development of education in Britain over the past 40 years. The continuing success of the Dartington programme results in no small measure from the initiative, integrity and, one should add, native wit of Roger Bullock.

REFERENCES

Brown, E., Bullock, R., Hobson, C. and Little, M. (1998) *Making Residential Care Work: structure and culture in children's homes*, Aldershot, Ashgate.

Bullock, R., Little, M. and Mount, K. (1995) *Matching Needs and Services: the audit and planning of provision for children looked after by local authorities*, Dartington, Dartington Social Research Unit.

Bullock, R., Little, M., Ryan, M. and Tunnard, J. (1999) *Structure, Culture and Outcome: how to improve residential services for children*, Dartington, Warren House Press.

Crick, B. (1998) *Education for Citizenship and the Teaching of Democracy in School: final report of the Advisory Group in Citizenship*, London, QCA.

DES (Department for Education and Science) (1967) *Children and Their Primary Schools: a report of the Central Advisory Council for Education*, Plowden Report, London, HMSO.

DES (1975) *A Language for Life*, Bullock Report, London, HMSO.

DES (1977) *A New Partnership for Our Schools*, Taylor Report, London, HMSO.

DES (1986) *Education and Training: working together*, London, HMSO.

DES (1991) *You and Your Child's Education*, Parents' Charter, London, DES.

DfE (Department for Education) (1991) *Choice and Diversity: a new framework for schools*, London, HMSO.

DfE (1994) *Code of Practice on the Identification and Assessment of Special Educational Needs*, London, Department for Education.

DfEE (Department for Education and Employment) (1996) *Learning to Compete: education and training for 14–19 year olds*, London, HMSO.

DfES (Department for Education and Skills) (2003) *Every Child Matters*, Cm. 5860, London, The Stationery Office.

Inman, S., Buck, M. and Burke, H. (1998) *Assessing Personal and Social Development: measuring the unmeasureable?*, London, Falmer Press.

Kidel, M. (1990) *Beyond the Classroom: Dartington's experiments in education*, Bideford, Green Books.

Lambert, R. and Millham, S. (1968) *The Hothouse Society: an exploration of boarding-school life through the boys' and girls' own writings*, London, Weidenfeld & Nicolson.

Lambert, R., Millham, S. and Bullock, R. (1970) *A Manual to the Sociology of the School*, London, Weidenfeld & Nicolson.

Lambert, R., Millham, S. and Bullock, R. (1975) *The Chance of a Lifetime? A survey of boys' and co-educational boarding schools in England and Wales*, London, Weidenfeld & Nicolson.

Little, M., Madge, J., Mount, K., Ryan, M. and Tunnard, J. (2001) *Matching Needs and Services,* 3rd Edition, Dartington, Dartington Academic Press.

Millham, S., Bullock, R. and Cherrett, P. (1975) *After Grace – Teeth: a comparative study of the residential experience of boys in approved schools*, London, Human Context Books.

Millham, S., Bullock, R. and Hosie, K. (1978) *Locking Up Children: secure provision within the child care system*, Farnborough, Saxon House.

Mittler, P. (2000) *Working Towards Inclusive Education: social contexts*, London, Fulton.

National Commission on Education (1993) *Learning to Succeed*, London, Heinemann.

Skidelsky, R. (1969) *English Progressive Schools*, Harmondsworth, Penguin Books.

Tomlinson, S. (2001) *Education in Post-Welfare Society*, Buckingham, Open University Press.

Warnock, M. (1978) *Special Educational Needs: report of the Committee of Inquiry into the Education of Handicapped Children and Young People*, Warnock Report, London, HMSO.

4

CHILDREN IN RESIDENCE

Roger Clough

DARTINGTON MEMORIES

My first contact with the group that was to become the Dartington Social Research Unit (DSRU) was about 35 years ago. I had completed a Postgraduate Diploma in Social Administration at the London School of Economics (LSE) and was working in a senior boys' approved school. Royston Lambert and Spencer Millham (1968) had just produced *The Hothouse Society*. Dipping into the book at any place today reminds me why I had been excited by the book. It draws heavily on writing from boys and girls at different schools; it uses formal documents, such as rules, house books and minute books; and it includes observations from the authors. It encapsulates a style of research that captures people's experiences, using these as a basis for understanding the processes that took place, as reflected in chapter headings such as: the pattern (of life); a place in the sun – power; the outside world; the inner world; the underworld; adaptations and verdicts.

The ideas and the analysis included in this book were an important contribution to understanding life in boarding schools. Moreover, relying heavily on writing from the pupils, the book is both immensely revealing and powerful. The *New Statesman* said it was 'touching, sometimes funny, usually dignified'. A similar comment was to be found in *The Listener*: 'Much of the writing is so frank, spontaneous, heartfelt that it's a marvel to read.' Since its move to Dartington, the Unit has maintained its interest in what in education is termed 'boarding' and in social care is known as 'residential living'. Two features that stand out in *The Hothouse Society* have marked Dartington's approach to residential child care: the first is that of drawing on sociology to interpret what happens in residential homes; the second is the willingness to listen to children's accounts of their experiences. Amid changing fashions in research and changing constraints from central government, Dartington has maintained the richness of its approach.

And so to the second book from the Dartington Unit that I take off my bookshelves, *After Grace – Teeth* (Millham *et al.* 1975a). It, too, was soundly theoretical, yet beautifully written.

Forty Years of Research, Policy and Practice in Children's Services.
Edited by N. Axford, V. Berry, M. Little and L. Morpeth.
© 2005 John Wiley & Sons, Ltd. ISBN 0-470-01219-6.

By the time it appeared in 1975 I was a Lecturer in Residential Care at Bristol Polytechnic. I used the book extensively in encouraging students to search to understand residential living. I remember, without referring to the book, the devastating way in which Spencer, Roger and Paul Cherrett unpicked events. They described the casual way in which, at some schools, the boys were allowed free time to do what they want after tea. Rather than seeing this as a liberal approach, and therefore a positive, they claimed that, in the context of the rest of the life of the regimes, this laissez-faire approach meant that the boys were free to impose their worlds, which in the worst schools conflicted with the stated goals of the school. The boys' world, they argued, had to be fragmented to prevent such conflicts.

Sub-culture would have been a common theme in those days in sociological writing, found in what I would term the LSE school of writing on residential establishments, such as Terence and Pauline Morris's work on prisons and what were then termed subnormality hospitals (Morris and Morris 1963; Morris 1969). The Dartington team translated this into the subtler 'informal world'. It is fascinating to see that recent work from Dartington still holds to the importance of culture in understanding what makes a place work well. But more of that later.

In *The Hothouse Society* we learned of the ways in which some schools engender immense commitment from their pupils. *After Grace – Teeth* showed that, in some approved schools, the goals of the school matched those of the young people and their parents. The authors had looked at different kinds of goals in the schools: *instrumental* ('skill acquiring'), *expressive* ('things worthy in themselves, like self-discipline') and *organisational* ('concerned with the maintenance and survival of the institution') (p. 57). The places that worked best were those where the parents and young people were convinced that they provided instrumental benefits as well as the other goals. This is a notable finding, especially given the way the emphasis on instrumental skills was downplayed in residential children's homes for 20 to 30 years. The former approved schools had aimed to provide some training in skills, whether in the classroom at junior schools or in trade-training for older pupils. There were understandable reasons why many contended that the focus on trade-training was too often irrelevant to the modern job market and that it did not recognise the importance of expressive goals.

Yet the Dartington study showed that learning to do things made sense to many young people. Today there is recognition of the importance of educational skills, although other instrumental skills still have less emphasis. Indeed the critical strategy seems to be to create an environment in which the instrumental, expressive and organisational are all valued and encouraged to flourish. The danger of focusing on one element is illustrated by considering the changing fashions in how places prepare young people for life after the residential home. At various times there have been after-care officers and support social workers to help young people manage to find and hold a job and to cope with their housing arrangements. As part of such arrangements there would have been attempts to find supportive landladies. More recently the emphasis has been on the teaching of life skills: learning to cook, to wash clothes, to manage money and so on. These are important – but there is too little understanding of the experience of living *outside* the residential home. For example, the reasons that many adults do not cook and eat well have far more to do with feelings of loneliness and lack of pleasure at eating on one's own. The instrumental skill of learning to cook will not result in sensible, inexpensive eating unless people learn how to be on their own – an expressive goal.

Three topics from Dartington's work already highlighted illustrate factors that remain central to understanding life in residential establishments, and thus for thinking about practice: (i) the questioning of the laissez-faire approach shows that residential living has to be structured; (ii) the recognition of the informal worlds of children and staff is illustrative of the fact that what happens is determined by the informal as well as the formal; and (iii) their highlighting of instrumental skills is not only valuable in its own right (showing that such skills matter) but also in that places that want their influence to extend beyond the period of residence must capture the hearts and minds of the children and, preferably, their families. We could add that staff have an obligation to get beyond their own experiences and aspirations to open doors for young people.

THE 'STEAMPRESS MODEL'

In the 1960s, places where people lived in large groups away from their own families had become fashionable places to study. In part this was explained by the ease of access for researchers: the population under the microscope was, in many ways, captive. However, the study was driven also by a reforming zeal to examine, and then expose, the impact of institutions on the lives of the people who lived there, whether described as inmates or, more recently, residents. (Difficult as it may be, I use the term 'institution' in a neutral sense, descriptive of a building used by an organisation, and without the overtones implicit in the word 'institutional'.)

In a seminal work, *Institutional Neurosis*, Barton (1959) contended that living in an institution created problems over and above those for which the person had moved to the establishment: it created 'institutional neurosis', which, in effect, became a disease that was more difficult to treat than the original problem. A couple of years later, Goffman (1961) (drawing, it should be noted, on autobiographies and other accounts of life in very large residential establishments) claimed that such places set out to strip people of their identity and impose the lifestyle of the new organisation. The ideas are central to understanding of residential living in the second half of the twentieth century but no doubt today would be dismissed by many as unsound in terms of research methods.

Goffman epitomises the dilemmas in thinking and analysis regarding residential homes. His description of processes has been fundamental in shaping the way others have thought about residential living. The places he used as a basis for his study were very large, up to 1000 or more residents, and were closed to the outside world to a far greater extent than most residential establishments. For me the deep understanding contained in his work helps to explain the experience of residents in small residential units – for example, the way private life is lived to some extent in public or the way behaviour is interpreted in the light of the staff's perception of the overriding problem. And I have no doubt that the analysis of life in institutions contained in his and others' work has played a significant part in moves to humanise residential establishments and, with that, to ensure that lifestyles were more responsive to individuals. Yet Goffman's work, simplified into certainties rather than processes, has been taken by many to mean that residential places are bound to produce negative experiences. Goffman's rich understanding results in a climate in which, for many, any option is to be preferred to a residential home.

It is in this climate that Dartington has sought to understand and describe both what happens in residential child care establishments and the reasons why some places are more successful than others. This search to understand has been part of an important British approach to the study of residential homes that has developed from the 1970s onwards. Captured in *Varieties of Residential Experience* (Tizard *et al.* 1975), there has been a determination to try to understand not what drives all residential places in the same direction but what makes them differ from one another. Previously, what the authors termed the 'steampress model' had looked for similarities between places and ended up forcing establishments into moulds:

> Most previous research on residential establishments and their functioning, has started, not from the obvious fact of institutional variety, but from the equally obvious fact that the members of any class of institutions tend to resemble each other. (p. 3)

The Dartington team wrote two chapters for the book, outlining an approach to comparing residential homes and setting out an analysis of the processes involved in socialisation within homes (Millham *et al.* 1975b, 1975c). At the heart of Dartington's approach is a belief that it is possible, initially, to show the ways in which places are different from one another and then to set out the factors that lead to the best outcomes. Their demonstration of this through their work for nearly 40 years is both their hallmark and among their most valuable contributions to residential child care research.

Alongside this they have held to a belief that residential places may not only be necessary as a fallback when all else fails, but may also be good places in which to live. By way of contrast, much research into residential establishments has betrayed an underlying belief that such places intrinsically provide negative experiences. The Dartington team's intertwining of, first, a belief (based on research experience) that residential homes can provide high-quality experiences for children and young people (Bullock *et al.* 1994) *and*, second, evidence as to why places work differently from one another, has been the backbone of residential child care research in the UK. Indeed, the Department of Health's overview of research into residential child care, *Caring for Children Away from Home* (DoH 1998), stresses that residence should be seen as part of the continuum of care; it is not something to be prevented per se (as has often been argued) but rather one of numerous means of interrupting the development of children's social and psychological problems and helping children to develop better coping strategies.

It remains a matter of conjecture as to why so many people take a firm stance either that residential homes should all be closed or that they can provide life-enhancing experiences. I remember discussing this at a seminar in the Dartington grounds and we mused on whether people's own life experiences of family, boarding or group living coloured such beliefs.

RESIDENTIAL CHILD CARE RESEARCH IN THE UK

In an overview of residential child care research, Roger Bullock and his colleagues (1993) suggest that in the first period, from 1960 to 1975, the focus was on understanding processes within regimes in terms of the factors I have noted: what explains their 'ethos' and culture, their impacts on staff and residents and the importance of informal cultures. In the second period, 1975 to 1992, they identify a shift to looking at the functions of residential care for the wider child-care system. There had been some interest early on in outcomes, as evidenced in *After Grace – Teeth*, which looked at success rates in approved schools in terms both of non-reconviction, an official measure, and the impact on young people's commitment and behaviour. The study of outcomes became more important as this period came to an end. Anyone familiar with the drive from 1993 to the present day towards creating what has been termed 'evidence-based practice' will know of the increasing demand to look not just at what happens (the processes) but also at the outputs and outcomes. Can, or does residential care make any difference to children's well-being? Does one residential establishment achieve more, or less, in terms of outcomes than another?

Dartington's own view, based on their long history in research, is that residence can make substantial differences to children's lives for the period that the young people live at the establishment. Their work has been important in demonstrating that residential places often manage to hold highly troubled and troublesome children more effectively than the settings from which they have come; further, they may also help children to develop their own coping strategies. What is far more difficult to show is the longer term impact when the child leaves the home.

I have referred above to *Caring for Children Away from Home* (DoH 1998). Covering 12 linked studies commissioned during the period 1995 to 1998, this overview searches for common themes, testing conclusions among researchers and practitioners. What stands out is the importance to effective residential care of, first, leadership style and, second, clarity of objectives, with there being agreement on objectives both within the staff team in the establishment and with the external management of the home. The third critical element to creating a good residential life is that of culture, and here the review drew heavily on work from a Dartington team that included Roger (Brown *et al.* 1998):

> The culture inside residential centres is an ingredient of good outcomes. Getting staff to agree on certain tasks is likely to produce a healthy home, which in turn will produce better results for the residents.
> (DoH 1998, p. 32)

> Culture can be measured in several ways. [The study by Brown and her colleagues] took a series of tasks most likely to occur in a children's home, such as a parent's visit, a child's refusal to go to school or an attack by one resident on another, and asked staff how they would respond. Three patterns of response were identified:
>
> • staff responded differently, signifying the lack of a cultural response
> • staff agreed with each other about what they would do, but suggested an unhelpful course of action; a negative culture
> • staff agreed on largely helpful responses; a positive culture.
> (DoH 1998, p. 50)

One of the difficulties of studying residential homes in the UK is that there have been huge changes in both the use made of residential homes and the size and structure of homes. Consequently, it is not possible to compare studies of residences today with those of even 20 years ago, let alone the 1970s. In brief, what might be termed 'children's homes', that is, the less specialist type of residence, have become smaller, with some 'homes' now having one young person resident and a team of staff providing 24-hour cover. By contrast, what is called 'fostering' has changed too: there are more foster carers taking several children, more taking children with greater degrees of disturbance and more who are paid rather than receiving an allowance. The boundary with residential care is somewhat blurred, and the core difference seems to be that in foster homes the house where the children live is the home of the foster carers.

The numbers of young people in residence has dropped dramatically in the last 30 years. Gooch (1996) has shown that there were 128,000 children aged 0–18 in residence, a 45 per cent fall since Moss's (1975) earlier survey.

However, this fall has been greatest in children's homes, provision for children with disabilities and independent boarding schools but is less for special education and hospitals. Figures have increased for youth custody. The 1996 figures for children aged 0–18 in residential establishments in England and Wales are set out in Table 4.1.

Table 4.1   Children in residential establishments in England and Wales, 1996

Context	Number (thousands)
Children's homes	7
Boarding special schools	21
Provision for disabled children	2
Young offender institutions	2
Boarding schools (not special)	84
Hospitals	12
TOTAL	**128**

Source: Gooch (1996).

More detailed information for Wales illustrates the changes: 123 local authority children's homes in 1980 drop to 29 in 2001; the number of places falls from 1,664 to 203; and the numbers of residents on 31 March of the respective years drops from 1,329 to 161. Of course, these figures list the numbers only in local authority homes.

Another way of looking at the changes is to show the pattern of placements in different years, again using Wales as an illustration (Table 4.2). In addition to the declining number of placements overall between 1980 and 2001, the figures show that the number of children in community homes has declined sharply over the same period (from 1,445 to 211), while the number in foster care and being placed for adoption has increased considerably.

In spite of changes it is fair to assume that the Social Services Inspectorate's summary of the conditions for good practice has remained true throughout:

> the effectiveness of staff in those homes where good practice was observed was based on clear leadership, organised and consistent ways of working, and clarity of purpose.
> (SSI 1993, p. 31)

Table 4.2   Children looked after by local authorities by placement, 31 March in respective years, Wales*

Placement	1980	1992	1997	2001
Foster placement	1,709	2,038	2,303	2,690
Community homes	1,445	468	232	211
Private or voluntary homes	153	20	5	24
With parents or family	1,207	380	289	408
Placed for adoption	—	82	93	176
Retained, detained or other compulsory order	—	—	—	73
Independent accommodation	88	96	106	52
Other placements	259	77	262	83
Total	**4,861**	**3,161**	**3,290**	**3,644**

*In the UK the term 'looked after children' has become the shorthand for 'children and young people who are looked after by the local authority on behalf of the state'.
Source: National Assembly for Wales (2004).

THE STRENGTHS AND LIMITATIONS OF RESEARCH KNOWLEDGE

There is a solid body of research evidence about residential child care, built over the experience of 40 years. What do we know from this? What are the uncertainties?

One very important feature of residential child care history that has not been mentioned so far in this review is the revelation of abuse in child care establishments of all sorts. There have been two different types of inquiry into allegations of abuse. In the first, events at a particular place are examined at around the time of the allegation. Examples of this are what became known as the Pin Down Inquiry (Levy and Kahan 1991) and numerous agency investigations into their own establishments. More media attention has been given to the second type of inquiry, namely the huge investigations of abuses that took place many years previously and over a large number of establishments. The North Wales Inquiry is an example of such an investigation (Waterhouse *et al.* 2000).

The reason for writing here about the known abuse of young people in residential homes is not to evaluate the quality of the investigations. (For an examination of the costs and benefits of inquiries, see the study by Corby (2004) of the North Wales Inquiry.) Rather, my purpose is to acknowledge that the views held about the quality and use of residential care are in part shaped by a recognition that young people have been damaged in the places that were designed to look after them. It is hoped that current practices and safeguards – for example, in terms of staff selection and access for children to people outside the home – will minimise the likelihood of young people being abused today. There is no research, however, into levels of abuse in residences today, with most of the current investigations concerning allegations of abuse in the past.

There is a further important factor that influences views about the quality of residential child care. There are repeated governmental references to the numbers of children who have been looked after by local authorities who either face later problems, for example in terms of criminal convictions, or who seem not to have been sufficiently helped, for example in terms of educational performance (e.g. SEU 2003). There are dilemmas here in attempting to reach conclusions about the quality of provision: the children and young people who go to residential homes are likely to be those facing what are seen as the most intractable problems. A realistic appraisal of residential care should set the predictions for a child's future when he or she moves into a residential home against the child's state when he or she moves out. There is also a need for more control group studies, similar to those in the early 1970s that allocated young people to contrasting regimes within single establishments (e.g. Bottoms and McLintock 1973; Cornish and Clarke 1975). Instead, assessments are typically made on the basis of blunt instruments such as the numbers of GCSEs passed at the age of 16.

What we do know from research, and have discussed earlier in this chapter, are the factors that seem to be prerequisites to successful outcomes. For example, we know that the quality of the relationship between carer and child is critical to success, a feature that many adults looking back at their lives in residential homes have identified as important. When Roy Parker (1988) summarised the research findings, he noted that the information from various studies suggests that different regimes have a differential effect on children's behaviour, with the best results achieved by child-oriented rather than institution-oriented practices:

> [In] . . . retrospective accounts provided by adults and young people who had been in care it is the sense of receiving understanding, sympathetic, comforting and individual attention which stands out as the hallmark of the experiences which they cherish. (p. 111)

> Establishments do 'best' when the children feel they are cared for, listened to and responded to in a quiet, sympathetic, and consistent fashion. (p. 115)

My own list of factors emerging from research that are intrinsic to resident-centred practice is as follows:

- The starting point is an attempt to understand the resident: this is an active search . . . The daily life within the home is built from an attempt to produce systems that best match residents' wants and needs.
- There is time within the daily routine to listen to individual residents.
- Residents are involved in negotiations about life in the establishment.
- Staff worry about residents: they are concerned for residents, hold on to their interests and continue to think about what will work best for them, even when they are not with residents.
- Residents must feel that they are at the centre of life in the home, that their interests and well-being matter to staff . . .
- The key to good experience for the residents is that they feel they matter, that they are cared for and cared about.
- In effect, the experience of the resident should be at the heart of practice.

(Clough 2000, pp. 88–90)

Whitaker and her colleagues similarly state that good practice includes:

- being ready to listen, both to the evidently momentous and to the apparently mundane;
- being sensitive to a young person's readiness, or not, to talk and to share feelings and experiences;

- combining non-verbal or symbolic forms of caring with verbal, explicit ones;
- noticing good or admirable behaviour and crediting a young person for it;
- marking special occasions in a young person's life with a celebration.

(Whitaker *et al.* 1998, p. 170)

However, while it is possible to identify the characteristics that mark an establishment as likely to work well, there is very little research into how such factors are created. Thus, it is possible to state, for example, that good residential care demands high-quality leadership and positive relationships between staff and young people but we know little about what creates and maintains such positive relationships. Is it the personalities of staff and, if so, what are the key aspects, or is it the styles of regime? Is it the type of support systems for staff or, perhaps, the coherence of the institution's goals? Of course, the creation of positive relationships may be multi-causal – a combination of personality, approach within the establishment, coherence of objectives and support for staff. Overall it is fair to state that if residential practice is to improve we need better evidence of *how* to do things, so building on knowledge of *what* to do.

Addressing the gap is important. Staff work in a volatile environment. The research gives clues about what produces these factors, in particular the need to ensure that there is congruence between the goals of those inside the establishment and managers. There is further evidence in the work on cultures, demonstrating the importance of staff responding to situations in similar ways. It is possible, then, to develop styles (or cultures) in which staff are able to learn and adopt responses so that, in effect, they can say: 'In these circumstances, this is what we do here.'

One of the ways in which it would be expected that staff learn strategies for working in difficult situations is through training, yet there is no evidence from research that the proportion of qualified staff in a home correlates with outcomes, either for the home or for the children. Having been involved for a large part of my working life in training residential staff, as well as in research, I find the lack of such evidence alarming. Given that in any other profession that demands skills from staff it is presumed that training is essential to maintaining standards and best practice, the findings concerning residential homes are, indeed, bizarre. At least two factors may be at work. First, the courses may not train staff well for residential work. There has been great uncertainty for many years in the UK about the best way to train residential child care staff: it is widely accepted that the social work qualification has not been well suited to residential work, with few courses offering specialist teaching in the area. Some people would consider the alternative training route via National Vocational Qualifications (NVQs) and their Scottish equivalents (SNVQs) to be based too much on practice and competence, with insufficient focus on theories or the research evidence. Second, it may be that training does influence staff practice but that other factors, such as leadership and congruence of objectives, have far greater impact: 'good enough' trained staff may not function well in a negative culture.

Clearly, then, there is need for further work examining the best ways to train staff and for evaluations of the outcomes of training. We cannot afford to stop at a position where all we know is that training appears to have no impact on the quality of provision. At the very least it is arguable that training matters to the extent that at least a core of staff are trained or people are trained to a certain threshold: below these levels the quality of service and outcomes may deteriorate considerably. Further, given the importance of the task, we need to discover both what best equips people for residential work *and* what is the impact of relevant training.

A further area for research consideration is the size of home (in terms of the number of residents). The working presumption of many is 'the smaller, the better', with a study by Sinclair and Gibbs (1998) indeed suggesting that smaller homes performed better than larger ones. However, the conclusion needs further examination. In a review of the literature Chipenda-Dansokho and Bullock (2003) claim that the Sinclair–Gibbs research is the only major study providing evidence in support of smaller units and argue that a 'model that considers the size in the context of institutional aims and structures is ... a more fruitful approach to understanding the significance of size in service development' (p. 66).

It is possible that very small homes, not part of the Sinclair–Gibbs research, may create their own set of problems, for example in that the behaviour of any one child has a dramatic effect on the life of the establishment, and is less easily contained by a wider stability. Again, this is an area where we need to know more, including the impact of the lifestyle of a one-bedded home on a young person in terms of daily living pattern and lack of contact with other young people.

RESEARCH AND PRACTICE

The Dartington Unit has been one of the more important forces in the UK in residential child care research. It was one of a small number of units that for many years were funded on a rolling programme by the Department of Health (and preceding bodies). In this, the Unit has been at the heart of a very significant programme of research sponsored by central government. The culmination of this was the previously mentioned overview of UK research into residential child care (DoH 1998), in which Michael Little (then co-director at Dartington with Roger) played a central role in testing findings from different research studies and writing up the key conclusions. The research programme was designed to influence not only government policy but also the direct practice of those who ran residential homes, worked in them or placed children and young people in them.

The changing use of residence in the holding and treatment of children and young people in the UK, in particular the huge drop in the use of residential homes, has had far more to do with economics and climate of opinion than it has with research evidence. Residential establishments are costly; such costs, policy-makers have argued, could be reduced if more children were fostered or lived at home. This picture of the residential home as last resort is driven by an attempt to try less costly options first, regardless of the best match between the child and the type of intervention. The climate of opinion on residential homes has developed from information about terrible abuse in some homes, coupled with the half-truths about institutionalisation referred to earlier. It is correct that many, perhaps most, very large residential establishments developed depersonalised styles as a means of coping with numbers of residents. It is correct also that in some smaller residential homes the lifestyle has focused on the interests of the institution rather than that of the individual.

There are few examples, then, of research evidence being used to drive national or local strategies to develop the types of residences wanted. Instead, there has been too much reliance on generalisation and half-truth to back changes in practice. If, in the future, policies are to be based on evidence, then the starting point has to be a review of the total population of children and young people (again locally or nationally) in order to identify the numbers who need special help. This is likely to reveal heterogeneous patterns of need, with discrete groups of children whose needs may be met by different types of residential and other provision (see, for example, Bullock *et al.* 1995). It is at that stage that the evidence should be called in of what works, not just in residential provision but also in related services such as fostering and mental health. Most commentators agree that this would result in some young people being provided with a specialist residential placement earlier than is common, with others receiving appropriate assistance in non-residential settings.

It is worth reflecting briefly on how research is conveyed so as to influence policy-makers. The Dartington team's belief that rigorous research must include the feelings of those who are studied has held firm throughout the life of the Unit, even when others would have bowed to prevailing fashions that saw truth only in numbers. Indeed, for me the essence of its work is contained in an ability to capture the positive experiences of children, as well as the structural factors that militate against success. In the mid-1990s, Michael Little with Siobhan Kelly (1995), a teenage girl in a therapeutic institution, wrote *A Life Without Problems?* The book uses Siobhan's diaries and experiences to explain what happens at the Caldecott Community. The blurb on the back cover states: 'The central scientific concern is with outcome. The book asks "does any good come of the great efforts invested in tragic young lives?"' Towards the end the researchers write:

> We cannot capture the different emotions of Siobhan, her foster parents and the researcher. It was an extremely difficult process which taught us a great deal more about Caldecott and the lives of the children it shelters. It also reminds us that taking the child's view seriously is time-consuming and needs very careful preparation, understanding and interpretation. (p. 191)

At the end Siobhan rereads her own diary and has a conversation with the researcher. She states that so often therapists only want to focus on sex, and that she was conscious of what she told people and what she did not:

> The things you miss in this book are all the normal bits that happen to people of my age. Like, I haven't heard from my friends for ages, and I don't know whether anybody likes me at the moment. That's my main worry. And my exam results tomorrow. (p. 192)

Of course, changing policy and practice also depends to some extent on the way that research findings are communicated. I have never known whether it is the Dartington air or the process for selecting staff that has resulted in producing such people as Spencer (Millham) and Roger, who are amazing raconteurs. In formal lectures and in informal discussions, their repertoire of stories has held many an audience captivated. Indeed, it may be that their skill in telling a story has meant that people who might be hostile to what they have to say have been charmed.

CONCLUSION

My most recent knowledge of Roger's work is when collaborating with him and Adrian Ward on a study for the National Assembly for Wales (Clough *et al.* 2004):

> to consider the purpose and future shape of residential care services for children in Wales with the aim of establishing a cogent theoretical basis and strategic direction for the development of an effective, quality service.

Our task was to present a report on what is known from research about what works in residential practice, which was followed by a paper outlining the purpose and future shape of residential care in Wales, with proposals for change for consideration. Roger contributed the breadth of his knowledge of research, his conclusions as to what evidence emerges from research and his analysis of the ways in which local authorities have to look at their child populations to plan services. He argued that local authorities did not make full use of the data they had (or should have) and consequently did not know enough about what was happening in their own services. As we presented our material to an expert seminar, he asserted his belief in the value of residential care and in the potential to develop systems that would result in better placements for children and young people.

So, the spirit of the Dartington Unit lives on: good research is needed so that we can know what is happening; such research must be used to plan far more assertively for children and young people; drifting, and dealing with problems as they emerge, is too casual a way of dealing with children's hurt.

REFERENCES

Barton, R. (1959) *Institutional Neurosis*, London, Wright.

Bottoms, A. and McClintock, F. (1973) *Criminals Coming of Age*, Oxford, Heinemann.

Brown, E., Bullock, R., Hobson, C. and Little, M. (1998) *Making Residential Care Work: structure and culture in children's homes*, Aldershot, Ashgate.

Bullock, R., Millham, S. and Little, M. (1993) *Residential Care for Children: a review of the research*, London, HMSO.

Bullock, R., Little, M. and Millham, S. (1994) 'Assessing the quality of life for children in local authority care or accommodation', *Journal of Adolescence* 17 (1), 29–40.

Bullock, R., Little, M. and Mount, K. (1995) *Matching Needs and Services: the audit and planning of provision for children looked after by local authorities*, Dartington, Dartington Social Research Unit.

Chipenda-Dansokho, S. and Bullock, R. (2003) 'The determinants and influence of size on residential settings for children', *International Journal of Child and Family Welfare* 6 (3), 66–76.

Clough, R. (2000) *The Practice of Residential Work*, Basingstoke, Macmillan.

Clough, R., Bullock, R. and Ward, A. (2004) *Review of Fostering and Residential Care: Literature Review*, Cardiff, National Assembly for Wales http://www.childrenfirst.wales.gov.uk/content/placement/index-e.htm [accessed 13 August 2004].

Corby, B. (2004) 'The North Wales Tribunal of Inquiry', in Stanley, N. and Manthorpe, J. (eds) *The Age of the Inquiry: learning and blaming in health and social care*, London, Routledge.

Cornish, D. and Clarke, R. (1975) *Residential Treatment and its Effects on Juvenile Delinquency*, London, HMSO.

DoH (Department of Health) (1998) *Caring for Children Away from Home: messages from research*, Chichester, John Wiley & Sons.

Goffman, E. (1961) *Asylums: essays on the social situation of mental patients and other inmates*, New York, Anchor Books.

Gooch, D. (1996) 'Home and away: the residential care, education and control of children in historical and political context', *Child and Family Social Work* 1 (1), 19–32.

Lambert, R. and Millham, S. (1968) *The Hothouse Society: an exploration of boarding-school life through the boys' and girls' own writings*, London, Weidenfeld & Nicolson.

Levy A. and Kahan B. (1991) *The Pindown Experience and the Protection of Children*, Stafford, Staffordshire County Council.

Little, M. with Kelly, S. (1995) *A Life without Problems? The achievements of a therapeutic community*, Aldershot, Arena.

Millham, S., Bullock, R. and Cherrett, P. (1975a) *After Grace – Teeth: a comparative study of the residential experience of boys in approved schools*, Brighton, Human Context Books.

Millham, S., Bullock, R. and Cherrett, P. (1975b) 'A conceptual scheme for the comparative analysis of residential institutions', in Tizard, J., Sinclair, I. and Clarke, R.V.G. (eds) *Varieties of Residential Experience*, London, Routledge & Kegan Paul.

Millham, S., Bullock, R. and Cherrett, P. (1975c) 'Socialisation in residential communities: an illustration of the analytic framework previously presented', in Tizard, J., Sinclair, I. and Clarke, R.V.G. (eds) *Varieties of Residential Experience*, London, Routledge & Kegan Paul.

Morris, T. and Morris, P. (1963) *Pentonville: a sociological study of an English prison*, London, Routledge & Kegan Paul.

Morris, P. (1969) *Put Away: a sociological study of institutions for the mentally retarded*, London, Routledge & Kegan Paul.

Moss, P. (1975) 'Residential care of children: a general overview', in Tizard, J., Sinclair, I. and Clarke, R.V.G. (eds) *Varieties of Residential Care Experience*, London, Routledge & Kegan Paul.

National Assembly for Wales (2004) *Personal Social Services Statistics Wales 2003: SSDA 903: Children Looked After*, Cardiff, National Assembly for Wales http://www.lgdu-wales.gov.uk/eng/pss.asp?cat=201&year=2003 [accessed 13 August 2004].

Parker, R. (1988) *Residential Care: the research reviewed*, London, NISW.

SEU (Social Exclusion Unit) (2003) *A Better Education for Children in Care*, London, Office of the Deputy Prime Minister.

Sinclair, I. and Gibbs, I. (1998) *Children's Homes: a study in diversity*, Chichester, John Wiley & Sons.

SSI (Social Services Inspectorate) (1993) *Corporate Parents: inspection of residential child care services in 11 local authorities, November 1992–March 1993*, London, Department of Health.

Tizard, J., Sinclair, I. and Clarke, R.V.G. (eds) (1975) *Varieties of Residential Experience*, London, Routledge & Kegan Paul.

Waterhouse, R., Clough, M. and le Fleming, M. (2000) *Lost in Care: report of the tribunal of inquiry into the abuse of children in care in the former county council areas of Gwynedd and Clwyd since 1974*, London, The Stationery Office.

Whitaker, D., Archer, L. and Hicks, L. (1998) *Working in Children's Homes: challenges and complexities*, Chichester, John Wiley & Sons.

5

REFORMING JUVENILE JUSTICE

MOVES IN THE RIGHT DIRECTION?

Henri Giller

In the 40 years that Roger has been active in the field of social research significant changes have taken place in the arena of juvenile justice in England and Wales. This chapter seeks to examine the extent to which those changes have been influenced by three themes that are the hallmark of Roger's work and that of the Dartington Social Research Unit, namely:

- the impact of research on policy and practice developments (Bullock 1989);
- the appreciation of the need for a 'whole system' approach to social interventions (Bullock *et al.* 1993);
- a practice context in which services are matched to needs (Bullock *et al.* 1995).

RESEARCH, POLICY AND PRACTICE

The terrain of the juvenile justice system has changed vastly since the 1970s when the seminal Dartington texts *After Grace – Teeth* (Millham *et al.* 1975) and *Locking Up Children* (Millham *et al.* 1978) first appeared. At that time the research community was heavily engaged in disentangling the dual effects of the partially implemented *Children and Young Persons Act 1969*, which sought to institute an hegemony of social welfare within the criminal justice arena, with the continuing impact of a retributive sentencing philosophy as actioned by many of the traditional sanctions available to juvenile court magistrates (Bottoms 1974). The analyses provided by these two texts illustrated clearly the impact that a fragmented system could have on young people's lives, shaping (potentially positively, but often negatively) care careers and all too frequently facilitating the moving on and ultimate rejection of children and young people by the system. Both works highlighted the potential of the criminal justice and welfare systems to effect change in the lives of young people,

Forty Years of Research, Policy and Practice in Children's Services.
Edited by N. Axford, V. Berry, M. Little and L. Morpeth.
© 2005 John Wiley & Sons, Ltd. ISBN 0-470-01219-6.

but they also demonstrated that such outcomes had to be strived for and managed. Above all, the texts elevated the concept of a child's 'career' within social welfare services and the need to conceptualise how the actions of social institutions and their agents could shape and mould its development.

While initially these insights had a limited impact in the policy arena, for practitioners the lessons of career management and a whole systems approach rapidly took root. The 1980s were characterised by a managerial strategy in juvenile justice, which witnessed the emergence of a raft of tactical approaches that sought to minimise the potential harm that the system could do to a young person (Morris and Giller 1987). Diversion, 'down tariffing', seeking the least restrictive alternative and striving for 'custody-free zones' were all approaches that were both widely adopted and significantly implemented, so leading to:

- an expansion of pre-court diversion decisions;
- a separation of welfare from criminal justice processes to reduce the 'unintended consequences' of benign intervention; and
- a significant reduction in the use of custody for young people.

As has been well documented, however, these attainments alone could not resist two realms of influence – the political and the financial – that radically transformed the juvenile, now youth justice, system in the 1990s (Newburn 1997). On the political front the impact of the Bulger case – in which two 10-year-olds murdered a toddler – and the ensuing demonisation of delinquents meant that an increasingly punitive rhetoric pervaded the policy agenda. In the financial arena the work of the Audit Commission (1996), under the banner of *Misspent Youth*, raised fundamental questions about:

- our commitment to prevention;
- our engagement with evidence-based practice; and
- our awareness of value for money.

Each of these themes has a significant resonance in the work of Roger and the Dartington Research Unit. Conceptualising and managing the whole system may be a necessary condition for effective practice, but in and of itself it is not a sufficient condition. Social policy is shaped by many forces – practicalities, economics and public opinion – as well as by socio-legal factors and research evidence. Although a sound and logical framework to underpin practice is essential and fruitful, as is shown by the England and Wales *Children Act* 1989, on its own it is insufficient to determine what happens to young offenders. Intolerant public opinion and a diminished welfare perspective have refocused the perennial welfare justice dilemma posed by serious young offenders, especially as the current government has made crime reduction one of its priorities.

In addition to raising these issues, *Misspent Youth* provided the opportunity to raise a further theme characterised by the work of the Dartington Unit, namely the (negative) impact of the fragmented responsibility for young offenders across the agencies of government (national and local) which had, or should have had, responsibility for meeting their needs in an holistic manner. This fragmentation – with responsibilities distributed across the Home Office, the Department of Health, the Lord Chancellor's Department and the Department for Education and Skills – had a long and enduring history and its impact had been documented lucidly by Roger and his colleagues in their work on approved schools (Millham *et al.* 1975) and latterly community homes with education on the premises.

The political response to *Misspent Youth*, in particular that of the Labour Party – initially in opposition and latterly in government, as embodied in the White Paper *No More Excuses* (Home Office 1997) and subsequently the *Crime and Disorder Act* 1998 – provides the current policy context within which to evaluate the enduring contribution of Roger and his colleagues.

FROM JUVENILE TO YOUTH JUSTICE

The *Crime and Disorder Act* 1998 provided for the first time in law in England and Wales a unifying statutory objective for the youth justice system, namely the prevention of offending, and introduced two crucial institutional changes to effect that legislative intent: the introduction of a Youth Justice Board (YJB) for England and Wales and the requirement for each Local Authority Chief Executive to establish a local multi-agency Youth Offending Team (YOT) to discharge the functions of the legislation. It is through these two new institutions that we need to examine the translation into policy and practice of the three themes that were laid out at the start of this chapter.

The YJB was established as an 'arm's length' agency from central government (i.e. Home Office) although responsible to it. It consists of 11 members, whose backgrounds and experience reflect the full range of needs and agencies experienced by young people likely to come within the ambit of the youth justice system. Significantly, the first Board Chair was Lord (Norman) Warner, previously director of social services for Kent and subsequently adviser to Labour on youth justice matters when they were in opposition, and the first Chief Executive was Mark Perfect, one of the lead investigators of the Audit Commission in the *Misspent Youth* review.

The Board has a number of statutory responsibilities, including:

- ensuring that the performance of the YOTs is consonant with the objectives of the legislation;
- requiring an annual plan from YOTs to demonstrate how their responsibilities will be discharged;
- assuring government that adequate funding is being provided locally to meet those functions;
- supplementing the funding where necessary by the implementation of specific initiatives; and
- being responsible for the usage and performance of the secure estate (that is, secure accommodation for juveniles in child care and prison department establishments).

In discharging these responsibilities, particularly in the arena of YOTs, the YJB has clearly begun to demonstrate the impact of the three themes of Roger's work, both strategically and in action. For example, the YJB has adopted an active performance management approach, with all YOTs required to operate to a three-year set of performance measures organised in terms of a threefold agenda (YJB 2001a).

1. The reduction of youth crime:
   – the reduction of the number of young offenders committing burglary, vehicle crime and robbery locally;
   – the reduction of reoffending rates (by 5 per cent over a 2001 baseline) by December 2004.
2. The engagement of appropriate people in the youth justice process:
   – to increase the use of restorative justice approaches to 80 per cent of disposals by December 2004;
   – to increase the level of victim satisfaction with the process to 70 per cent being 'satisfied' or 'very satisfied' with the process by December 2004;
   – to increase parental satisfaction with the process to 70 per cent being 'satisfied' or 'very satisfied' by December 2004.
3. The identification and response to the range of needs experienced by young offenders:
   – ASSET assessments to be undertaken in 100 per cent of cases where young people are being considered for or are engaged in final warnings, community penalties or custody (ASSET is a framework both for making assessments and for producing aggregated data for information and management purposes);
   – the education, training and employment needs to be met in 90 per cent of cases being supervised by YOTs by December 2004;
   – the accommodation needs of young offenders to be met in 100 per cent of cases where subject to a community intervention or released from custody by December 2004.

The YJB requires all YOTs to produce an annual Youth Justice Plan, which must include a report on their progress towards meeting those performance requirements and identify strategic actions that will be addressed in the forthcoming planning period (YJB 2002a). In addition, the YJB has established a minimum dataset to which all YOTs must adhere by providing the Board with quarterly and annual statistical returns on their performance (YJB 2002b). This minimum dataset not only monitors the business of YOTs but also contains proxy measures of their relative effectiveness by way of a reoffending cohort drawn from each area (from those warned or sentenced between October and December each year) followed up over a period of 24 months.

In the arena of the secure estate it would be accurate to say that the Board has been less robust in its performance management approach. To date, the main focus has been to have service providers (be they the Prison Department or private contractors) report on contract compliance and to reward them financially according to performance. Only recently has the Board begun to look at the outcomes produced from the secure estate and to examine the integration (or lack of it) with community-based services. Once again, this echoes a theme from Roger's work, namely the effort required to institute change within the custodial care sector and the significant work needed to develop continuity of care and support pathways across the institutional and community domains.

As for the YOTs, there has been rapid and significant development since their formation in 1998. Currently some 154 YOTs operate across England and Wales, all having multi-agency and multidisciplinary contributions from police, social work, probation, education and health. Despite a common statutory framework, the deployment of YOTs has – inevitably perhaps – varied. A review report in 2001 on the findings from Youth Justice Plans noted three structural models operating (YJB 2001b):

- a geographically distributed generic service;
- a functionally distributed service; and
- a geographically distributed specialist service.

Even within this short timescale the functions attributed to the YOTs have been expanded, most noticeably with the introduction in 2002 of the Referral Order. The requirement for each YOT to have in place a Referral Order Co-ordinator has frequently added to the range of functional specialisms that YOTs have identified, notably bail support and restorative justice. But the scope of YOTs has not only been determined by factors of geography and function. Different areas have also taken different views on the scope of the work of the YOTs. Some have confined their remit to the specific statutory duties identified in the *Crime and Disorder Act* 1998 for those offenders formally apprehended and put within the youth justice system. Others have sought to develop a Youth Offending Service (YOS) with a remit for prevention, a crime and disorder reduction strategy as it applies to young people, substance misuse prevention and a range of allied initiatives that seek to impact upon social exclusion. An exceedingly interesting research brief would be to determine the relationship between the scope of such services and their impact in reducing crime and disorder.

THE IMPACT OF YOUTH JUSTICE INITIATIVES

As for the impact of YOTs, evidence is beginning to emerge on a range of key issues. With respect to the prevention of youth crime (i.e. pre-formal engagement in the youth justice process) – a key weakness of the previous juvenile justice process according to *Misspent Youth* – the engagement of YOTs has varied widely. While all YOTs have received ring-fenced monies for specific initiatives from the YJB, for example for the Summer Splash holiday activities programme, mainstream preventative initiatives have often been spearheaded by other units or funding streams, in particular the Sure Start and Children's Fund programmes. More worryingly, recent research into the response of YOTs, the police and social services to under-age offenders demonstrates that, at present, these young people stand a real risk of falling between perceived boundaries of agency responsibility (Giller 2003). Often YOTs confine their jurisdiction to those formally in the youth justice process (apprehended offenders aged 10 or over) while social services give no a priori status to these children as 'children in need', assuming that the social workers they fund and second to YOTs will identify and respond to such needs in appropriate cases.

It remains to be seen whether or not a more integrated response is engendered with Local Authority Chief Executives in England and Wales being encouraged by central government to implement a comprehensive preventative strategy to respond to the needs of children that face social exclusion, including the needs of offenders and pre-offenders. At present, the omens are not entirely positive in ensuring that YOTs are fully integrated into this process. For example, the initiative on Identification, Referral and Tracking (IRT) – now called

Information Sharing and Assessment (ISA) – from the Children, Young People and Families Directorate seemed to be launched in the face of, rather than in hand with, developments in YOTs. The IRT/ISA initiative requires the local implementation of a system to identify vulnerable children and to notify all relevant agencies of them, so encouraging a more co-ordinated response to the needs of children at risk of social exclusion. But by failing to provide a common definition of 'vulnerability' (each area is to reach its own locally relevant definition) or to scope the role and remits of agencies to provide an integrated response (e.g. case management and co-ordination roles) there is a serious risk that the needs of critical groups will be missed and that their social exclusion careers will continue to be addressed inadequately.

This issue is perhaps compounded when one appreciates that those most vulnerable to social exclusion often move between areas (due to homelessness or drifting lifestyles) and the boundaries of IRT/ISA in one area may not be exactly calibrated with those of its near or not-so-near neighbour. Moreover, the IRT/ISA initiative makes little or no cross-reference to the YJB initiative to encourage YOTs to establish Youth Inclusion and Support Panels (YISPs) to identify and respond to early age offenders (8–13 years). How YISPs will be integrated within a broader IRT/ISA strategy context will need careful local negotiation. It is hoped that by relocating responsibility for this initiative with the Department for Education and Skills there will be more proactive collaboration between responsible authorities within the context of the government's agenda for children's services *Every Child Matters* (DfES 2003) and the *Children Act* 2004.

Pre-court decision-making was intended to be fundamentally altered with the implementation of the *Crime and Disorder Act* 1998. The previous administratively regulated police cautioning system was to be replaced with a statutory scheme of reprimands (for minor first offending) and final warnings (for a second minor matter or a first apprehension for a mid-level offence). The pattern (often overestimated in its frequency) of providing young people with multiple opportunities to be diverted from the court system was to be broken. Moreover, the variation between police forces in their frequency of use of diversion decisions was to be reduced. YOTs were envisaged to have a significant role in what hitherto was usually a police-determined decision, both in the assessment of a young person's suitability for final warning and in the delivery of final warning interventions. As if to reinforce this message the YJB, early in its existence, stipulated in a performance measure that YOTs should deliver intervention programmes in 80 per cent of final warnings by December 2004.

In practice, not all of the legislative intent is being realised. While the rate of pre-court decisions over all youth justice decisions remains at 51 per cent, as with practice prior to the implementation of the change, the composition of those decisions is such that 34 per cent are reprimands and 16 per cent are final warnings. The aspiration of reducing variations between police forces in the use of pre-court decisions seems to have been somewhat thwarted. On recent figures some 40 percentage points separate the highest pre-court decision-making force from the lowest. YOTs are well on the way to delivering interventions in 80 per cent of final warning cases, although at a rate of cases much fewer than initially anticipated. Moreover, research into the initial implementation of the final warning process demonstrated that YOTs were frequently not engaged by the police in the assessment and decision-making process (Giller and Murray 2002), necessitating a change in the guidance on final warnings in January 2003 (Home Office and YJB 2003). Nevertheless, pre-court decisions remain an effective intervention for the early onset of offending. Using the reoffending cohort study currently run by all YOTs, some 77 per cent of offenders given a final warning do not reoffend over 24 months.

With respect to court interventions, the emerging evidence is that YOTs have gained a credibility and identity of confidence with courts. The introduction of the Referral Order, of course, has had a significant impact on the volume of cases requiring a court-based intervention. In 2002 some 23 per cent of court decisions were Referral Orders (Table 5.1) and during 2003 a whole micro-system of adjudication via Youth Offender Panels was established. While the development of Referral Order infrastructure has been an outstanding success, results as to its impact on offending are awaited.

Table 5.1   Distribution of sentence decisions 2002

Sentence decision	Proportion (%)
First tier penalties (of which 23% were Referral Orders)	71
Community penalties	22
Custodial penalties	8

Many of the newer orders introduced by the *Crime and Disorder Act* 1998 have not super-seded the more traditional orders and disposals available to courts. Indeed, the conditional discharge, which many foresaw as being abolished by the changes in legislation, continued to be used in excess of 8,000 cases in 2002. Restorative justice approaches, much heralded with the change of legislation, seem initially to have focused mainly on first-tier orders, although evidence is emerging of their wider use as part of community penalties.

It is with the use of custody and the secure estate, however, that the least movement or change is apparent and about which most concern has been expressed. Some 8 per cent of young people sentenced in courts currently receive custody decisions (about 7,000 young people per year) (Table 5.1) and the emerging evidence shows:

- misunderstanding by courts as to the level and quality of education and training provided in a Detention and Training Order;
- significant under-performance in aspects of the mandatory requirements of secure estate contracts; and
- non-integration of the role and work of the secure estate and YOTs.

While the YJB has committed itself to reducing the use of the secure estate, both with respect to remands and sentences, there is still a considerable distance to travel if these targets are to be met. Moreover, as with earlier research, the evidence continues to demonstrate significant variation in court cultures with respect to reliance on custody and the fact that, to date, neither the YOTs nor the YJB has found a strategy to break that culture.

With respect to the delivery of orders and programmes by the YOTs, the current initiatives of the YJB (2002) to implement an Effective Practice Quality Assurance (EPQA) process very much reflect the three themes of Roger's work mentioned at the start of the chapter. The Board has produced more than a dozen Effective Practice Guides covering significant elements of the YOT agenda, including remand management, offending behaviour programmes and the swift administration of justice. Each guide has been derived from a review of available research, with Web technology enabling YOT staff to access the source research reviews behind the Guide précis. A process of 'quality assuring' the delivery of effective practice has now commenced. YOT managers have been asked to self-assess their YOT on a number of practice areas prioritised by the YJB, namely final warnings; assessment and planning; education, training and employment; and parenting. These self-assessments have been evaluated by the Board and an agreed programme for performance improvement negotiated with each YOT. This programme of EPQA will continue to roll out in the coming years, with follow-up evaluations of the implementation of performance improvement programmes being undertaken within each YOT.

This strategy, based on research and effective practice, is currently being extended to the secure estate. While the YJB continues to exhort courts and the judiciary to restrain their custodial ambitions, the EPQA initiative seeks to develop effective regimes from within in order to reduce the demand for such services.

CONCLUSIONS

I began this analysis with a question about the extent to which juvenile justice in England and Wales has been informed over the recent past by three hallmark themes of Roger's work:

- the impact of research on policy and practice development;
- the appreciation of the need for a whole system approach to social interventions; and
- a practice context in which services are matched to children's needs.

Overall, I believe we can discern some distinct improvements in the way in which policy and practice have responded to the themes highlighted at the opening of this chapter. While the political dimension of youth justice remains as high, if not higher, than 40 years ago, the knowledge-base of what works and the knowledge of stakeholders have increased immeasurably (see, for example, Rutter et al. 1998). Awareness of criminological understanding and the impact that youth crime and the risk of youth crime have on developmental careers and social exclusion is now widespread at politician, manager and practitioner level. In no small measure the work of Roger and his colleagues at the Dartington Social Research Unit has been a significant beacon in illuminating an important area of social policy.

But how strong has this influence been? Initially, I think the Dartington Unit would have preferred to keep young offenders in the child welfare system, as their work has always emphasised the background characteristics and needs common to young offenders and disadvantaged children and adolescents. A separate system with its own staff training and assessment procedures for young people who happen to commit an offence seems illogical but, as explained, is politically more acceptable. Nevertheless, if separate career routes for children with many common needs cannot be avoided, the ethos and composition of YOTs is more to Dartington's taste. Multidisciplinary work, prevention strategies and community support are possible and emphasised within this approach.

This approach has been vindicated in the Audit Commission (2004) report *Youth Justice 2004*, which has evaluated the work of YOTs and reviewed their progress in the light of the earlier ambitions expressed in *Misspent Youth*. The Audit Commission is very complimentary, concluding that the 'new system is a considerable improvement on the old one' (p. 2). Young offenders are more likely to receive an intervention, the process is quicker, magistrates are more satisfied and offenders are more likely to make amends for their behaviour. On process developments, there is a recommendation for greater use of the community-based intervention ISSP (Intensive Supervision and Surveillance Programmes), an area in which Dartington research can be seen as influential. The Unit undertook a randomised-controlled trial evaluation of an early scheme in Kent (Little *et al.* 2004). The caution included in the sentence in the Audit Commission's report 'ISSPs are a more constructive and considerably cheaper option for persistent young offenders than a spell in custody, but they cannot be expected to reduce custody on their own' (p. 4) reflects the conclusions of the Dartington study.

One area that must be disappointing for Roger and his colleagues, however, is the high number of young people in secure settings. There has been a considerable increase since *Locking Up Children* was published (Millham *et al.* 1978) and the issues raised in that study continue to cause concern – high cost, abuse, poor outcomes, criminal cultures, over-representation of black and minority ethnic groups, and so on. Recent inquiries into the deaths of young people in custody, the poor management these have revealed and the concerns expressed by respected public figures, such as the Archbishop of Canterbury, may improve things but the political context for reforms in this area remains inauspicious.

But to end on a more upbeat note, the national coverage and good information systems provided by YOTs could help to respond to some of the themes that Dartington has long highlighted in relation to children's services. These include: consistency of service delivery to young people presenting similar needs; the balance between outcomes for children and families and performance management; how a multi-agency team can work effectively; the optimal arrangements for inter-agency collaboration; and the identification of children at risk of exclusion or with other pressing needs. As yet, authoritative lessons from YOTs cannot be drawn, but these wider spin-offs should inform the development of children's services as experience accumulates.

REFERENCES

Audit Commission (1996) *Misspent Youth: young people and crime*, London, Audit Commission.
Audit Commission (2004) *Youth Justice 2004: a review of the reformed youth justice system*, London, Audit Commission.
Bottoms, A.E. (1974) 'On the decriminalisation of the English Juvenile Court', in Hood, R. (ed.) *Crime, Criminology and Public Policy*, Oxford, Heinemann.
Bullock, R. (1989) 'Social research', in Kahan, B. (ed.) *Child Care Research, Policy and Practice*, London, Hodder & Stoughton.

Bullock, R., Little, M. and Millham, S. (1993) *Residential Care for Children: a review of the research*, London, HMSO.

Bullock, R., Little, M. and Mount, K. (1995) *Matching Needs and Services: the audit and planning of provision for children looked after by local authorities*, Dartington, Dartington Social Research Unit.

DfES (Department for Education and Skills) (2003) *Every Child Matters*, Cm. 5860, London, The Stationery Office.

Giller, H. (2003) *Information and Action on the Offending Behaviour of Children Under the Age of Criminal Responsibility: findings from a survey of police forces, YOTs and social services departments*, Unpublished report, Northwich, Social Information Systems.

Giller, H. and Murray, C. (2002) *Final Warning Implementation in 18 Police Force Areas*, Unpublished report, Northwich, Social Information Systems.

Home Office (1997) *No More Excuses: a new approach to tackling youth crime in England and Wales*, Cm. 3809, London, Home Office.

Home Office and YJB (2003) *Final Warnings Scheme: guidance for the police and youth offending teams*, London, Home Office.

Little, M., Kogan, J., Bullock, R. and Van der Laan, P. (2004) 'ISSP: an experiment in multisystemic responses to persistent young offenders known to children's services', *British Journal of Criminology* 44 (2), 225–240.

Millham, S., Bullock, R. and Cherrett, P. (1975) *After Grace – Teeth: a comparative study of the residential experience of boys in approved schools*, London, Human Context Books.

Millham, S., Bullock, R. and Hosie, K. (1978) *Locking Up Children: secure provision within the child care system*, Farnborough, Saxon House.

Morris, A. and Giller, H. (1987) *Understanding Juvenile Justice*, London, Croom Helm.

Newburn, T. (1997) 'Youth, crime and justice', in Maguire, M., Morgan, R. and Reiser, R. (eds) *The Oxford Handbook of Criminology*, 2nd Edition, Oxford, Oxford University Press.

Rutter, M., Giller, H. and Hagell, A. (1998) *Antisocial Behaviour by Young People*, Cambridge, Cambridge University Press.

YJB (2001a) *Corporate Plan 2001–2004*, London, Youth Justice Board.

YJB (2001b) *Findings from the Youth Justice Plans 2001/02*, London, Youth Justice Board.

YJB (2002a) *Youth Justice Plans 2002–2005*, London, Youth Justice Board.

YJB (2002b) *Youth Justice Board Counting Rules*, London, Youth Justice Board.

YJB (2002c) *Effective Practice Quality Assurance*, London, Youth Justice Board.

6

YOUNG OFFENDERS, MENTAL HEALTH AND SECURE CARE
A LIFE HAPPY THEREAFTER?

Sue Bailey

Wherever there are descriptions of the legal frameworks that apply to young offenders, theories of residential care relevant to detained young people and innovative, evidence-based thinking in the field of services for highly vulnerable adolescents, the name of Roger Bullock appears. His clear thinking, wisdom and patience have greatly influenced many who work in the mental health and youth justice fields.

Traditionally, health and mental health research, including child mental health, has focused on particular groups of children or specific disorders. The work of the Dartington Social Research Unit has provided an important impetus in helping child and adolescent mental health services (CAMHS) research to move from a sometimes tunnel vision approach to the complex panorama of children and their needs.

DEVELOPMENTS IN CHILD AND ADOLESCENT MENTAL HEALTH SERVICES

This much more encompassing view of child mental health was acknowledged by the NHS Health Advisory Service (1995) in its pivotal review of CAMHS in the UK, *Together We Stand*. For the first time, this iterated a strategic framework for the complex, systemic dynamics involved in the delivery of a comprehensive service. It brought together and clarified the various roles and interactions between the layers of the CAMHS service, defined its component parts and showed how effective multi-agency partnerships and communication could become a reality. The strategic four-tier framework is especially useful for complex, partnership-based, systemic services like CAMHS and has been adopted by the Audit Commission as a baseline for future planning.

Forty Years of Research, Policy and Practice in Children's Services.
Edited by N. Axford, V. Berry, M. Little and L. Morpeth.
© 2005 John Wiley & Sons, Ltd. ISBN 0-470-01219-6.

The tiered framework is intended, first and foremost, to be a strategic and planning tool. Its second purpose is to improve communication between participants involved in providing mental health services for children and adolescents. Only in third place does it act as a blueprint for how services should be delivered. The importance of this framework is that it promotes a better focus on the service functions required of mature, effective and efficient CAMHS by offering a model that spans the agencies involved and their working practices. The tiered approach has also created a common language for discussing services. This has enabled policy-makers, strategists, managers and practitioners to engage with an aspect of mental health service provision that was previously little understood and poorly resourced, with a growing gap between its potential and its capacity to deliver.

Thus the tiered approach:

- focuses on strategy rather than operational or organisational matters;
- relates to functions that are intended to meet the needs of the population at risk;
- denotes the nature of the service that children and young people are assessed as requiring; and
- is intended to promote flexible working patterns, which focus on the needs of children, young people and their families.

Tier 1 describes the frontline of service delivery. Tier 1 staff are not necessarily trained as mental health specialists but, by virtue of their first contacts with and their continuing responsibilities for young people and/or their families, they are well placed to recognise, assess and intervene with children's mental health problems. Tier 1 staff include GPs, health visitors, school nurses, teachers and other school staff, non-specialist children's social workers, foster carers and many non-statutory sector workers.

Tier 2 is the first line of specialist services. The staff include members of CAMHS, those working in education support services, including educational psychologists and specialist teachers, specialist children's social workers as well as some employees of voluntary organisations.

Tier 3 is the second line of specialist CAMHS and involves specifically trained professionals working together to provide a specialist mental health service for young people. Services at this level comprise both generic specialists and more focused services. Some young people and their families may require access to Tier 3 services as a consequence of the complexity of their need, the concentration of skill required by professionals or the crucial nature of the multidisciplinary and/or inter-agency planning needed to deliver an effective intervention. This tier also includes a variety of specialised clinics, day-care facilities, units in schools, fostering programmes and family centres.

Tier 4 services are highly specialised. They may not need to be available in every district but local specialist CAMHS will require predictable access to them. They include in-patient psychiatric services for children and adolescents and highly specialised clinics that can only be supported on a regional or national basis.

In addition to this strategic framework, a further significant development for child and adolescent mental health provision in recent years has been the emphasis on needs-led, evidence-based provision. This is manifested in the report *Right Start* (DoH 2003) and the establishment of a National Service Framework (NSF) for children that encompasses not only child health but also child mental health. This document constitutes a long-overdue recognition of what has been obvious to researchers at Dartington and elsewhere for many years, namely that nothing matters more to families than 'the health, welfare and future success of their children'. The NSF for children sets out a challenging agenda with three key objectives: to put children and their families at the centre of care; to develop effective partnerships so that the needs of the child are always considered; and to deliver needs-led services.

The task of implementing this agenda is not insignificant. Children and young people make up around one-fifth of the population of England. They have legally enforceable rights as children and their families have the right to have their family life upheld and respected. In designing and delivering services, providers must accommodate the needs of:

- 12 million children;
- 400,000 children in need;
- 60,000 looked-after children;
- 320,000 disabled children;
- 600,000 live births a year;
- one million children with mental health disorders (reflected in Chapter 7 of *Right Start*).

Thus, the importance of meeting the needs of all children, including those children in the youth justice system, is firmly acknowledged.

YOUTH JUSTICE SERVICES AND WELFARE NEEDS

The introduction to the evaluation of the Medway Secure Training Centre for young people (Hagell *et al.* 2000) describes the changing pattern of custodial options for and attitude towards young offenders in the UK over two centuries. In doing so it illustrates how concerns about the welfare needs of such young people have fluctuated. During the early nineteenth century, punishment and retribution dominated the approach to youth crime. The first penal institution reserved exclusively for male juvenile offenders opened at Parkhurst on the Isle of Wight, reflecting the emergence of childhood as a distinct social and legal category.

Following the *Youthful Offenders Act* 1854, reformers such as Mary Carpenter established a series of 'reformatories' as an alternative to youth imprisonment. Along with the industrial schools, they were expanded in the late nineteenth century following the *Gladstone Report* of 1895.

By the early twentieth century, elements of welfare, punishment and treatment were contained within legislative and juvenile justice policy, with the first *Children Act* 1908 (The Children's Charter) creating a distinct system of separate juvenile courts and abolishing the imprisonment of children under 14 years. The *Prevention of Crime Act* 1908 introduced Borstal training for young offenders aged 16 to 20 and a period of supervision in the community after release. Following the Maloney Committee Report of 1927, the approach to young people and crime became more firmly based on the welfare of young offenders and on treatments to reform them. The *Children and Young Persons Act* 1933 firmly embedded welfare principles in legislation with the opening of 'approved' or reform schools for young offenders and run by local authorities or voluntary organisations. Five years later, however, the changing emphasis in the punishment of young offenders was reflected in the recommendations of the *Departmental Committee on Corporal Punishment* 1938.

In the *Criminal Justice Act* and the *Children Act* (both 1948) attempts were made to prevent the placement of neglected children alongside offenders in approved schools. Local authority children's departments were established with their own resources for residential care and the *Children and Young Persons Act* 1963 raised the age of criminal responsibility from 8 to 10 years. However, the 1950s and 1960s saw a parallel increase in the number of young offenders sent to Detention Centres.

In 1964 the first of several 'secure units' opened for children aged 10 to 18, and they became the responsibility of social services departments. Stemming from this development a 'youth treatment service' with special secure provisions for disturbed young people was formulated, with 'intermediate treatment' as an alternative to custody. This involved support, supervision and activities for children living at home and remaining at school. Symbolically, responsibility for local authorities and therefore approved schools passed from the Home Office to the Department of Health.

In the *Children and Young Persons Act* 1969 approved schools were abolished and replaced by a system of local authority community homes with education (CHEs). These provided open and closed residential facilities for children and young people aged 10 to 18, including convicted offenders and other children in care. These new establishments set out to incorporate a child-centred regime, appropriate to individual welfare and treatment needs. The 1970s, although seeing a sharp decline in the use of care orders, saw the overall use of custodial sentences for juveniles increase from 3,000 in 1970 to 7,000 in 1978. Secure care provision was also growing and two Youth Treatment Centres, St Charles and Glenthorne, opened to provide specialised secure facilities for highly disturbed young people aged 10 to 18. These were some of the institutions studied by Roger and his Dartington colleagues (Bullock *et al.* 1998), research that still provides an important steer to current research and service development.

As many of us were starting our practitioner lives in our chosen field, we encountered a welcome emphasis on diversion from court and custody and the expansion of intermediate treatment programmes and intensive probation initiatives. It soon became clear in establishing this provision that children and young people had complex needs that required an integrated approach from health, including mental health services, and youth justice.

Legislation in the 1980s helped this development. The *Criminal Justice Act* 1982 introduced further restrictions on the use of custody for young offenders over 15 and extended the range of non-custodial options. The *Criminal Justice Act* 1988 merged Youth Custody Centres and Detention Centres into Young Offender Institutions and the *Criminal Justice Act* 1991 introduced new youth courts, bringing 17-year-olds within the ambit of juvenile justice law and policy for the first time. Custodial sentences for young offenders were further restricted to categories of serious offences and the UK government ratified the United Nations *Convention on the Rights of the Child* in the same year.

However, the mid-1990s saw a growing disillusionment with diversion from custody as recorded youth crime continued to rise. The popular press began to highlight persistent young offenders, with the juvenile justice system refocusing towards punishment, retribution and deterrence. In the *Criminal Justice and Public Order Act* 1994 Secure Training Centres for persistent young offenders aged 12 to 14 were introduced. Increases in the use of custody for young offenders were also apparent. The late 1990s saw an exceptional period of restructuring and overhaul of the system, including: a new statutory aim, the creation of the Youth Justice Board (YJB), the introduction of the Detention and Training Order, the replacement of the Secure Training Order, a new range of non-custodial sentences, an increase in the extent of criminal responsibility by children and the abolition of *doli incapax* for children aged 10 to 14.

Despite this mixed bag of reforms, the emergence at the dawn of the new millennium of an NSF for children and the rolling out of programmes from the YJB meant that the integration of service delivery was starting to be a fact rather than a vision. The child is seen as an individual rather than as flotsam and jetsam being buffeted through a system by the prevailing winds of policy and/or service change and there are now joint meetings between the Department of Health and the YJB with the described aim of meeting the health care needs of young people in the youth justice system.

CHILDREN IN RESIDENTIAL CARE

In their review of the research on residential care for children, Bullock and his colleagues (1993) delivered a scholarly analysis of studies undertaken before and after 1975, a turning point year with the publication of *Varieties of Residential Experience* (Tizard *et al.* 1975). The Dartington review set out longstanding research knowledge in the fields not only of delinquency but also of the mental health and social well-being of young people detained in locked institutions. It showed that young offenders and others with complex social and mental health needs shared common life pathways.

But the benefits of residence for the children were less clear. Bottoms and McClintock (1973) found no obvious differences in the subsequent nature and extent of criminality between two matched groups of 250/300 boys, one placed in a traditional Borstal – characterised by a rigid regime and activities in large groups – and the other experiencing a more experimental regime that stressed the individualisation of training. Similarly, when Cornish and Clarke (1975) followed up boys considered suitable for a therapeutic unit but allocated randomly to two contrasting regimes – one orthodox and the other therapeutic – they found few differences in subsequence reoffending that could be attributed to the different approaches.

There were also some enquires as to whether offenders were fundamentally different from other children. Gilbert (1972) studied girls aged 14 to 16, comparing 400 in approved schools with 200 in a secondary modern school in order to examine differences in background characteristics and factors relevant to delinquency. There were many similarities in the girls' backgrounds although the study demonstrated that the offenders had poor discipline from mothers, displayed greater anomie, perceived their parents' relationships with them differently and were from a lower socio-economic background.

In the early 1970s, the Dartington Unit undertook a comparative study of 18 approved schools for boys, examining their intake and stylistic variety and the care careers of the boys up to two years after leaving (Millham *et al.* 1975). It classified regimes into 'junior training', 'senior training', 'therapeutic', 'campus' and 'family group'. Outcomes for boys while resident varied considerably according to regime but the effects on later delinquency were much less marked. The regime differences only accounted for a 10 per cent variation in reoffending rates, much of which was due to boys' behaviour while there. The study also examined the informal worlds of the boys and staff to identify conditions that reinforced or challenged institutional goals, finding that in the less successful institutions there was clear evidence of a criminal, antisocial subculture. Similarly, in an intensive study of boys and staff at a boys' approved school, Tutt (1974) showed that tension and conflict existed where care and custody aims were concerned. Staff and boys adapted to achieve a *modus vivendi*. All of the studies outlined in this section laid the foundation for further work on the effects of interventions and the different career routes followed by children with similar needs.

THE CONTRIBUTION OF DARTINGTON RESEARCH

I became aware of the Dartington Social Research Unit in the course of working with Norman Tutt on estimating the number of children detained in the jurisdictions of health care, education and custody, prior to the introduction in 1983 of legislation on secure ac-commodation. This awareness became crystallised when I started to visit and give clinical opinions on young people detained in the St Charles and Glenthorne Youth Treatment Cen-tres, which in turn led to a longstanding, productive and, from my point of view, empowering relationship with Roger and his colleagues. This provided me with a bedrock from which to develop the early descriptive research studies of Adolescent Forensic Mental Health Ser-vices and continues to influence the current research programme carried out in collaboration with the University of Manchester, initially with the late Professor Richard Harrington.

At least five contributions by Dartington to the subject of this chapter may be identified. First, and drawing on previous work, Little and Bullock (2004) cut through the administrative policy and professional jargon to challenge the jurisdictions of health and justice to come together to delineate effective needs-led services for children with complex needs, some of whom present a high risk to others by virtue of conduct disorder and/or more formal mental disorder. Without dismissing the value of diagnosis, they rightly point to the importance of the professional, administrative and legal frameworks in which the young people's problems are addressed. They reiterate the sometimes understandable frustration, particularly on the part of social workers, that despite the young person's displaying an array of bizarre behaviours, the child and adolescent mental health assessment will read 'not formally mentally ill', with the result that the client is not viewed as suitable for hospital treatment. They point out that a feature of young people who become potential candidates for long-term security is their tendency to present problems that cannot be met effectively by a single agency or intervention. The serendipitous nature of the career routes of these children is also highlighted. Children enter one system and stay within it when their needs would be better met by another.

Second, the Dartington Unit has long stressed the need for a common language in children's services, not only between professionals and policy-makers but also involving the young people and their families and carers. As well as aiding inter-agency collaboration, this is intended to help to understand what happens to young people passing through administrative and legal systems.

Two dimensions of troubled children's lives have been used by the Dartington Unit in successive studies. One is 'life route' – the decisions that a young person and his or her carers make that affect the young person's life chances. In order to make an accurate prognosis about outcomes, it is necessary to compile a picture that begins at birth and covers all areas of a child's life. Events in one area, such as living situation, can affect others, for example family and social relationships. The concept of life route is an important and helpful conceptualisation for mental health workers because it incorporates the influence of the individual's personality on conduct. For very difficult young people, behavioural patterns reflect pathological conditions, such as conduct, emotional or mixed disorders, and pressing problems of running away, violence and offending need to be taken into account in any assessment. The other dimension is 'process', defined as the decisions made by professionals or courts in response to the young person's life route and which affect his or her life chances. Whether an adolescent is picked up by education, child guidance, social or health services will certainly make some difference to his or her long-term experience and possibly to outcomes.

This approach incorporates the background, circumstances, needs and pathologies of young people and their families as well as the interventions fashioned to ease difficulties. As such, it brings together two streams of research that are rarely connected. With so many variables contributing to an outcome, it helps if the interaction between the decisions of the child and family on the one hand and those of support agencies on the other is subsumed under the single term 'career route'. Decisions made at successive moments in a career will influence what happens subsequently. 'Career routes', so defined, are a useful way of categorising the situations of children and young people in need.

A third contribution of the Dartington Unit relates to the prediction of young people's life trajectories. The very difficult young people referred to welfare and control agencies for help will follow several different career routes and the subsequent classification developed by Dartington (see below) provides more than a taxonomy: it has predictive value, encouraging us to state within a reasonable margin of error what a troubled adolescent's future life chances will be. Prediction is a notoriously complicated process in child care, especially in view of those individuals who display risk factors but do not succumb to the behaviour being predicted – 'false positives' in research parlance. Predicting the future for young people known to be very difficult, however, is somewhat easier since the starting point is the high-risk case already known to welfare or control agencies (Little 2002).

The Dartington study of long-stay secure treatment units in England identified five groups of young people (Bullock *et al.* 1998):

(1) those long in local authority care who exceed the capabilities of good open residential provision;
(2) those long dealt with by special education, school psychology and mental health services;
(3) those previously unknown to control and welfare agencies whose behaviour deteriorates in mid-adolescence;

(4) those who commit a one-off grave crime;
(5) persistent delinquents who also commit a serious offence.

Such a classification would be of limited interest if the five groups had no predictive power but, with a reasonable degree of confidence, Bullock and his colleagues are able to say what a long-term state care case (group 1) or an 'adolescent eruptor' (group 3) will be doing in two or five years' time. There is some indication about where they will be living, what kinds of family and social relationships they will enjoy, how much trouble they will get into and whether they will go to school, get a job, fall ill or move about. Further, they argue that, once known to health, education and social services, most cases behave predictably and that this information can be used to design an effective response to young people's problems.

The fourth perspective offered by the Dartington work concerns the need for a systematic method to achieve effective services accurately targeted at the right children. Little and Bullock (2004) rightly stress that much has been written about linking the concepts of needs, threshold, services and outcome, and note that some research teams have worked closely with local authorities to put these ideas into practice. The aim of these exercises is to encourage agencies to move from offering isolated initiatives to ones that prioritise risk, introduce eligibility criteria, encourage practitioners to respond creatively to the needs of children and families and adopt a perspective that sees all services as integral to a continuum, each part of which is useful to different individuals at different moments in their care careers.

Although this has been a principle of child protection for some time, it has been a late arrival to the scene of dangerous, high need adolescents. This may be because it is not easy to achieve. Children's marginality is frequently accompanied by their notoriety: any single individual can encompass both welfare and justice concerns. All too often, such young people have been marginal to available interventions and the specialism of the specialist centres becomes their ability to 'pick up the pieces' as opposed to delivering validated therapy. This finding resonates with the responsibilities that have been placed upon community adolescent forensic services across the UK. Moreover, the public consensus is that the young person should be locked up, even though he or she is usually a victim of abuse and disadvantage. Hence, the high proportion of young people with learning difficulties and mental health disorders in detention.

The fifth contribution of Roger and his colleagues relates to what happens to young people after they leave care or detention. It is sobering to note that the environment to which young people return remains depressingly constant and is a reminder of the importance of education, housing and employment opportunities for those who are disadvantaged (Little and Bullock 2004). Whilst aiming to state that outcomes are moderately good and predictable, follow-up studies of leavers from long-stay Secure Treatment Centres urge cautious optimism. A positive situation of the ages of 18–21 is no indication of 'a life happy thereafter'. Many young people have stored up problems of health or isolation that revisit them later and many are settled in happy domestic relationships that come under strain in subsequent years. Most of the grave offenders have been law-abiding but still have to be considered a long-term risk to the public.

The relative lack of scientific and practice knowledge about what happens to disordered young people between the ages of 18 and 30 is striking. In the past, researchers and professionals have tended to view young adults as merely adolescents writ large, focusing on unfinished tasks, such as educational underachievement, and failing to look to the future and encourage what will help them as adults, such as late entry into continuing education or social skills to stay in work. Little and Bullock (2004) ask for more evidence to be extracted on how careers develop, whether or not protective factors continue to operate and how long the effects of treatment last. They say that only by looking at what happens in the very long term can we know whether the cautious optimism resulting from achievements to date is well founded.

IMPROVING THE MENTAL HEALTH OF YOUNG OFFENDERS

Looking at the progress since the early 1990s in meeting the mental health needs of young offenders, we have come some way down the road of reform. In a previous work (Bailey 1992), I noted that mental health services for juvenile offenders would need to function effectively within a complex, ever-changing system. This requires being alert to the total clinical profile of the individual and not just referred offence behaviour, being proactive in multi-agency liaison and treatment programmes and making the best use of scarce research resources. At the time, the increase in violent acts committed by adolescents together with concern about the quality of care and treatment offered to juvenile offenders had caught the attention of the public and politicians, leading to persistent demands for action. The challenge was to bring together the various agencies involved to deliver integrated care.

Heightened concern at this time was epitomised by Leibling's (1991) comprehensive study of suicide and self-injury amongst young offenders. As well as describing the components that made up the vulnerability and situational triggers, their varying contribution to individual crises and their possible protecting agents, she made suggestions for the safer care of juveniles in custody. In 2004, levels of suicide in youth custody remain high, although there has been much work on how to meet young people's needs safely, for instance by improving health provision in the establishments and transferring health responsibility in prisons to the National Health Service (NHS). By 2006 all local Primary Care Trusts in England will be commissioning health services for prisons in their area. We have also seen the development of forensic secure mental health beds, now nationally commissioned. Indications of this change include the current provision of NHS beds in Newcastle and Manchester, the opening of a 24-bed unit in Birmingham (incidentally, on the old Glenthorne Youth Treatment site) and plans for developing similar provision in London and the South.

Other developments aimed at improving the mental health of young offenders concern practice and training. The YJB has complemented its assessment tool (ASSET) with a mental health screening tool for use by youth justice workers (YJB 2003). I developed this by me with colleagues working in Manchester and it is used in training health workers in Youth Offending Teams and staff in Youth Offender Institutions and local authority secure children's homes.

Mental health awareness training has also been rolled out into the youth justice system. Under the umbrella of the NSF for children, the Children's Care Group Workforce Team and the Mental Health Care Group Workforce Team are collaborating to develop strategies to deliver a 'fit for purpose' workforce that can take a developmental approach to working with young people wherever they are in the system. Child and adolescent mental health development workers are now in place and can act as facilitators to improve joint working and local access to services through the use of generic mental health workers based in CAMHS and/or in Youth Offending Teams.

Research is contributing to the improvement of services. This is apparent in several areas. In a review of the literature, I have brought together findings on the background, nature, assessment, treatment and outcomes of those young people who have committed grave crimes (Bailey 1997a). The review cites Boswell (1995), who describes vividly the prevalence and nature of abuse and loss in the lives of such offenders, as well as research on the nature of the medical, legal, clinical, assessment and treatment interventions with adolescents who murder (Bailey 1996, 1997b). It also examines the challenges of working directly with sadistic and violent young people using verbal and non-verbal therapies and the psychosocial characteristics of juvenile sex offenders (Dolan *et al.* 1996).

Parallel to these developments, Loeber and Hayes' (1997) description of developmental pathways to aggression in adolescence and adulthood is being refined. Cicchetti and Newcombe (1997) have highlighted the importance of developmental psychopathology as the bridge across fields of study that span the life cycle and have clarified the process underlying adaptation and maladaptation, as well as the best means of preventing or ameliorating psychopathology. The application of this approach to the field of adolescent offenders offered a positive way forward for future research. Thus, by the turn of the millennium, psychosocial and biological factors placing young people at risk of offending and of developing mental health problems were well established in the national and international literature (Bailey 1999).

Also by this time, Dartington's book about the care careers of very difficult adolescents, *Secure Treatment Outcomes*, had been published, exploring the concepts of career prediction, protective factors and chains of effects (Bullock *et al.* 1998). A major international research review of antisocial behaviour by young people appeared in the same year (Rutter *et al.* 1998), while in the USA Kazdin and Weiss (1998) provided an important review offering a framework to help practitioners to consider and develop their own treatment interventions and monitor progress. The availability of official statistics and the increasing quality and sophistication of research data, particularly the longitudinal studies, meant that research could now inform both policy-makers and practitioners about those interventions most likely to reduce reoffending rates in young people and have a positive impact on their mental health.

Following on from these epidemiological and needs surveys of young people referred to CAMHS, specific studies were undertaken in the field of child and adolescent forensic mental health. These revealed a lack of appropriate services to meet the needs of young people at the interface of mental health and criminal justice, a situation already highlighted in Dartington's work and developed further in the specific field of mental health by Kurtz and her colleagues (1998). This major national survey highlighted the perceived extent and severity of psychiatric disorders among young people placed in different secure provision, whether in social care or penal establishments. It stressed the wish of non-health professionals to receive training, consultation and liaison services both from CAMHS and the then evolving specialist adolescent forensic mental health services.

At this time research opportunities arose for me to work more closely with the Department of Child and Adolescent Psychiatry at Manchester University, the team led by the late Professor Richard Harrington. With like-minded practitioners and researchers in Manchester, we paralleled some of the thinking of the Dartington team with the development and validation of the Salford Needs Assessment Schedule for Adolescents (Harrington *et al.* 1999; Kroll *et al.* 1999). This provided the starting point for a series of research projects looking at the mental health needs of young people in the criminal justice system, both within Youth Offending Teams and Secure Units. We utilised this schedule not only in dissemination to increase understanding of the mental health needs of young people in the criminal justice system but also to develop mental health screening tools and frameworks for intervention. The studies included the *Mental Health Needs of Boys in Secure Care for Serious or Persistent Offending*, the first prospective longitudinal study of its kind (Kroll *et al.* 2002).

CHALLENGES FOR RESEARCH, POLICY AND PRACTICE

Having recently completed a review of the research literature in the field of young offenders and mental health (Bailey 2003), I can see how far we have travelled over the last 20 years. Certainly we have a rapidly developing knowledge base about the life routes of these young people. It remains to be seen, however, if the increasingly promising findings from evaluations of prevention, early intervention and treatment programmes delivered to children and adolescents in the context of families, communities and institutions can reduce the burden on adult mental health, social care and criminal justice services. A further challenge is how best to engage children and families that are hostile or difficult to reach.

Key longitudinal studies continue also to inform what programmes should be taken forward and what this means to society in financial and human costs (Farrington 2002; Moffitt *et al.* 2002). The ongoing Dunedin and New Zealand Study of young people, led by Moffitt and her colleagues (2002), is testing and refining a developmental taxonomy of antisocial behaviour and is making challenging recommendations about interventions for all aggressive children and adolescent offenders. Smith and McVie (2003) are engaged in the early stages of an innovative longitudinal study in Edinburgh that concentrates on transitions and personal transformations during adolescence, integrating explanations at the levels of the individual and the social ecology.

The search for the Holy Grail of what turns a child with difficulties into an adult with an antisocial personality disorder continues, as does the search for the most promising early interventions. Reflected in recent research conducted by Little and Bullock (2004) around specific interventions, the literature suggests that the most promising interventions need to be multi-modal, intensive, well-structured and lengthy, and include multi-systemic therapy, functional family therapy, treatment foster care, multi-modal cognitive behavioural packages and some therapeutic communities.

Research needs to cover detailed assessments of the characteristics of the individual at the outset of an intervention and at long-term follow-up of a treatment series if it is to detect the stage at which additional intervention is required and the effects of additional top-up interventions. Other necessary conditions for improving mental health services for young offenders are clear definitions in research of risk and protective factors, detailed descriptions of interventions, methods of identifying high-risk adolescents and ways of ensuring that troubled adolescents are perceived as a priority rather than a last resort (Bailey 2002). This should include not only interventions directly with adolescents to reduce reoffending, in the context of evidence-based provision, but research into policy development itself.

The single most important challenge to all researchers, policy-makers and practitioners is how to provide a workforce that is 'fit for purpose' and empowered through education and knowledge. Central to this process is how to garner the views of the young people themselves about what interventions work for them, how the intervention should be delivered and how they can be involved in research projects. In the field of public education, for instance in the Royal College of Psychiatry's project Changing Minds Campaign – Cycles of Understanding, the challenge is to provide innovative ways of enabling young people to interact with professionals and so become levers for change in terms of their own reduction of reoffending and mental health promotion.

CONCLUSION

The research of Roger Bullock and his colleagues at Dartington into difficult-to-manage children, young offenders and their mental health will live on in the work of those who continue to develop the ideas discussed in this chapter. From the patience and time he has given to practitioners like me, whom he has helped to become active in research, we can now hopefully begin to see the long-term benefits of evidence-based practice in the lives of the most marginalised and alienated young people in society – young offenders with mental health problems.

Research over the last 20 years in the speciality of child and adolescent forensic mental health has put us in a position to develop an effective model for delivering forensic CAMHS. Research is now able to inform planned programmes of clinical work, suggest long-term outcomes and incorporate the children's views of their world and treatment experience. This will have to include the difficult moral dilemmas posed by the real world of limited finances for services. More challenging will be research and development that looks not only at what works but also how it engages reluctant children and families. We may also have to live with a society and government that may pass judgement on whether it is all worth it. Research into the process of care, linking inputs to outputs and costs with effectiveness – including the effect on demand for specialist CAMHS by Youth Offending and Children's Looked After Teams – will help guide what we hope will be ethical and safe future practice.

REFERENCES

Bailey, S. (1992) 'Delinquency in context', *Current Opinion in Psychiatry* 5, 778–782.
Bailey, S. (1996) 'Adolescents who murder', *Journal of Adolescence* 19, 19–39.
Bailey, S. (1997a) 'Adolescent offenders', *Current Opinion in Psychiatry* 10, 445–453.
Bailey, S. (1997b) 'Sadistic and violent acts in the young', *Child Psychology and Psychiatry Review* 2 (3), 92–102.

Bailey, S. (1999) 'The interface between mental health, criminal justice and forensic mental health services for children and adolescents', *Current Opinion in Psychiatry* 12, 425–432.

Bailey, S. (2002) *Antisocial Personality Disorder: children and adolescence*, Expert Paper, NHS National Programme on Forensic Mental Health Research and Development, London, Department of Health.

Bailey, S. (2003) 'Young offenders and mental health', *Current Opinion in Psychiatry* 16, 581–591.

Boswell, G. (1995) *Violent Victims: the prevalence of abuse and loss in the lives of Section 53 offenders*, London, The Prince's Trust.

Bottoms, A. and McClintock, F. (1973) *Criminals Coming of Age*, Oxford, Heinemann Publications.

Bullock, R., Little, M. and Millham, S. (1993) *Residential Care for Children: a review of the research*, London, HMSO Publications.

Bullock, R., Little, M. and Millham, S. (1998) *Secure Treatment Outcomes: the care careers of very difficult adolescents*, Aldershot, Ashgate.

Cicchetti, D. and Newcombe, B. (1997) 'Conceptual and scientific underpinnings of research and developmental psychopathology', *Development and Psychopathology*, Special Edition, 9 (2), 189–472.

Cornish, D. and Clarke, R. (1975) *Residential Care and Its Effects on Juvenile Delinquency*, London, HMSO Publications.

DoH (2003) *Getting the Right Start – National Service Framework for Children: emerging findings*, London, Department of Health.

Dolan, M., Holloway, J., Bailey, S. and Kroll, L. (1996) 'The psychosocial characteristics of juvenile sex offenders', *Medicine, Science and the Law* 36, 343–352.

Farrington, D.P. (2002) 'Key results from the first 40 years of the Cambridge study in delinquent development', in Thornberry, T.P. and Krohn, M.D. (eds) *Taking Stock of Delinquency: an overview of findings from contemporary longitudinal studies*, New York, Kluwer Academic Publishers.

Gilbert, J. (1972) 'Delinquent "approved school" and non-delinquent "secondary modern" girls', *British Journal of Criminology* 12, 325–356.

Hagell, A., Hazel, N. and Shaw, C. (2000) *Evaluation of Medway Secure Training Centre*, London, HMSO Publications.

Harrington, R.C., Kerfoot, M. and Verduyn, C. (1999) 'Developing needs-led child and adolescent mental health services: issues and prospects', *European Child and Adolescent Psychiatry* 8, 1–10.

Kazdin, A.E. and Weis, Z.J.R. (1998) 'Identifying and developing empirically supported child and adolescent treatment', *Journal of Consultant Clinical Psychologists* 66, 19–36.

Kroll, L., Woodham, A., Rothwell, J. *et al.* (1999) 'The reliability of the needs assessment schedule for adolescents', *Psychological Medicine* 29, 891–902.

Kroll, L., Rothwell, J., Bradley, D., Shah, P.E., Bailey, S. and Harrington, R.C. (2002) 'Mental health needs of boys in secure care for serious or persistent offending: a prospective longitudinal study', *The Lancet* 359, 1975–1979.

Kurtz, Z., Thornes, R. and Bailey, S. (1998) 'Children in the criminal justice and secure care systems: how their mental heath needs are met', *Journal of Adolescence* 21, 543–553.

Leibling, A. (1991) *Sentenced to Death? Suicide and Self Injury Amongst Young Offenders in Custody*, London, Routledge.

Little, M. (2002) *Prediction: perspectives on diagnosis, prognosis and interventions for children in need*, Dartington, Warren House Press.

Little, M. and Bullock, R. (2004) 'Administrative frameworks and services for very difficult adolescents in England', in Bailey, S. and Dolan, M. (eds) *Adolescent Forensic Psychiatry*, London, Arnold.

Loeber, R. and Hayes, D. (1997) 'Key issues in the development of aggression and violence from childhood to early adulthood', *Annual Review of Psychology* 48, 371–410.

Millham, S., Bullock, R. and Cherrett, P. (1975) *After Grace – Teeth: a comparative study of the residential experience of boys in approved schools*, Brighton, Human Context Books.

Moffitt, T.E., Caspi, A., Harrington, H. and Milne, B. (2002) 'Males on the life-course-persistent and adolescent-limited antisocial pathways: follow-up at age 26 years', *Development and Psychopathology* 14 (1), 179–207.

NHS Health Advisory Service (1995) *Child and Adolescent Mental Health Services – Together We Stand*, London, HMSO.

Rutter, M., Giller, H. and Hagell, A. (1998) *Antisocial Behaviour by Young People*, Cambridge, Cambridge University Press.

Smith, D.J and McVie, S. (2003) 'Theory and method in the Edinburgh study of youth transitions and crime', *British Journal of Criminology* 43,169–195.

Tizard, J., Sinclair, I. and Clarke, R.V.G. (eds) (1975) *Varieties of Residential Experience*, London, Routledge & Kegan Paul.

Tutt, N. (1974) *Care or Custody: a study of boys' approved schools*, London, Darton, Longman & Todd.

YJB (2003) *Screening for Mental Disorder in the Youth Justice System*, London, Youth Justice Board.

7

STABILITY THROUGH ADOPTION
FOR CHILDREN IN CARE
SOME MESSAGES FROM RESEARCH

June Thoburn

INTRODUCTION

Adoption is not an area of child welfare research in which Roger Bullock has 'majored', but his work has had an important impact on the way in which other researchers have looked at adoption as an appropriate placement for some of the children in care who cannot return safely to their parents. He has done this in three ways. First, his work on young people in residential settings has indicated that a 'care career' lacking in stability can result in some very troubled young people finding their way into closed residential or custodial settings: *After Grace – Teeth* (Millham *et al.* 1975) (incidentally, as one of my colleagues would say, a book title 'to die for').

Second, Roger's work on children going home has demonstrated that adoption will be a placement of choice for only a minority of children coming into care, since most will sooner or later go back home or to home environments – *Going Home* (Bullock *et al.* 1993) and *Children Going Home* (Bullock *et al.* 1998). This work also gave pointers to the circumstances when going home would be most fraught with difficulty and adoption should be seriously considered.

Third, and the area that has had most impact on my own research, is his work on contact and other links between children in long-term care and their family members. This theme has permeated his writing but there were some particularly powerful messages about how to make contact work (or not work) in *Lost in Care* (Millham *et al.* 1986). Roger's ability to bring this broader child welfare perspective to adoption research made an important contribution to the researchers' workshops at Dartington that were part of the lead-up to Roy Parker's overview of Department of Health commissioned studies on adoption, *Adoption Now: messages from research* (DoH 1999).

Forty Years of Research, Policy and Practice in Children's Services.
Edited by N. Axford, V. Berry, M. Little and L. Morpeth.
© 2005 John Wiley & Sons, Ltd. ISBN 0-470-01219-6.

In this chapter I shall concentrate on adoption for children in care in the UK. I use the term 'in care' because that has been the agreed term for most of Roger's research career, and 'children looked after' is clumsy and will have little meaning for Roger's overseas readers. After looking at the sorts of children who are adopted from care, I shall move on to look at what we know about outcomes and the factors associated with better or worse outcomes for the different groups of children. I shall focus on the two themes where Roger's work has most relevance and where there is disagreement between researchers about how findings should be interpreted in practice: the respective places of long-term/permanent foster care and adoption as 'routes to permanence' (Thoburn and Rowe 1985) and the impact on stability and long-term well-being of continuing contact with birth family members. The chapter ends with some thoughts about changes that may result from the implementation of the England and Wales *Adoption and Children Act* 2002. As well as drawing on my own research and that of colleagues at the University of East Anglia and elsewhere, my thinking has been influenced by my work as an expert witness in complex adoption cases – an activity which Roger also undertakes, so that we have been able to discuss the particular challenges involved.

WHICH CHILDREN ARE ADOPTED FROM CARE?

The first point to make is that there have been many changes in the characteristics of children placed for adoption during Roger's career. The 1950s and 1960s saw the peak of placements of very young children at the request of their parents; very few children were placed from care without parental consent, and adoptions from care that did happen were mainly by foster parents already caring for the child. That started to change with the publication of Rowe and Lambert's (1973) seminal work *Children Who Wait*, which had a major impact on the *Children Act* 1975. That Act made it more possible for children to be adopted from care, usually following the termination of parental contact.

Since then, the adoption of relinquished infants has declined and the majority of adoptions are of children in care, mostly against the wishes of their parents. The 1975 Act, and research from the USA that indicated that it was possible to successfully place older children who might have been in care for many years, coincided with the move to close children's homes and rely more heavily on foster care. Many of the children placed for adoption in the 1970s and 1980s (including many of African-Caribbean origin and mixed heritage who were previously considered 'unadoptable') had spent many years in children's homes. Many were 'lost in care' and had long been out of contact with birth parents. This is in contrast to those being adopted from care since the 1990s, very few of whom will have been in care for very long periods of time and even fewer of whom will have lived in residential care for more than a few weeks as a transition placement. Having been in care for shorter periods, they are more likely still to have links with birth parents and, for some, the importance of causing additional harm through the loss of these links has been recognised by a higher frequency of adoption with continuing birth family contact.

It is therefore very important, when considering adoption outcome research, to take account of the date when a particular cohort of children joined their adoptive families and the implications in terms of the likely characteristics of the children and their pre-adoption experiences. A range of child characteristics may have an impact on whether or not the placement is successful. Because of the very different pre- and post-adoption careers of children placed as infants and those placed when older, they need to be considered separately. It is now an accepted fact that the adoption of an infant can be a solution for only a tiny minority of the involuntarily childless. Very few (if any) UK infants are now placed directly for adoption by voluntary adoption agencies without first coming into care, and very few adopted children (somewhere between 200 and 300 in England each year) are infants placed at the request of their parents (Ivaldi 1998, 2000; Neil 2000).

However, this is not the whole picture as far as the adoption of infants is concerned, since increasing numbers are now coming into care following 'pre-birth' child protection conferences. From a cohort of nearly 300 infants and toddlers placed for adoption when under 4 years old, Neil (2000) concluded that they fell into three groups: around a third (mostly very young) were 'relinquished'; around a third were more complex cases but ultimately the case was not contested in court; and around a third were adopted from care against the wishes of their parents. In 2001, 3,400 of the 58,700 children and young people in the care of English local authorities were placed with their prospective adopters and only 210 of these were under 1 year of age. Of the 1,600 children in care whose legal status was 'freed for adoption' only 80 were aged under 12 months. When we look at the 3,100 actually adopted during the year, 200 were adopted under the age of 12 months (National Statistics and Department of Health 2002).

In response to the Prime Ministerial initiative (PIU 2000), after a long decline in numbers adopted, the number and proportion of children adopted from care is rising. This rise is accounted for by rising numbers of children placed between the ages of 1 and 5. In the 1980s and 1990s the face of adoption changed with the reporting by voluntary and some local authority adoption agencies of their successes in the placement for adoption of older children with complex histories and difficulties. Although some in these age groups are still being adopted (often by the foster parents with whom they have lived for some time) it is to the placement of younger children that attention has primarily turned. (In 1996, 28 per cent of children placed for adoption from care were aged 5 or over, and in 1998 this had dropped to 21 per cent.)

Although statistics are improving with the publication of annual adoption figures (National Statistics and Department of Health 2003), it is not easy to tell the age at placement since children already living with the foster families who decide to adopt them (14 per cent of those 'placed for adoption' in 2001) are recorded as 'placed' at the date that a decision was taken that this was in their best interest and not the date they actually joined the family. A child recorded as placed for adoption at the age of 8 may actually have been living with the prospective adopters (the current foster carers) since the age of 8 weeks.

The largest group of children adopted from care, then, are those who came into care as pre-schoolers. Of these, the majority will have spent some time with their parents. Most will have suffered the adverse impact of being separated from a parent with whom they had at least a beginning attachment and many will have been exposed to adverse circumstances, often including maltreatment, neglect and/or multiple parenting. Once in care, some will be placed with a foster carer who subsequently applies to adopt (including a small number of infants involved in the 'concurrent planning' pilot schemes evaluated by Monck *et al.* (2003)) or spend a month or so with a short-term foster carer before joining an adoptive family. At the other end of the continuum, children may have been exposed to multiple changes of carer, possibly including return home to a birth parent or relative before returning to care as happened to some of the children in the Dartington *Going Home* studies. These children will join their new families when older and a substantial proportion will have emotional and behavioural problems resulting from these experiences.

Other groups of children placed from care for adoption include a small number coming into care when older, many of whom will have suffered severe trauma including physical and sexual assault and serious neglect resulting from living with a parent with severe mental health or addiction problems, domestic violence or frequent moves within the family. Some of these will be the older members of sibling groups and will have played a quasi-parenting role to their younger brothers and sisters. The placement of sibling groups poses considerable dilemmas and has been researched in separate studies (Mullender 1999; Rushton *et al.* 2001) or as a subcategory in more general cohort studies (Fratter *et al.* 1991; Thoburn *et al.* 2000). Other groups for whom different variables need to be considered when researching process and outcome are children with disabilities, and children of minority ethnic origin.

THE PLACEMENT AND SOCIAL WORK PROCESSES

While some researchers look only at outcomes, or look for associations between child and family variables and outcomes, most consider whether some aspects of process are associated with more or less successful outcomes. The placement process can be considered in terms both of the decisions taken and also the approaches to helping the different members of the 'adoption triangle' at different stages in the life history of the adoptive and birth family.

The main decisions taken are:

- Should this child be placed with a permanent substitute family?
- Should the placement be made via adoption or as a foster placement (possibly leading to a Residence Order – or now, Special Guardianship Order)?
- Should the child be placed with a sibling or separately from siblings?
- What sort of contact should there be with parents, relatives, siblings or previous carers?
- What sort of family will have the best chance of meeting the child's needs?
- What sort of financial support will be needed by whom (for example, help to parents to retain contact, adoption allowances or one-off grants)?

Throughout the 'life history' of what has been referred to as the adoptive kinship group (encompassing the child's kin by birth and by adoption, whether or not they are in contact) questions will arise as to how best to help, support or provide therapy to adults and children, whether additional help is needed with education and whether additional assistance and advice are needed with health problems or disabilities.

The other side of the decision-making process is what sort of families should be encouraged to come forward to adopt children from care, how should they be assessed, approved and trained, and what processes are going to result in the most appropriate match between the hopes, capacities and skills of the new parents and the needs of the children?

HOW DO WE MEASURE 'SUCCESS' AND HOW SUCCESSFUL IS ADOPTION?

A range of research outcome measures is to be found. The most frequently used, especially in the larger cohort studies, is whether the placement lasted or disrupted within varying lengths of time. In some US research, and more recently in UK policy documents, achieving legal adoption is used as the measure of success. This results in higher reported 'success rates' than for those studies that follow through for a period of years after legal adoption. The UK government is aware of the limitations of this approach and is consulting on ways of measuring adoption outcome in the long term (as they are able to do with foster care since these children remain within the system).

At the moment the only 'official measure' routinely available is whether children come into care from adoptive families, but this hides the number of cases when, for example, adopters struggle on and the placement breaks down in adolescence without the child coming back into care. In any case, 'starting to be looked after [in care] from an adoptive family' is not a reliable measure of adoption breakdown, as it is not routinely recorded whether the family from which the child comes into care is an adoptive family.

Other researchers consider well-being as an outcome measure. In recent years these have been influenced by the work initiated at workshops at Dartington led by Roy Parker and resulting in the *Looking After Children* dimensions of well-being (Parker *et al.* 1991). Subjective measures, such as the satisfaction of adopted people and adopters, are available from some small-scale qualitative studies and some postal surveys. Very rarely are data collected on the well-being or satisfaction of birth parents or relatives.

Using disruption rates as a measure, studies that have followed up large enough cohorts of children placed for adoption from care with families not previously known to them conclude that the 'breakdown rate' for children placed past infancy is around 20 per cent (Barth and Berry 1988; O'Hara and Hoggan 1988; Thoburn 1990; Fratter *et al.* 1991). However, this figure can be seriously misleading, since outcomes will differ for different groups of children. Also, by definition, by the time we can estimate long-term success, especially for children placed when young, we will be considering the policy and practice of some 15 to 25 years previously. Much may have changed in the meantime, both in respect of the children needing placement and the policies and practices in use.

Age at placement is a 'proxy' variable for many other characteristics that are found in more or less successful adoptions. Thus, if the placement of infants under 6 months is being considered, the disruption rate is likely to be under 5 per cent, while, for children placed between the ages of 10 and 12, it is likely to be around 50 per cent. Studies that look at the 'satisfaction' of adopters and adopted adults with the experience of growing up adopted show less variation, with around 80 per cent of adopters and adopted young people being generally satisfied with the experience and 20 per cent expressing dissatisfaction.

When those adopted as infants express dissatisfaction, it is usually around questions of identity and not knowing why they were adopted (Howe 1992, 1996; Howe and Feast 2000).

VARIABLES ASSOCIATED WITH OUTCOME

Child and Birth Family Variables

As indicated above, the variable most strongly associated with placement success or breakdown is the age of the child at placement. Once over 6 months, the risks increase, but it is also important to note that some older children do well and that there are success stories in respect of young people placed even in late adolescence. Similarly, some young people placed as infants do not thrive emotionally in adoptive placements. Children who are known to be emotionally or behaviourally disturbed at the time of placement are more likely to experience placement breakdown, as are children who have a history of maltreatment prior to placement (Fratter *et al.* 1991; Gibbons *et al.* 1995; Rushton *et al.* 1995; Quinton *et al.* 1998). A 'softer' variable identified by some researchers is that children and young people who do not want to be in this placement, or who do not want to change their legal status to that of adoption, are more likely to experience placement breakdown. I have referred to this as the 'cutting your losses' factor, although it is important to make a distinction between wanting to find a place in a new family and attitudes towards continuing contact with birth family members (Thoburn 1996; Thoburn *et al.* 2000). Some will only be willing to 'cut their losses' on the first family if they can go on having contact with them – a point to which I will return. To give an example, a teenager well settled in her new family said:

> I don't hate my mum. I suppose I love her because she is my mum. We used to get on sometimes, and sometimes we never used to. I'm glad we didn't stay with her.

Adoptive Family Variables

Looking at easily measurable characteristics such as age or marital status is not particularly helpful when reaching conclusions about the sorts of families who are most likely to be successful adopters for children in care. Some studies of long-term foster families have concluded that having a birth child close in age to the adopted child is associated with less successful placement. The good news is that a very wide range of parents can be successful adopters. Successful families describe a wide range of motivations. What seems to be important is that self-directed motives, such as wanting to become a parent, are combined with an element of altruism (showing up in the ability of the parents to empathise not only with the child but also with his or her biography, and thus to develop an understanding of the problems in the birth family which led to the need for placement). Other characteristics identified by researchers as important are: enjoying spending time with children and being family-centred; being highly sensitive towards the emotional life of the child; accepting the child for who he or she is; being sensitive and proactive around birth family issues; and providing active parenting in respect of education, activities and life skills.

The Crucial Importance to Success of the Matching Decision

Although post-adoption support and appropriate and appropriately timed therapy can make a difference when adoptive families are under stress, my research on adoption leads me to the conclusion that the most crucial part of the social worker's role is finding the placement that has most chance of meeting all the child's identified needs. This will include the ability to empathise with the child, and having the skills and competence to meet any special needs associated with the child's physical or learning disability or emotional or behavioural problems. Finding a family that can keep a sibling group together, if that is considered to be in their interests, and finding a family of a similar ethnic background and culture, are also important aspects of securing the best possible fit between the new family and the child. It will also mean finding a family that is comfortable with the legal status that is most appropriate to the child's wishes and circumstances and new parents who are able to facilitate appropriate continuing contact with birth parents, adult relatives, siblings and previous carers to whom the child has become attached.

The Impact on Adoption Outcomes of Continuing Birth Family Contact

Most studies that have looked at this question conclude that being placed with at least one sibling is associated with the placement lasting into adulthood. When siblings are separated, quantitative and qualitative studies indicate that there is an association between continued contact with siblings and more successful outcomes (Fratter et al. 1991; Rushton et al. 2001). It is also clear that, in the vast majority of cases, this is what children want; indeed they long for it if it is denied them.

Most children also want to stay in contact with birth parents, relatives, friends and former foster parents (Thomas and Beckford 1999). A recently conducted survey of the views of over 700 children in care, including some whose adoptive placements had broken down, demonstrates how often children's wishes are not respected when it comes to contact. When asked if they saw enough of the family members with whom they wanted to remain in contact, 39 per cent reported that they had insufficient contact with their mothers, 60 per cent with their fathers, 37 per cent with siblings and 49 per cent with other relatives (Timms and Thoburn 2003).

Recent studies of adoption practice indicate that some form of direct or indirect contact between the birth and adoptive families occurs in over 80 per cent of cases (Lowe and Murch 1999; Neil 2000). However, the research on contact after adoption often does not state clearly enough the form that contact takes. Studies that have specifically considered whether some form of direct post-adoption contact with birth parents had an impact on rates of disruption have concluded that it is either a protective or a neutral factor (Fratter et al. 1991; Sellick et al. 2004). In the UK, direct post-adoption birth family contact is most likely to be arranged in respect of children placed when over the age of 3 or 4, whereas indirect 'letter-box' contact is most likely for the youngest children (Neil 2000). However, research from the USA, where continuing contact with birth parents happens more frequently for infants, indicates that it is most likely to be a positive factor and present few, if any, problems for those placed when young (Grotevant and McRoy 1998). Qualitative studies, involving interviews with adopters and with adopted young people, indicate that post-adoption contact does not impede the growth of attachments and that it can lead to some adoptive parents having a greater sense of entitlement to be the child's parents (Neil 2004; Smith and Logan 2004).

Clearly, there are cases when post-adoption contact is either inappropriate or likely to be harmful. These include cases where the child is consistently saying that he or she does not wish to go on seeing the parent or relative, or children demonstrate by their behaviour that they are afraid of the parent. The research on adoption with contact was debated in articles by Quinton and his colleagues (1997), Ryburn (1997) and Quinton and Selwyn (1998).

Long-Term Foster Care or Adoption?

A recent study by Lowe and Murch (2002) found that long-term fostering rather than adoption was more likely to be the eventual outcome for children who could not safely go home if they: were over 4 years of age; had emotional or behavioural problems; were of minority ethnic origin; had a history of physical or sexual abuse; and were attached to their short-term foster carers. Foster care was also more likely if a previous attempt at reunification with birth parents had been unsuccessful. Thoburn and her colleagues (2000) found that ethnic minority parents were more likely than white parents to opt for long-term fostering rather than adoption. That study found that African-Caribbean parents in particular were more likely to encourage continuing contact with birth parents after placement and to say that one of the reasons why they preferred to foster was that it did not feel culturally appropriate for them to sever links totally between children and their relatives by birth.

The policy and practice literature, qualitative data and data from court cases indicate that, for 20 years or so, long-term fostering has, for most authorities, either been discounted as a 'permanence option' or been seen as very much second best. For children under 10 years, a long-term foster home is usually not sought unless the child remains adamant that he or she does not wish to be adopted or an attempt to find an adoptive family has been unsuccessful. Yet this position is not supported by evidence from research. Disruption studies with sufficient numbers to control for age and other mediating variables conclude that, when like is compared with like, there is no difference in breakdown rates between those placed for adoption and those placed in foster families with the intention that they will become long-term members of the foster family (Thoburn 1990; Fratter et al. 1991; Sellick et al. 2004). When young people, adopters and foster parents are interviewed in the course of (usually smaller scale) studies, it is clear that some prefer and are more satisfied with being an adoptive family and others prefer the foster care route to family formation. The following comment from a young woman who joined her long-term foster family when aged 10, and who was adamant that she would not have wanted to be adopted, shows the potential complexity of young people's attitudes:

> I didn't want people to think that they were our real mum and dad, but at the same time I wanted them to think that we were just family instead of being adopted. When I talk to people about Annie it's easier to refer to her as my auntie. They know she is not my mum. When I was little I was teased about being fostered – they used to think we were adopted – like we had some kind of disease.

The conclusion I draw from a range of studies is that, for some children and some families, only adoption will be appropriate; for some children and some families, only foster care will be appropriate; and for the majority in the middle, what is needed is a family that can meet their needs and where they can put down roots, knowing that they are not going to be moved on. For these children, looking at the same time for either an adoptive or a permanent foster family will be the approach most likely to avoid unnecessary delay and avoid children feeling let down if what they are told is the 'best option' – adoption – does not materialise.

The research evidence in support of this conclusion has been available for at least 10 years, but this is an area where it has not been heeded, as the push to achieve adoption targets has kept long-term foster care off the permanence agenda. Similarly, in the drive to increase adoptions, Neil's (2000) research and my work as an expert witness indicate that findings on the importance of placing siblings together and of birth family contact are often not taken on board. Children's needs for contact can all too easily be placed at the bottom of the 'hierarchy of need' because it is believed that meeting these needs will hinder the search for an adoptive family or delay placement.

Variables Concerning Social Work and Other Services

Messages from research about the sort of social work service that birth and adoptive families and adopted young people find helpful have much in common with findings from general research on social work effectiveness. Social workers need to be well informed, especially about the special issues around adoptive family life and the special needs of the child. They will offer support to the adopters in dealing with difficult behaviour, and managing contact and liaison with schools, but will leave the adopters 'in the driving seat'. They must be reliable and accessible and establish a relationship of trust. When the child needs specialist therapy, whether because of physical disabilities or educational or emotional problems, the social worker must engage energetically with the adopters in seeking out the sort of help that makes sense to family members.

Prior to placement, the main role of the social worker is to provide information to the child about what is happening and to undertake relationship-based work to help the child to make sense of why he or she can no longer live with the birth family. This will contribute to an assessment of the child's needs and wishes – essential at the matching stage to ensure that important needs are met by the new family. When deciding how to work with the child and young person after adoption, partnership with the new parents is essential. Sometimes workers will provide one-to-one work with the child, but more often they will work through the adopters.

Work with the birth parent at the time of placement has to involve the provision of a combination of support, information and advocacy. Often, the role of the social worker will be to ensure that these services are provided by a worker from a voluntary agency, or a lay advocate working with the parents' solicitor. Although 'grief work' may be helpful after the legal processes are completed and the pattern of contact with the agency and the child and adoptive family has settled down, in the early stages of placement and during the court processes, parents rarely find 'counselling to cope with loss' helpful, yet this is often all that its offered. Its refusal is often seen as a sign that the parents will be 'uncooperative' and therefore that direct contact will be inappropriate. There is very little research on what helps birth relatives, but the research available indicates that birth parents and relatives rarely receive the sort of service that they find helpful (Neil 2003).

SOME REFLECTIONS ON THE IMPACT OF THE *ADOPTION AND CHILDREN ACT* 2002

Although the legislative framework for adoption has now been set, much detail remains to be filled in by guidance and judicial interpretation. The interplay between human rights legislation and the *Adoption and Children Act* 2002 will be of crucial importance to children, adopters and birth parents. Although the child will be a party (and a Children's Guardian will be appointed) when a Placement Order is made giving permission for the child to be placed for adoption without the consent of the parents, it appears that the child will not normally be a party in the final adoption hearing. It is not clear whether birth parents, who retain parental responsibility despite having lost their right to oppose the adoption, will be able to get legal help to give their views to the court on whether the particular adoption plan is appropriate for their child. They may, for example, have strong views about the splitting of siblings when the care plan called for them to be placed together.

The way in which these issues of representation are decided will give a strong message about how policy-makers and child placement agencies are resolving the tension between the need to place a child quickly (and meet government targets on adoption) and the need to place the child with a family that has the best possible chance of successfully meeting his or her needs. If the child is not represented there will be no opportunity for those familiar with research to present expert evidence (as Roger has done to some effect in the past) on, for example, the likely impact on the child of being separated from siblings and having infrequent or no contact with them. Speed is clearly of crucial importance for an infant, and the question of matching is usually less complex than for an older child. But for older children, undue haste can lead to important needs not being met, thus increasing the risk of placement breakdown. The crudity of the targets in terms of time between the different stages of the process pays little heed to research that would point to a very different set of 'time-limits' for children of different ages.

The new legislation brings adoption into line with the *Children Act* 1989 as the child's welfare is the paramount consideration. But there is a complex interaction between wishes, needs and welfare. In the cases of the many children in care who need placement, there can be legitimate debate about the priority to be given to different aspects of welfare. For example, is it always better for a child to be adopted rather than to remain in a stable long-term foster home, even when no adopter can be found who is willing to meet the child's expressed need to continue to see his or her mother and siblings? With a shortage of adopters, especially for older children, we can quickly get into a situation where the wishes of the prospective adopters not to facilitate direct contact between the child and members of the birth family take precedence over the child's wishes to continue to see them. Can a child's needs be said to be met if strongly held wishes are overruled? What justifies the overruling of children's clearly and consistently expressed wishes?

The vigilance of the caring professions will be needed as much as it ever was to ensure that, in a climate of targets and shortage of resources, the adoption and child placement services keep children's needs and wishes at the top of the policy and practice agenda. Moreover, researchers who have Roger Bullock's talents for observing and communicating the impact of policy and practice on the lives of children and parents are as necessary now as they have been throughout his career. I end with a quotation from a young woman who responded to the *Your Shout!* survey (Timms and Thoburn 2003):

> See what decision the child wants to make before you jump to things, think about what the child wants, it could come out good in the long run . . .

REFERENCES

Barth, R. and Berry, M. (1988) *Adoption and Disruption: rates, risk and responses*, New York, Aldine de Gruyter.

Bullock, R., Little, M. and Millham, S. (1993) *Going Home: the return of children separated from their families*, Dartmouth, Ashgate.

Bullock, R., Gooch, D. and Little, M. (1998) *Children Going Home: the re-unification of families*, Aldershot, Ashgate.

DoH (Department of Health) (1999) *Adoption Now: messages from research*, Chichester, John Wiley & Sons.

Fratter, J., Rowe, J., Sapsford, D. and Thoburn, J. (1991) *Permanent Family Placement: a decade of experience*, London, BAAF.

Gibbons, J., Gallagher, B., Bell, C. and Gordon, D. (1995) *Development after Physical Abuse in Early Childhood*, London, HMSO.

Grotevant, H.D. and McRoy, R.G. (1998) *Openness in Adoption: exploring family connections*, Thousand Oaks, CA, Sage.

Howe, D. (1992) 'Assessing adoptions in difficulty', *British Journal of Social Work* 22 (1), 1–15.

Howe, D. (1996) *Adopters on Adoption*, London, BAAF.

Howe, D. and Feast, J. (2000) *Adoption, Search and Reunion: the long-term experiences of adopted adults,* London, The Children's Society.

Ivaldi, G. (1998) *Children Adopted from Care*, London, BAAF.

Ivaldi, G. (2000) *Surveying Adoption*, London, BAAF.

Lowe, M. and Murch, M. (1999) *Supporting Adoption: reframing the approach*, London, BAAF.

Lowe, N. and Murch, M. with Bader, K., Borkowski, M., Copner, R., Isles, C. and Shearman, J. (2002) *The Plan for the Child: adoption or long-term fostering*, London, BAAF.

Millham, S., Bullock, R. and Cherrett, P. (1975) *After Grace – Teeth*, Brighton, Human Context Books.

Millham, S., Bullock, R., Hosie, K. and Haak, M. (1986) *Lost in Care: the problems of maintaining links between children in care and their families*, Aldershot, Gower.

Monck, E., Reynolds, J. and Wigfall, V. (2003) *The Role of Concurrent Planning: making permanent placements for young children*, London, BAAF.

Mullender, A. (ed.) (1999) *We Are Family: sibling relationships in placement and beyond*, London, BAAF.

National Statistics and Department of Health (2002) *Children Adopted from Care in England: 2000/2001*, London, Department of Health.

National Statistics and Department of Health (2003) *Children Adopted from Care in England: 2001/2002*, London, Department of Health.

Neil, E. (2000) 'The reasons why young children are placed for adoption: findings from a recently-placed sample', *Child and Family Social Work* 5 (4), 303–316.

Neil, E. (2003) 'Accepting the reality of adoption: birth relatives' experiences of face-to-face contact', *Adoption and Fostering* 27 (2), 32–43.

Neil, E. (2004) 'The contact after adoption study: face-to-face contact', in Neil, E. and Howe, D. (eds) *Contact in Adoption and Permanent Foster Care*, London, BAAF.

O'Hara, J. and Hoggan, P. (1988) 'Permanent substitute family care in Lothian – placement outcomes', *Adoption and Fostering*, 12 (3), 35–38.

Parker, R.A., Ward, H., Jackson, S., Aldgate, J. and Wedge, P. (1991) *Assessing Outcomes in Child Care*, London, HMSO.

PIU (Policy Innovations Unit) (2000) *The Prime Minister's Review of Adoption*, London, The Cabinet Office.

Quinton, D. and Selwyn, J. (1998) 'Contact with birth parents in adoption: a response to Ryburn', *Child and Family Law Quarterly* 10 (4), 349–361.

Quinton, D., Rushton, A., Dance, D. and Mayes, D. (1997) 'Contact between children placed away from home and their birth parents: research issues and evidence', *Clinical Child Psychology and Psychiatry* 2 (3), 393–413.

Quinton, D., Rushton, A., Dance, C. and Mayes, D. (1998) *Joining New Families: a study of adoption and fostering in middle childhood*, Chichester, John Wiley & Sons.

Rowe, J. and Lambert, L. (1973) *Children Who Wait*, London, ABAFA.

Rushton, A., Treseder, J. and Quinton, D. (1995) 'An eight-year prospective study of older boys placed in permanent substitute families', *Journal of Child Psychology and Psychiatry* 36 (4), 687–695.

Rushton, A., Dance, C., Quinton, D. and Mayes, D. (2001) *Siblings in Late Permanent Placement*, London, BAAF.

Ryburn, M. (1997) 'In whose best interests? Post-adoption contact with the birth family', *Child and Family Law Quarterly* 53, 53–70.

Sellick, C., Thoburn, J. and Philpot, T. (2004) *What Works in Adoption and Foster Care*, Barkingside, Barnardos.

Smith, G. and Logan, J. (2004) *After Adoption: direct contact and relationships*, London, Routledge.

Thoburn, J. (1990) *Success and Failure in Permanent Family Placement*, Aldershot, Gower/Avebury.

Thoburn, J. (1996) 'Psychological parenting and child placement', in Howe, D. (ed.) *Attachment and Loss in Child and Family Social Work*, Aldershot, Avebury.

Thoburn, J. and Rowe, J. (1985) 'Routes to permanence', *Adoption and Fostering* 9 (1), 50–54.

Thoburn, J., Norford, E. and Rashid, S. (2000) *Permanent Family Placement for Children of Minority Ethnic Origin*, London, Jessica Kingsley.

Thomas, C., Beckford, V. with Murch, M. and Lowe, N. (1999) *Adopted Children Speaking*, London, BAAF.

Timms, J. and Thoburn. J. (2003) *Your Shout!*, London, NSPCC.

8

GOING HOME OR STAYING AWAY

WHAT IS BEST FOR LONG-STAY FOSTER CHILDREN?

Ian Sinclair

INTRODUCTION

Should long-stay foster children go home? The answer, of course, is that it depends. What is thought best must vary with the child and also with the priorities of those making an assessment. This chapter sets out to explore these complexities. In doing so it builds on one of the more influential streams of work of the Dartington Unit.

The nature of the Unit's influence bears, perhaps, a moment's reflection. Like other units involved in social research, this one finds things out. Its influence, however, depends on more than simply its findings. Typically these come packaged and enlivened by jokes, historical allusion, the telling turn of phrase. The medium is less than the message but is nevertheless an important part of it. So it is that the title *Lost in Care* has carried an emotional punch which is more than the statistical findings that underlie it.

Roger Bullock's part in this impressive output is perhaps more difficult to discern. The Unit's publications are usually co-authored. Only the most advanced textual critic would be able to identify sentences drafted by Roger or by other hands. And so for my picture of him I have had to rely on his talks. These I have unfailingly found witty, perceptive, enlightening and wise. One of the instructions to those preparing papers for this festschrift is that the odd funny story about Roger would not come amiss. Certainly I can remember funny stories that Roger himself has told. I know, however, of none about him. Thoughtful, discreet and kindly, he is for me the author of jokes and certainly not the butt of them.

That said, there is reason for thinking that Roger is interested in the topic of the chapter. He is the senior author of the Unit's two main publications on going home from the care system. Most of the Unit's work since its pioneering forays into the public school system have had to take seriously the relationship between a child or adolescent's life when placed

Forty Years of Research, Policy and Practice in Children's Services.
Edited by N. Axford, V. Berry, M. Little and L. Morpeth.
© 2005 John Wiley & Sons, Ltd. ISBN 0-470-01219-6.

away from his or her family and the family itself. So, in a festschrift in his honour it is not inappropriate to look at:

- the Dartington Unit's account of the relationship between the child looked after in the care system and his or her birth family;
- how far research on longer staying children in the care system bears out or modifies these conclusions;
- the implications of the above for policy practice and research.

In this exploration I will rely particularly on research that my colleagues and I have just completed on children in foster care at a particular point in time (Sinclair *et al.* 2004a, 2004b). The nature of the sample explains most of any apparent differences between the conclusions I reach and those reached by the Dartington Unit. The latter focuses on all those who enter the care system. Depending on the date of the study, between a half and two-thirds of those who enter the care system go home within 6 months and the majority of these do so within 4 weeks. It is likely that ideas about this whole group will differ in emphasis from ideas directed at the much longer staying group who are picked up by sampling those in the care system at a particular point in time.

BIRTH FAMILIES AND LOOKED AFTER CHILDREN: THE DARTINGTON WORK

In their book *Going Home* (Bullock *et al.* 1993), Roger and his colleagues set the experience of removal and return in the context of the Second World War. They link the difficulties of return to those foretold by Winnicott when wartime evacuees were returning to their families. In this way they call attention to the impact of impersonal forces (for example, war and the policy decisions of governments) on the very personal relationships of children and their families.

This context for viewing the experience of children is to my mind of a piece with the evocative title *Lost in Care* (Millham *et al.* 1986). It picks up themes in the dreams and quotations with which Roger and his colleagues illustrate their book: the children's need for an explanation of why they were removed, their fear that their parents were lost or damaged. It picks up, too, the striking image of the 'river of rootless adolescents'. Deliberately, perhaps, this image recalls *The Waste Land:*

> A crowd flowed over London Bridge, so many,
> I had not thought death had undone so many.
> (Eliot 1999)

This, too, was a conscious quotation from Dante, a vision of the souls of the damned.

This imaginative approach to the experience of children in the care system is rhetorical. It is designed to persuade. 'Lost in care' resembles other key phrases – 'shock and awe', 'twilight housing' and a 'land fit for heroes' come to mind. It encapsulates an emotion and implies an approach; it does not summarise evidence but rather asks us to look at it in a certain way. Nevertheless the phrase is not, in my view, illegitimate. The view compels precisely because it picks up something important about the way these children and young people see the world. It inclines us to do everything possible to return them to the lost Eden of their families.

Such myths may well be an essential part of an effective policy process. Over the past 40 years or so three major strands of thought have dominated policy on children in the care system. First, there has been the rise of the belief that family care is best. This has led to a dramatic reduction in the proportion of children looked after in residential as against foster care. Second has been the growing belief that children are best looked after in their own families and that any separation from family should, if possible, be brief. Third has been an increasing commitment to the idea that delinquency and a failure to attend school are best seen either as the result of some kind of deprivation – and hence dealt with as a child care problem – or as a temporary adolescent aberration which does not call for heavy-handed legal intervention.

The pictures behind these strands are, in a sense, myths, albeit myths that partake of some truth. They call up images of loving foster families, forbidding residential establishments, families struggling against hardship and essentially innocent children. They determine action. In particular, the belief that 'birth family' is best has meant that effectively children are now looked after in the care system for any length of time only if they lack a family (as in the case of unaccompanied asylum seekers), have been subject to very severe abuse or have fallen out with their families to the extent that they cannot live together.

These myths may also lead to potential contradictions. At the moment, for example, children are only looked after in residential care if they are seen as very difficult indeed. This is the consequence of a family ideology which both restricts the use of residential care and emphasises the need for residential units to be as small as possible. As a consequence of these trends, residential care continues to be extremely expensive (somewhere between £1,200 and £1,600 per week per place) and takes up more than half the money available for looked-after children. This, in turn, reduces the money available for 'family style' care in long-term foster placements and increases the pressure to return foster children home. So, one set of pressures selects a group of children for whom return home is likely to be difficult. Another set of financial and ideological pressures encourages it.

For these reasons myths need to be balanced with analysis and evidence. Policy should not be purely sentimental. It should depend on more hard-headed and detailed arguments, and these are also provided by the Dartington Unit. The crunch argument is that the vast majority of children, according to the Unit upwards of 87 per cent, will eventually return to their families. As the Unit also pointed out, the time that they are away from their parents is marked by considerable upheaval, not least the arrival or departure of step- or real siblings and of transient adult males. These changes must make the apparently inevitable return more difficult and less likely to succeed. So it is logical to accelerate what must, in any case, be. Policy should be based on returning children as quickly as possible to the families of their birth.

The Unit places these arguments in the context of other pressures. As is well known, frontline staff, faced with a limitless well of child need, give priority to children in need of 'protection'. Despite these priorities, very few – perhaps about one in seven – of those about whom child protection concerns are raised actually make it to a child protection conference. Very few indeed – perhaps around 5 per cent – are actually removed from home as a result. At present looked-after children consume around two-thirds of the money spent by social services on children (for more precise estimates see Sinclair and Gibbs (2002)). So in equity there is a strong argument for refocusing the resources of social services departments away from looked-after children and towards the very much larger numbers who are in some sense 'in need'. If this is to be done, the rapid and efficient rehabilitation of looked-after children is a necessary part of the policy.

How, then, is this policy of rehabilitation to be implemented? In considering this issue, the Unit leans – as others have done before – on the strong correlation between a looked-after child's contact with his or her birth family and return home. In its own study (Millham *et al.* 1986) it showed that contact was much more common among children who had recently been placed than among those who were still looked after 2 years later – an effect which the figures suggest reflected the greater likelihood of those with frequent contact returning home rather than a drop in the frequency of contact over time. The Unit also made important distinctions between formal and informal barriers to contact. Informal barriers include the attitudes of foster carers. Formal ones are pre-eminently prohibitions on contact and the effects of distance from home. The greater the distance from home the lower the frequency of contact is found to be.

Return home is not, in itself, sufficient. It also needs to be in the interests of the child. In its exploration of what might promote these interests, the Unit has examined both activities in the care system and the activities of social workers both during and after the period a child is looked after. These interests have preoccupied it at rather different periods in its history. Its study of the long-term effects of care has largely been conducted in relation to residential care. Its exploration of social work and the natural history of return has been more recent. This later work has taken in the whole care system. As most of those looked after are fostered it has inevitably focused most on foster care.

The work on the long-term effects of residential care suggests to me two conclusions. First, the maintenance of changes depends to quite a large degree on the way a child or young person is treated on return to his or her home. Second, lasting changes in young people occur in part because of changes in the way they see themselves and consequential changes in the way others interact with them and see them. This view contrasts with a perspective based on a narrow interpretation of social learning. The latter would suggest that young people learn specific behaviours and attend selectively to the cues which prompt them and the rewards that flow from them. This learning can be studied without reference to the way the behaviour fits in with the young people's view of themselves or the way others view them.

I will return to these theses later. For the moment I need only note the evidence for them from the Unit's own work. A key emphasis has been the need to take account of the children's subsequent environments. In the Unit's work on return they emphasise that this is something that needs to begin the moment a child enters the care system. It is at this point that the family may either keep open a place for the child to return to or effectively begin to close it down. More generally, they have emphasised the influence of broader social forces – for example, the way in which children's careers subsequent to leaving the care system have depended on the kinds of jobs available to them. In their study of two secure units they found that one had significantly better results in terms of reconviction and other measures of social adjustment than the other. The secure units differed in a variety of ways – not least in their espousal of a basically psychoanalytical as against a learning theory approach. The Unit explains the differences in outcomes on the basis that one secure unit had developed a way of working with families which the other had not (Bullock *et al.* 1998).

Their work on the relationship between outcomes and meaning is illuminated by an early controversy concerning reconviction. Some had argued that this was simply a matter of social learning. Young people learned to behave in a delinquent way because this was a logical response to their situation and they were 'rewarded' for doing so. The success of residential establishments in changing this pattern would depend on whether these provided alternative and competing responses to these difficulties (e.g. work skills as a way of acquiring reputation and money) and on whether these were rewarded after the young person left (e.g. whether work was available). In contrast to this, the Unit argued – correctly in my view – that much depended on whether young persons changed their view of themselves and on how they were seen by and interacted with others. For example, it was not only important that work was available to them but also that they saw themselves as workers, and that key figures in their world treated them as such.

This earlier work on the long-term effects of care complements the later study of social work and the natural history of return home. In the latter the focus is on the birth family, the social worker and the child's interactions with these. Little is said about the foster or residential home and their effects. The main conclusions are that successful return home is a process which, as discussed above, needs to start from the moment a child begins to be looked after. Much depends on the symbols of belonging. Children who have their own room with their own things kept for them are more likely to make a successful return. Purposeful social work which keeps these places open, focuses on barriers and proceeds in a committed, planned way is essential for success. Subsequent to arrival there is a process of accommodation, often a quarrel and achievement of a *modus vivendi* that is much helped by success in roles outside the home – a job held down or success at school.

This work on the natural history of return is in a sense the culmination of the Dartington Unit's research on the relationship between looked-after children and their birth families. As we have seen, the contributions of the Unit to this topic are wide and varied. In my view they include the following:

- a perspective – an imaginative and compelling insight into the way we should view the experience of being looked after;
- a policy steer – arguments which emphasise the inevitability and appropriateness of policies designed to return children home within the shortest practicable time;
- practice priorities – the identification of practices which are, in Dartington's view, likely to further the policy of rehabilitation;

- exploration of effects – findings which bear on the long-term effects of being in care on subsequent events;
- accounts of the natural history of return and of the kind of practice likely to promote successful return.

How far does the Unit's work on these issues fit with other research?

BIRTH FAMILIES AND LOOKED-AFTER CHILDREN: OTHER RESEARCH

There are few, if any, direct contradictions between the work of the Dartington Unit and that of others. Other studies, however, do emphasise different points. The result, I think, is a tension or dilemma. The points that Dartington has emphasised are true. The inferences they draw from them are plausible. At the same time there are other points to be made and other plausible inferences that could be drawn. Most of this tension centres on the issue of how desirable or otherwise it is to return looked-after children to their families. I will look first at this and then at the evidence on contact and the long-term effects of care.

Home or Away – What Do Foster Children Want?

One point on which both Dartington and other researchers agree is that the great majority of looked-after children want to remain connected to their families. The acid test here is whether they want to be adopted. In our study (Sinclair *et al*. 2004a, 2004b) very few did – probably around 1 in 10 of those over 5 years of age. Most of the others had never entertained the idea of adoption. Those who have been forced to consider it were often passionately opposed to it.

The desire not to be adopted was quite compatible with a wish not to live with their birth family. We asked the children what they wanted to do. The majority of those replying said that they wanted to stay on with their current foster carers until they were over 18. A sizeable minority (between 40 and 50 per cent) wanted to remain until they were over 18 or 'for ever'.

These wishes were quite compatible with a wish to see more of their family. Contact with family has risen substantially in recent years – a tribute to the impact of the Dartington ideas. In our study nearly half (44 per cent) of the sample were in at least weekly contact with at least one member of their family (other than cohabiting siblings) when we first met them. So, frequent contact with family, a common desire for more family contact and a common wish to remain with birth family suggests both a need for and a preoccupation with some accommodation between the birth family and the current foster family.

In practice, children seemed to desire one of four possible adaptations:

- to return to the birth family with little or no contact with the foster family which was either disliked or seen as a threat to family relations;
- to return to the birth family accompanied by frequent contact with the foster family;

- to remain with the foster family while having continuing contact with the birth family;
- to remain with the foster family with as little as possible contact with a birth family that was feared, disliked or otherwise seen as preventing the child from getting on with her or his own life.

The case studies suggested that these adaptations were pursued with varying degrees of ambivalence. Some children wished to return to parents who wanted them. Others wanted to return to families who continued to abuse them and who blew hot and cold over whether they wanted them at all. Some were clear that they loved their family or members of it but had nevertheless come to the conclusion that their family's life was not for them. In these cases some wanted continuing contact – sometimes to enable them to keep an eye on their feckless parents. Others wanted to cut their ties and forget their past. One child was fed up with her social worker's wish to dwell on the past: 'I want my foster mother to adopt me. Nobody ever talks to me about that.'

These findings are elaborations rather than contradictions of those of earlier studies. Most admissions to the care system are voluntary. It may be objected that there is often little choice. If parents and children did not agree, compulsion would be used. Nevertheless others have found that requests for accommodation often fit the wishes of both parents and children. In the study by Packman et al. (1986) most parents in some sense wanted those admissions that were voluntary. Even where compulsion was used, around 50 per cent of parents eventually admitted that removal to the care system had been a good idea. A central idea in the study by Fisher et al. (1986) of short-term admissions was that separations of children and family had always been common and were seen as a way in which families managed rather than as the antithesis of family bonds.

Home or Away – What Are the Effects of Return?

So far this evidence suggests the need for a differentiated account of the relationship between foster children and their families. It is a matter of horses for courses, not of 'family good, foster care bad': different things work for different children. Disturbingly, however, birth families in our study seemed, on average, to have a negative impact on rehabilitated children. The findings also need to be associated with findings on the effects of return home. At the end of 3 years, 16 per cent of our sample were with their birth families. A rather higher proportion (23 per cent) had returned there at some point but had either moved on or returned to the care system. Those who returned to their families seemed to do worse at school, were more likely to be re-abused, and exhibited more behavioural problems than those who did not. These effects did not apparently reflect the characteristics of the children themselves. Certainly they were not surprising in the light of our case studies. These illustrated successful returns but also ones in which children were pressed by their mother to sleep with their stepfather, told by their mother that her suicide attempts were the child's fault, and expected to take responsibility for their mother's mental health.

This evidence is not unique. Barbara Tizard (1977) demonstrated the superior results of adoption over return home among children placed early in residential nurseries. Surprisingly, even at the age of 8, the admittedly small group of children still in residential care ($n = 7$) were doing better on the criteria used than those with birth families. In keeping with this finding there is at least some evidence that among children who enter the care system, those who stay longer tend to do better in various ways – being more likely to thrive psychologically (Hensey *et al.* 1983) and physically (King and Taitz 1985) if younger, and less likely to be involved in delinquent or other difficult activity if older (Zimmerman 1982; Minty 1987, 1989; Taussig *et al.* 2001). Children who return from residential homes to families that are 'disharmonious' or otherwise difficult often do badly there (Sinclair 1971, 1975; Quinton and Rutter 1988) although they may do comparatively well away from home (Sinclair 1971, 1975). By contrast, children removed from appalling conditions often do surprisingly well, a point made – albeit not totally consistently, since much depends on age and so on – by studies of children brought up by animals, locked alone in rooms or chained to radiators for years at a time (e.g. Koluchova 1976; Skuse 1984).

What Are the Effects of Contact?

In keeping with these results our study also put contact between child and birth family in a more equivocal light than is currently fashionable. Most children wanted more of this contact than they received. Nevertheless they could distinguish between types and purposes of contact and they did not necessarily wish to see all the members of their family. So a child might want to see more of her grandmother, be happy to see her mother with supervision, wish never to see her stepfather again, and be happy to have telephone contact with a sibling in Scotland but not to have to have the trouble of going up to see her. As others have found, foster carers were somewhat ambivalent about contact. In theory they knew that they should approve of it. In practice they approved of it when it seemed to be working well. They also commonly found that contact was not working well. They complained of its effect on the children and its unreliability and of the way the parents might use it to set the children against them, undermine discipline, or upset routines.

Statistically our study provided strong support for three of the Dartington Unit's theses. Contact with family was strongly associated with return home. Distance between birth family and foster family was strongly associated with low contact. Prohibition of contact between any family member and a child was strongly associated with low contact. Interestingly neither prohibition nor distance was in any way related to the likelihood of return home. Of itself this tends to suggest that frequency of contact per se is not the cause of return. If this was the case one would expect that, for example, those at considerable distance from home would be less likely to return simply because the frequency of contact was less. So other variables, for example the prior attachment of both birth family and child (Cleaver 2000), may determine both frequency of contact and the likelihood of return.

One striking piece of evidence from our study suggested that in certain circumstances contact could be harmful. We compared the apparent effects of 'unrestricted contact' – where no member of the family was prohibited from seeing the child – with those of restricted contact – where there was a prohibition of at least one member of the family. In cases where there was no strong evidence of abuse prior to placement there was no difference in outcome between these two groups. However, in cases where the social worker said there was strong evidence of prior abuse, this was not so. In the short run the placements of such children were three times more likely to disrupt (33 per cent compared to 11 per cent) over 14 months. In the longer term (3 years) these children were more likely to be re-abused. This was partly because some of them were re-abused on contact and also because they were more likely to go home where re-abuse was – as we will see – more prevalent.

These findings on the potentially negative effects of contact are in keeping with the more cautious approach towards it of recent researchers. Schofield and her colleagues (2000) found that contact was 'problematic' in almost all her cases. Similarly, Farmer and her colleagues (2001), in their study of adolescent fostering, found problems over contact in all but five out of 68 cases. By the time of the second interview they assessed just over two-thirds (69 per cent) of their sample as having 'positive' contact with someone and just under two-thirds (63 per cent) as having 'detrimental' contact.

What Other Issues Affect the Outcomes of Foster Placements?

So, could the potentially harmful effects of contact and return be mitigated by 'treatment' or by more purposeful social work? In approaching this question it is useful to look at what seem to be the determinants of success in different settings. Our own study suggested that, in the case of foster care, there were four:

(1) the child – particularly whether he or she wanted to be in the placement and his or her problems with attachment;
(2) the quality of the parenting provided by the carers;
(3) relationships and contact with birth family; and
(4) the child's experience at school.

School, child and parent motivation and the quality of parenting seemed to be equally important when the child returned home.

These findings suggest that work on relationships with the birth family, the child's happiness at school and the reactions of foster carers to the child should all be important in ensuring success in foster care. Other findings were compatible with this. As already discussed, forbidding contact with certain family members seemed in some circumstances an effective strategy. Contact with an educational psychologist seemed the only form of 'therapeutic' intervention associated with the avoidance of short-term breakdown. The difficulty of the child led to breakdown only if it led (as could easily happen) to the foster carer's rejection of the child. Similar findings might be expected for birth families. We were, however, unable to look for them. This was partly for lack of numbers and partly because there was very little planned intervention after the child returned home.

At the most general level this suggests that outcomes depend heavily on setting. In particular, they depend on the degree to which a given setting provides supportive key relationships (e.g. with partner, parent, or birth family) and a supportive social setting which offers an enjoyable or meaningful role (school or work). They will also depend on the degree to which an individual has the attributes that enable him or her to use and encourage such support. These will include the individual's attachment status and his or her 'temperament'. Experience in one setting will only influence outcome in another if (a) work is done on that other setting to ensure that it is more adapted to the child, or (b) the experience enables the child to adapt better to the new setting, or (c) (preferably) both. (Interestingly in our study this paradigm seemed to hold good not only for those returning home but also for those starting to live on their own.)

How Does This Fit with Dartington Research?

In my view this paradigm is compatible with the following key strands of research:

- Rutter's theory of resilience, which emphasises the importance of school, key attachment relationships and the opportunity for a new start as determinants of escape from poor backgrounds (Rutter 1999; Gilligan 2000);
- findings from residential research, which has repeatedly emphasised the difficulty of ensuring that behaviour elicited in the residential setting is repeated on return home (Allerhand et al. 1966; Sinclair 1971);
- research on 'therapeutic foster care', which suggests to me that this should (a) take account of all relevant aspects of a child and her/his milieu, involving specialists as necessary and (b) is likely to work best if close attention is paid to the child's relationship with school and if birth parents as well as foster carers are trained in the same approach to the child (Chamberlain 1998; Clark et al. 1994).

In my view it is also compatible with the Dartington Unit's research. In particular it fits with:

- their emphasis on the continuing importance of family relationships within foster care (albeit I may think this less uniformly benign than they do);
- their suggestion from their secure unit research that work with the family may produce subsequent fruit;
- their concept of 'compatible roles', whereby a young person's success at school or work was seen as an important determinant of his or her successful return home.

The part of the Dartington research that is not picked up by this account relates to their emphasis on 'meaning'; that is, on the way individuals conceive of themselves in relation to others. On this I can only say that in my view there is no proof either way of its significance in relation to what happens to children in care, but my vote would be for the Dartington view. Two points can be made.

First, I do not think that a very narrow view of the transmission of learning from one setting to another can be maintained. In the early 1970s, for example, it was suggested that the relationship between absconding and subsequent offending occurred because absconders had to offend in order to survive while on the run. In my own work around that time I found that absconders from probation hostels were slightly more likely to be reconvicted subsequently if they were not convicted of another offence at the time of the absconding – not something that would have been expected if transmission was purely behavioural. I also found that absconders were more likely to re-abscond if they were taken back by a hostel that had a negative view of absconding, as evidenced by its reluctance to take many absconders back – something that would be expected from a perspective that emphasised interaction and meaning.

Second, the case studies in our recent research suggested that the crucial step for children in the care system was, as it were, to free themselves of their families. This did not necessarily mean that they rejected them. What was essential, however, was that they somehow moved on psychologically – ideally forgiving if not necessarily forgetting. Failure to do this meant that they ruminated on their families. Many returned to repeated abuse. Essentially they could not regard themselves as independent beings. The creative act of conceiving for themselves a positive identity separate from their families was something that could be enabled but not determined.

Overall, therefore, a full account of 'treatment' in the care system has to take account of children's key relationships, their social roles and their view of themselves. The latter is both dependent on these roles and relationships and capable of yielding a certain independence of them.

WHERE DO WE GO FROM HERE?

I have argued that a facile reading of the Dartington work might encourage too sanguine a view of the family relationships of looked-after children. In many ways many of these children would do better not to return home.

That said, to return home is what many of them want to do. Equally, there is a 'realpolitik' in the Dartington argument. Most are going back, in part because they have little social, economic or intellectual capital and, thus, few other options. Moreover, the system would not survive if they did not return home. There are simply not enough foster carers to offer long-term places to all those who enter. And, even if there were, our own work – like that of Rowe and her colleagues (1989) earlier – suggests that although the care system can offer long-term, quasi-adoptive placements, it rarely does so. Long-stays remain vulnerable to breakdowns, particularly in the teenage years. Very few of those who reach the age of 18 in the care system stay on with their foster carers.

So there is a dilemma. Children want to go home and will inevitably do so. Going home is very often bad for them. What is to be done? Four things can perhaps be suggested. First, ideological positions should soften. It should be realised that some children *do* have a better life away from home. There is scope for some increase in the number of children adopted from care – partly through greater decisiveness in the early years and partly through enabling adoptions by carers themselves.

Second, there should be more exploration of midway positions. Most children in the care system do not want to be adopted. Many, however, want either to stay with their carers on a long-term basis or to return home with close contact with them. There needs to be more exploration of the scope for enabling children to stay on with their carers or remain in touch with them on a long-term basis after 18. There also needs to be more exploration of the shared care relationship, which, it seems, is what many children want.

Third, there needs to be a more explicit acknowledgement that return home is dangerous and difficult for children. This might be obviated by (a) therapeutic foster care, perhaps on the model advocated above, or (b) increased support for families after the child has returned (arguably on a similar model), or (c) both.

Fourth, there needs to be an explicit acknowledgement that success will require additional resources and a willingness to experiment. At present there is not an 'off the shelf' model of intervention that will work. Without additional research and development this will remain the case. Any such model will, in the end, require investment. So, too, will any attempts to increase the permanence offered by foster care. How such an increase is to be made compatible with the manifold responsibilities of social services departments or children's trusts or the expensive anxieties of Lord Laming (2003) is fortunately not an issue for this chapter.

CONCLUSION

The Dartington Unit has made a major contribution to the study of return home. It is possible that, like the rest of us, they have been over-sanguine about birth families and insufficiently wary about contact. That said, they must be praised for their emphasis on the issue, their imaginative grasp of children's concerns, their ability to place these in a wide contact and their stress on the need to plan for returns that, in any case, usually occur. In my view the account of treatment and rehabilitation in their work is extremely important. The rest of us would do well to build on it. In this way we can continue to pay tribute to Roger, who, one hopes, will continue to work among us.

REFERENCES

Allerhand, M., Weber, R. and Haug, M. (1966) *Adaption and Adaptability*, New York, Child Welfare League of America.

Bullock, R., Little, M. and Millham, S. (1993) *Going Home: the return of children separated from their families,* London, Dartmouth.

Bullock, R., Little, M. and Millham, S. (1998) *Secure Treatment Outcomes: the care careers of very difficult adolescents*, Aldershot, Ashgate.

Chamberlain, P. (1998) *Family Connections: a treatment foster care model for adolescents with delinquency*, Oregon, Northwest Media Inc.

Clark, H., Prange, M., Lee, B., Boyd, L., McDonald, B. and Stewart, E. (1994) 'Improving adjustment outcomes for foster children with emotional and behavioural disorders: early findings from a controlled study on individualised services', *Journal of Emotional and Behavioral Disorders* 2, 207–218.

Cleaver, H. (2000) *Fostering Family Contact*, London, The Stationery Office.

Eliot, T.S. (1999) *The Waste Land and Others Poems*, London, Faber and Faber.

Farmer, E., Moyers, S. and Lipscombe, J. (2001) *The Fostering Task with Adolescents: report to the Department of Health*, Bristol, School for Policy Studies, University of Bristol.

Fisher, M., Marsh, P., Phillips, D. and Sainsbury, E. (1986) *In and Out of Care: the experience of children, parents and social workers*, London, Batsford.

Gilligan, R. (2000) *Promoting Resilience*, London, BAAF.

Hensey, D., Williams, J. and Rosenbloom, L. (1983) 'Intervention in child abuse: experience in Liverpool', *Developmental Medicine and Child Neurology* 25, 606–611.

King, J. and Taitz, L. (1985) 'Catch-up growth following abuse', *Archives of Disease in Childhood* 60, 1152–1154.

Koluchova, J. (1976) 'Severe deprivation in twins: a case study', in Clarke, A. and Clarke, A. (eds) *Myth and Evidence*, London, Open Books.

Laming, H. (2003) *The Victoria Climbié Inquiry*, Cm. 5730, London, TSO.

Millham, S., Bullock, R., Hosie, K. and Haak, M. (1986) *Lost in Care: the problems of maintaining links between children in care and their families*, Aldershot, Gower.

Minty, B. (1987) *Child Care and Adult Crime*, Manchester, Manchester University Press.

Minty, B. (1989) 'Annotation: outcomes in long-term foster family care', *Journal of Child Psychology and Psychiatry* 40 (7), 991–999.

Packman, J., Randall, J. and Jacques, N. (1986) *Who Needs Care? Social Work Decisions about Children*, Oxford, Basil Blackwell.

Quinton, D. and Rutter, M. (1988) *Parenting Breakdown: the making and breaking of inter-generational links*, Aldershot, Avebury.

Rowe, J., Cain, H., Hundleby, M. and Garnett, L. (1989) *Child Care Now: a survey of placement patterns*, London, BAAF.

Rutter, M. (1999) 'Resilience concepts and findings: implications for family therapy', *American Journal of Orthopsychiatry* 57, 316–331.

Schofield, G., Beek, M., Sargent, K. and Thoburn, J. (2000) *Growing up in Foster Care*, London, BAAF.

Sinclair, I. (1971) *Hostels for Probationers*, London, HMSO.

Sinclair, I. (1975) 'The influence of wardens and matrons on probation hostels: a study of a quasi-family institution', in Tizard, J., Sinclair, I. and Clarke, R. (eds) *Varieties of Residential Experience*, London, Routledge & Kegan Paul.

Sinclair, I. and Gibbs, I. (2002) 'Looked after children in the UK', in Bradshaw, J. (ed.) *The Well-being of Children in the UK*, London, Save the Children.

Sinclair, I., Wilson, K. and Gibbs, I. (2004a) *Foster Placements: why they succeed and why they fail*, London, Jessica Kingsley.

Sinclair, I., Baker, C., Gibbs, I. and Wilson, K. (2004b) *What Happens to Foster Children?*, London, Jessica Kingsley.

Skuse, D. (1984) 'Extreme deprivation in early childhood. I. Diverse outcomes from children from an extraordinary family', *Journal of Child Psychiatry and Psychiatry* 25, 523–541.

Taussig, H., Clyman, R. and Landsverk, J. (2001) 'Children who return home from foster care: a 6-year prospective study of behavioral health outcomes in adolescence', *Pediatrics* 108 (1), e.10 (Electronic article).

Tizard, B. (1977) *Adoption: a second chance*, London, Open Books.

Zimmerman, R. (1982) 'Foster care in retrospect', *Tulane Studies in Social Welfare* 14, 1–119.

9

CHILD PROTECTION
RESEARCH AND RESEARCHERS

David Berridge

I was both pleased and flattered to be asked to contribute to a book for Roger Bullock, whom I have known both professionally and personally for 25 years. Having enquired after his state of health and being reassured that we were indeed discussing a testimonial rather than an obituary, my next step was to consult the dictionary and discover exactly what a festschrift is. My enthusiasm and *camaraderie* were soon diminished by the realisation that I was down to write the section on the particularly complex and controversial topic of child protection. Roger certainly wouldn't be so foolish as to attempt to write a comprehensive account of the relationship between research, policy and practice in child protection in England and Wales since the 1960s and neither, therefore, shall I. Instead, I shall attempt to give some personal observations of key issues over that period, discuss the area of institutional abuse and make some links with the work of the Dartington Social Research Unit and, especially, Roger's own career.

During the 40 years under review, child abuse and child protection have come to occupy prominent roles in public life. They are major themes of media speculation and political concern. Children are scrutinised as never before. Whether one agrees with his argument or not, Frank Furedi's (2001) polemic on *Paranoid Parenting* was a book that needed to be written. It outlines the way in which parents today are bombarded with expert advice and their insecurity is heightened as babies and children are perceived to be constantly under threat from kidnap or assault. He concocts the term 'battery children' as a response to parental overprotection and argues that adults are increasingly scared of badly behaving children. Laurie Taylor and his son's (2003) contribution to the current debate on childhood (once again male authors, interestingly) was to pose the questions, 'Why is it that parents want to have children?' and 'What are children *for*?' (not a great boost to Taylor junior's self-esteem, presumably).

Forty Years of Research, Policy and Practice in Children's Services.
Edited by N. Axford, V. Berry, M. Little and L. Morpeth.
© 2005 John Wiley & Sons, Ltd. ISBN 0-470-01219-6.

Child abuse and child protection have also, as much as anything else, shaped the development of social work services and the social worker's role. The euphemism 'social care' has been introduced partly as a response to downplay social workers' role and significance, limit their professionalism and, perhaps, reduce expectations. Social workers continue to be castigated when errors of misjudgement are made, whether through under- or overreaction. Inquiry reports repeatedly chronicle problems of professional miscommunication and inter-agency division. Depending on one's perspective, these have been interpreted as intractable problems or incompetence. Lord Laming (2003), in his report into the murder of Victoria Climbié, usefully highlights the shared responsibility for the tragedy of local authority managers and political leaders, not just frontline workers on whom the spotlight usually falls. But initially let us consider more of the background.

CHILD PROTECTION SERVICES IN ENGLAND AND WALES

The development of services to protect children from abuse and neglect has been described in a variety of ways, influenced by observers' reading of history as well as by their professional and theoretical approach (Burke 1996; Parton *et al.* 1997). Prior to the Second World War, the voluntary children's societies, particularly the NSPCC (National Society for the Prevention of Cruelty to Children), were in the ascendancy. Their influence over definitions of, and responses to, abuse was significant. Emphasis was often on the criminal prosecution of abusers and permanent removal of children from home.

Following the Second World War, with economic expansion and growing social cohesion, there was greater emphasis on welfare, a belief in universal social services and an optimistic view of the state. There was growing (albeit short-lived) confidence in social science and the skills of social workers. Social Services Departments were established in 1971. It was generally assumed that the interests of the state and of social workers were the same as those of the people they were trying to assist. Under the influence of paediatricians such as Henry Kempe, who identified the 'battered baby syndrome', child abuse was seen as a disease seeking a cure and was medicalised. Improved diagnostic techniques, such as radiography, were used to recognise the symptoms of physical injury.

From the 1980s onwards these views were increasingly challenged and it was realised that social services were not operating exactly as intended. Child deaths, and the result-ing inquiries, continued (Reder *et al.* 1993). Feminists highlighted the level of violence in families, together with women and children's suffering (Parton and Parton 1989). These needed to be understood in the wider context of power inequalities and gender roles, not just individual pathology. Dartington's own contribution during this period was *Lost in Care* (Millham *et al.* 1986), part of the 'Pink Book' (DHSS 1985) series of studies, and influ-ence in developing the resulting *Children Act* 1989. *Lost in Care* was a detailed empirical study following-up over two years 450 children admitted to care in five local authorities. It revealed that children either left care early or stayed for a long period, not the more gradual exit pattern that would be expected. This pattern of departure was more likely created by the nature of social work intervention rather than reflecting children's needs or families' problems. Though continuing contact with birth parents was, in the main, beneficial to children, the care system made it difficult. Foster and residential placements were often unstable. Emergency measures (preceding current Emergency Protection Orders) were used too frequently and became self-fulfilling in terms of subsequent legal action. A significant minority of children unintentionally remained long term in care, without parental contact and living in unstable placements. Many of these were under the age of 11 and much of this child isolation was attributable to aspects of the care process, which was soon reformed.

But an event that proved a watershed in child welfare and child protection history was the experience in Cleveland, where over a six-month period some 125 children were diagnosed as being sexually abused by their parents, with most children being removed from their homes (Butler-Sloss 1988). There were several important features of Cleveland. For example, the allegations concerned *sexual* abuse, which broadened the dimensions of child abuse and touched on very private and intimate aspects of people's and families' lives. Interestingly, in Cleveland it was paediatricians who were prominent and, therefore, took the brunt of the blame rather than social workers. Furthermore, there was open disagreement about the diagnostic techniques that were used to attempt to prove that sexual abuse occurred. As well as the original mistreatment the children may have experienced, the report was highly critical of the repeated and insensitive interviewing to which children were subjected that inflicted further distress. But perhaps the most important feature of the Cleveland experience was that it involved a wide range of 'normal' families, not just the poor who are the usual targets of abuse investigations. With the exception of disabled children (Berridge and Brodie 1998, Chapter 8), affluent families do not usually experience child and family social work intervention but make their own arrangements.

The experience in Cleveland proved revealing. As a consequence, much effort was focused on how to avoid undue social work intrusion into family life. The *Children Act* 1989 gave this some priority: Section 1(5) makes what may appear the rather obvious point that a court shall not make a legal order unless it is preferable to making no order. The Act has many merits and broke much new ground (Packman and Jordan 1991). But it is unlikely that it would have been endorsed by Margaret Thatcher's strongly anti-welfarist and anti-public sector Conservative government unless it was perceived to be a reaction to Cleveland and to strengthen (middle-class) *parents'* (rather than children's) rights against social workers.

Parton and his colleagues (1997) have observed that since the 1990s we have in effect been left with a child *protection* system rather than one to combat child *abuse*. Indeed, the latter term is now infrequently heard. We return to this point later but there has increasingly been a managerialist emphasis on systems, procedures, assessments and case management rather than detailed work with children and families. Identifying, containing and managing *risk* are the watchwords. At long last there have been important developments in the field of child and adolescent mental health (Kurtz and James 2002; Payne and Butler 2003), including widening access, developing a stronger community rather than clinical focus and aiming to be more non-stigmatising. Yet it is by no means certain that we now have significantly better therapeutic services for abused and neglected children or violent adults. It will be interesting to observe the effects of the new government proposals for children's services in England and Wales outlined in *Every Child Matters* (DfES 2003), such as the Local Safeguarding Children's Boards and multidisciplinary Children's Trusts.

WHAT DO WE KNOW ABOUT PROTECTING CHILDREN FROM ABUSE AND NEGLECT?

In assessing developments in child protection over 40 years, what have we learned? First, some statistics. Commentators agree that a number of advanced industrial countries, including the USA, Canada and Australia, have experienced a considerable increase in the number of child abuse and neglect referrals. In the USA the rate more than quadrupled in 15 years. However, other European countries which adopt more of a family support approach, such as France, Germany and The Netherlands, have not been affected to the same degree (Corby 2000). Comparable statistics for Britain do not exist, as we quantify numbers of children named on child abuse registers rather than referrals, but it is also evident that the volume of child abuse work has grown very significantly. This does not, of course, necessarily mean that children's experiences have altered to the same degree, as there is a process of social construction in official statistics. About a third of the 220,000 or so children in need who receive a service at any one time from social services do so mainly because of concerns about abuse or neglect (DoH 2002). But it is clear that child protection work has come to dominate child welfare and that families are much less likely to receive a service when abuse issues are absent (DoH 2001).

One major lesson we have learned is that the child protection system is very inefficient in that only a minority of child abuse and neglect referrals are in fact substantiated. While over-reacting in this way may ensure better protection of children in the short term, such a low threshold comes at a heavy cost to the families involved and represents a waste of scarce resources. One key study by Gibbons and her colleagues (1995) tracked almost 2,000 children through the child protection system. About half of all referrals were unsubstantiated and barely one in seven was subsequently named on a Child Protection Register. Only 4 per cent were removed from home. The authors concluded that large numbers of cases were being drawn into the child protection system unnecessarily. Their broader needs tended to be neglected when it was decided that protective measures were not required.

Currently the most authoritative body of empirical research on child abuse is *Child Protection: messages from research* (DoH 1995), commonly known as 'the Blue Book'. Though an official publication, the research overview was produced by the Dartington Social Research Unit and partly written by Roger Bullock. This must have been a complex task: identifying the key messages from 20 studies and maintaining a degree of academic independence while satisfying the Department of Health and (Conservative) ministers post-Cleveland. The opening paragraphs ask specifically whether Cleveland social workers had been overzealous in their removal of children and contravened parents' rights.

The Blue Book develops a number of important themes from the programme of studies. It highlights that working in the field of child abuse is a difficult social work task and there are complex problems of definition. This sends an important message to politicians and the public at large but also to professionals, who need to approach the assessment of situations with great care. The overview raises the issue that any perceived inappropriate experiences involving children need to be set in the context of what happens within 'normal' families. The physical punishment of children is common throughout society. 'Sexual' experiences for children can also arise within families, such as seeing parents naked, bathing with parents or watching sexually explicit films and videos. From a sociological perspective, therefore, child abuse is not an absolute or unproblematic concept. This raises the notions of a continuum of behaviours and a threshold. Indeed, the Blue Book poses the question, how does society decide where the threshold is to be?

Linked to this is the parenting style that accompanies specific harmful acts, which give meaning to the violence. The Blue Book articulates the important idea that abuse is most harmful in particular circumstances:

> ...in families *low on warmth and high on criticism*, negative incidents accumulate as if to remind a child that he or she is unloved. (p. 19, my emphasis)

It is estimated that some 350,000 children experience this harmful combination of adversities each year.

Other important themes in the research overview include the problems in engaging families in the child protection process. A key factor in producing satisfactory outcomes is said to be the quality of relationships between parents and professionals. It also highlights that the discovery of new forms of abuse needs to be treated with caution, for example ritual or satanic abuse. But most importantly, perhaps, and the message on which the overview ends, is the need to emphasise the child's and family's overall needs rather than the abusive act per se. This is summarised succinctly in a paragraph that I have given to my students every year since:

> A more balanced service for vulnerable children would encourage professionals to take a wider view. There would be efforts to work alongside families rather than disempower them, to raise their self-esteem rather than reproach families, to promote family relationships where children have their needs met, rather than leave untreated families with an unsatisfactory parenting style. The focus would be on the overall needs of children rather than a narrow concentration on the alleged incident. (p. 55)

Hence, we need to reconsider the overall balance of services. This perspective has had a major influence on social work ever since, including, for example, the development conceptually and practically of services for 'children in need' (DoH 2002, Chapter 3) and a greater emphasis on interprofessional working and the contribution of agencies such as health and education (DoH 2001).

There are areas about which it would have been interesting to read more in the Blue Book, although some critiques dwell on limitations without giving equal attention to practical alternatives. Ultimately, of course, a research overview is only as strong as the group of studies on which it is based. Like its predecessors (DHSS 1985; DoH 1996, 1998a), the overview could have given more attention to ethnicity. Majority and minority ethnic groups experience the child protection and care systems differently (Owen and Farmer 1996; Barn *et al.* 1997) and this has important implications for children's welfare. In addition, it would be interesting to know how the processes operate whereby individual social workers make actual decisions about safeguarding children when faced with competing claims – for example, working alongside parents or protecting children (extreme cases) – and when situations are ambiguous (not unusual). There is also an apparent paradox when the Blue

Book argues for a 'lighter touch' to child protection while simultaneously reporting that between a quarter and a third of children were re-abused after they came to the attention of official agencies. The emphasis on parenting style potentially introduces value judgements and could discriminate against parents (mothers) living in poverty or with other stresses, which would influence the quality of child rearing they were able to provide. Farmer and Owen (1995) highlighted the iniquity of social services taking action based on innocent mothers' inability to protect children from violent partners. Interestingly, the Blue Book raises the class issue and states that we know little about middle-class parents who mistreat their children. There is also the surprising finding that adoptive (but not foster) families were as punitive towards children as birth families. Children, therefore, seem to be entitled to protection only if they live in the poorest social groups which are subjected to state surveillance. Cleveland's paediatricians transgressed these norms.

INSTITUTIONAL ABUSE

Though it was probably beyond its remit, and it is understood that strong research bids were not submitted, it is unfortunate that the Blue Book was unable to include discussion on children abused while living away from home, particularly in residential institutions. The same applies to its successor, the 'Green Book' (DoH 1998a). Institutional abuse mainly emerged into public consciousness in 1989 with reports of the 'pin-down' regime in Staffordshire, in which 132 children aged from 9 to 17 years had been confined to barely furnished rooms; made to wear night clothes during the day; and deprived of contact, education and sensory stimulus (Levy and Kahan 1991; Berridge and Brodie 1996). Systematic sexual abuse in residential care first came to light two years later when Frank Beck, who had been in charge of various Leicestershire children's homes between 1973 and 1986, was sentenced to life imprisonment on 17 counts of rape and other forms of sexual and physical assault involving children. A series of scandals has materialised since, involving the physical and sexual abuse of residents going back over 30 years. Although it is barely conceivable, Wolmar (2000) estimated that police investigations have occurred in over 500 residential institutions, with almost 10,000 allegations of abuse against over 1,500 perpetrators. Future generations will look back at the physical and sexual abuse in children's homes and residential schools as one of the greatest failures in social policy in the twentieth century.

Paradoxically, institutional abuse has been neglected as a research topic (Barter 1998). It is unclear why children should be more at risk in group settings than in, say, foster homes but at least we now have some evidence. Berridge and Brodie (1996) identified some common themes in management, policy and practice in early inquiry reports, including inadequate line management, unsatisfactory placement policies, poor staff training, a 'macho' culture and inadequate or no specialist external advice. This analysis has been developed and brought up to date by Colton (2002), encompassing events in North Wales (House of Commons 2000), to include shortcomings in staff recruitment, the development of inappropriate residential cultures and public ambivalence towards children in care. There is interesting earlier literature on the theme of violence without moral restraint (Wardaugh and Wilding 1993), which focuses on the neutralisation of moral concerns, the balance of power in organisations, the way in which the corruption of care is associated with particular types of work, 'management failure' and the nature of certain underprivileged client groups.

The unpalatable question for researchers, the author included, is how we missed the physical and sexual abuse that was occurring? I worked at the Dartington Social Research Unit with Roger Bullock and colleagues between 1981 and 1986 and can recall, in what must have been 1981 or 1982, attending an international conference in Paris at which Roger Singleton from Barnardo's spoke on the topic of institutional abuse. At the time it did not resonate with my experiences and observations in residential care, as community homes with education (CHEs) and other forms of total institutions run by social services were beginning to disappear. Allegations of sexual abuse at Kincora, the boys' hostel in East Belfast, surfaced in 1986 and have never been satisfactorily resolved, including any connections with Northern Ireland politics. I am unaware of any instances of physical or sexual abuse that have been reported at the group of 20 children's homes in each of which a colleague or I lived for a week in the early 1980s (Berridge 1985; Berridge and Brodie 1998). The skills that paedophiles used to befriend children and mislead management may have been used also to discourage researchers. Investigators have reported that, in retrospect, some of the high-profile abusers were evasive.

Another area of institutional abuse underestimated by researchers and policy-makers alike is peer violence (Cawson *et al.* 2001; Barter *et al.* 2004). A large-scale, national study of child maltreatment discovered that the most common source of distress for children was bullying and discrimination by other young people (Cawson *et al.* 2000). It also found that most child sexual abuse is perpetrated by someone close in age to the victim. Residential research may have erroneously assumed that children's (sub-) cultures were benign and/or weak. In many respects peer violence in children's homes resembles other experiences in the community, such as bullying at school. However, it causes much distress in children's homes as it can occur round the clock, it is misunderstood by staff and remedies are inadequate (Barter *et al.* 2004). Until recently, policy had little to say about the problem (Utting 1991, 1997; Warner 1992).

CONCLUSIONS CONCERNING CHILD PROTECTION

Rounding off the discussion, we have seen that child protection is a high-profile and complex topic. It appears to be a growing problem but, as with perceptions of crime and educational standards, moral panics are increasingly frequent in (post)modern society and there is a mismatch between public opinion and the nature of risk. Definitions of abuse are difficult and thresholds can be arbitrary. Indeed, what is 'normal' behaviour? Researchers have portrayed the child protection system as being inefficient: too many families are incorporated yet a significant minority of children are released only to be re-abused. As with most child and family social work, services are class-based. Institutional abuse took society and researchers alike by surprise. It has been, and may still be, a major problem although we now know some of the associated factors. Similarly, the extent and effects of peer violence in residential care and society generally have been underestimated as social problems.

If space permitted, or if someone else had been responsible for this chapter, there are many other relevant topics that could have been discussed (see also Corby 2000, Chapter 11). For example, we need to know more about the way in which the context of family life influences child abuse, particularly poverty, family stress and domestic violence. Though there have been some improvements, there is also concern about the way in which the legal system deals with child abuse matters, such as children's evidence and the prosecution of sexual abusers. Another area of investigation is society's attitudes to the physical punishment of the young and how this relates to child abuse. In addition, we need to consider gender socialisation in society, for example boys' and men's ideas of masculinity, and how this may be linked with violence. Being careful not to blame the victims, there is also a theme around the sexualisation of children in modern culture, which may influence abusers' attitudes. Further, there is a need to address the paucity of therapeutic services for the abused or abusers.

Other chapters in this book consider the subject in more detail but it is important to reflect on the extent to which the body of child welfare research over the past 40 years has influenced social policy. This is a difficult area: research may lead directly to change (as with adoption allowances (Hill *et al.* 1989)); be indirectly associated (as with the *Children Act* 1989); be unrelated to developments (the plethora of organisational reforms); or help to prevent changes occurring that may otherwise have been introduced (the privatisation or dismantling in the 1980s and early 1990s of social work services in England and Wales). The uneasy tension between child welfare research and policy may be particularly acute in child protection work, especially where the high-profile tragedies are concerned. For example, the murder in 1993 of the toddler James Bulger by two 10-year-olds received widespread attention from politicians and the media, and the knowledge base is rarely the primary consideration when such reverberations occur. Strengthening the relationship between research, policy and practice is a complex process, with key influences including the nature of professional cultures as well as the organisation of the civil service. Progress needs to take place simultaneously on several fronts.

At least at present we have a New Labour government that demonstrates a high commitment to children's social care (DoH 1998b), including its pledge to eradicate child poverty within a generation. But in other respects major social policy reforms have not been consistent with the academic consensus. Gilbert (2002) identifies remarkable similarity across the industrialised world in how governments have targeted and restricted access to welfare benefits. The welfare state has come under increasing criticism and, as the author succinctly puts it, safety nets have been replaced with trampolines. Free market economic theory has triumphed and *responsibilities* have been prioritised over *rights*. The USA has been in the vanguard of reform, despite having hardly an enviable record on public health and welfare, with the UK, as in foreign policy, in eager pursuit.

On social services specifically, Jordan and Jordan (2000) have outlined how New Labour's political philosophy of the 'Third Way', which they describe as 'tough love', has affected social work. They summarise this as a mistrust of the public sector generally and a preference for new agencies and roles – such as Sure Start or Connexions – to replace traditional social work functions. Most street-level, outreach support workers do not have training in social work, yet are discharging its previous responsibilities. Professional social work is thus being eroded. Furthermore, the approach to public sector management has been criticised by the think-tank Demos (Chapman 2002) as misunderstanding the way it operates and seeking to apply an outdated and inappropriate scientific management model. New Labour's preference for performance management through setting targets has been criticised as replacing politics with managerialism (Hutton 2002).

Whatever other improvements have occurred, this is the wider picture and most child welfare researchers over the past 40 years probably would not feel that their work during this period pointed in this direction. Politics and research will no doubt continue to have an uneasy relationship.

THE CONTRIBUTION OF THE DARTINGTON SOCIAL RESEARCH UNIT

But rather than bemoan aspects of the current situation, this book is to celebrate the major contribution to debates and the body of knowledge over the past 40 years of Dartington and, especially, Roger Bullock. It is difficult to separate Roger's influence for much of this time from that of his close colleague, Spencer Millham. As said earlier, I was very fortunate to have worked at Dartington in the 1980s and to have Roger and Spencer as mentors. Previously, when I was a student and (generally ineffective) residential social worker with adolescents, Dartington's books had pride of place on my shelf and influenced me probably more than any others. It is difficult to explain exactly why, but books such as *After Grace – Teeth* (Millham *et al.* 1975) and *Locking Up Children* (Millham *et al.* 1978) made sense to me and reflected the way I thought. (An exception, admittedly, was *The Manual to the Sociology of the School* (Lambert *et al.* 1970), which Spencer described certainly as the most boring book he had ever written, if not read, and his ultimate fantasy had been to set it to music.) I have always read Roger's books as soon as they have been published and before any others and am sorry to disappoint my many researcher friends in that none of your other works fall into this category!

So what is it exactly about Roger's and Dartington's research that appealed to me so much? It has been a salutary experience to reflect on what the characteristics are. First of all, I was attracted to the work because it was sociological. Much child welfare research in England is atheoretical (Trinder 1996) and seldom is it sociological. Sociological accounts are often absent in contemporary life or take pride in their theoretical incomprehensibility. The sociology of education has rather lost its way (Shain and Ozga 2001) and, for example, discussions of the educational underachievement of looked after children rarely highlight the previous social experiences that are largely responsible. A recent study demonstrated that the strongest factor associated with educational underachievement was childhood poverty (Bynner *et al.* 2002). Linked no doubt to this sociological perspective, Dartington's work often talked about social class (remember that?). It also pointed out the importance of history: children's services are strongly influenced by the past and we cannot fully understand, for example, services for looked-after children without an awareness of both the Poor Law and the strong historical theme of separation. Another aspect of Roger's work that appealed to me was that it was strongly child-centred. The case studies were a distinctive feature of the Dartington studies and, for some reason, I can still recall aspects of the Barton family (Millham *et al.* 1986) ('Brenda's first husband, Syd . . . died after 14 years of marriage while moving a wardrobe – "I knew it would happen if he didn't take the clothes out", volunteered

Brenda,' p. 67). Interestingly, I am attracted to Layder's (1994) theoretical work for similar reasons, in that it is sociological, incorporates dimensions of power and history and bridges the macro–micro gap ('disciplined eclecticism', p. 222).

Other important features of Roger's approach include the attempt to bring together research, policy and practice. A recent chapter on child protection (Bullock and Little 2002), for example, argues for a more evidence-based approach. There were numerous meetings and seminars at Dartington in the 1980s (and no doubt earlier and since) involving policy-makers and practitioners, in which research dissemination and related topics were on the agenda. Dartington thus anticipated, probably by at least a decade, debates about evidence-based practice and organisations such as the Social Care Institute for Excellence (SCIE). Furthermore, it was Roger's and Michael's [Little] direct influence that helped to spawn Research in Practice (based at Dartington) and Making Research Count, which I helped to found – two organisations that work to bring together more closely the worlds of research and practice in children's services.

Another distinctive feature of Roger's and Dartington's work was that it was always so well written. Its language was clear and expressive and there were references to novels, plays and poetry – *Lost in Care* opens with a quote from Oscar Wilde. It was also self-effacing. Child welfare researchers generally write well, unlike in some other disciplines, and I have always found this refreshing given the pomposity of some academics.

Humour was an important feature at Dartington. This has to be approached with caution as humour is a very personal matter; we tend to find different things amusing. It can also sit uneasily alongside aspects of child welfare and child abuse. No doubt it is at least partially a defence. Humour was an important antidote to the earnestness and self-importance associated with some aspects of the wider Dartington Hall Trust. Roger has amassed a wide repertoire of amusing anecdotes gathered from 40 years' research, as anyone who has heard him speak at a conference can testify. Loud laughter could frequently be heard in the Research Unit's offices, usually coinciding with one of Spencer's directorial visits. I recall the story of the American visitors who were rather amused on seeing the advertising slogan 'Nothing sucks like an Electrolux', or who were intrigued by the social work initiative providing home care for older people, called 'Knocking-up the elderly'. I remember Martin Haak who had put together the material for one of Spencer's lectures at an important Intermediate Treatment (IT) conference, and had erroneously packed one of his skiing videos rather than the IT film he was supposed to include. On return, Spencer described his experience and emotions in front of the large audience as the lights dimmed, the audience hushed and the skiers came into view.

CONCLUSION

The Dartington Social Research Unit was, and hopefully will continue to be, a unique institution. Under Roger's guidance it achieved high standards, retained the confidence of civil servants and practitioners alike, was a supportive and enabling environment to young researchers, crossed traditional academic and professional boundaries, and sought to represent effectively parents' and children's views. I have not alluded to Roger's personal interests, except to say that he is better at playing the piano than the cello. Finally, it was a cruel twist that we were to be deprived simultaneously of not one but two major institutions: in the same year that Roger retired the football team of which he is a devoted follower, West Bromwich Albion, were relegated from the Premiership, only to bounce back within a year. Presumably a stipulation of writing this book for Roger is that he doesn't do the same.

REFERENCES

Barn, R., Sinclair, R. and Ferdinand, D. (1997) *Acting on Principle: an examination of race and eth-nicity in social services provision for children and families*, London, National Children's Bureau.

Barter, C. (1998) *Investigating Institutional Abuse: an exploration of the NSPCC experience*, London, NSPCC.

Barter, C., Renold, E., Berridge, D. and Cawson, P. (2004) *Peer Violence in Children's Residential Care*, Basingstoke, Palgrave.

Berridge, D. (1985) *Children's Homes*, Oxford, Basil Blackwell.

Berridge, D. and Brodie, I. (1996) 'Residential child care in England and Wales: the inquiries and after', in Hill, M. and Aldgate, J. (eds) *Child Welfare Services: developments in law, policy, practice and research*, London, Jessica Kingsley.

Berridge, D. and Brodie, I. (1998) *Children's Homes Revisited*, London, Jessica Kingsley.

Bullock, R. and Little, M. (2002) 'The contribution of children's services to the protection of children', in Browne, K.D., Hanks, H., Stratton, D. and Hamilton, C. (eds) *Early Prediction and Prevention of Child Abuse: a handbook*, Chichester, John Wiley & Sons.

Burke, R. (1996) *The History of Child Protection in Britain*, Leicester, Scarman Centre for the Study of Public Order, University of Leicester.

Butler-Sloss, E. (1988) *Report of the Inquiry into Child Abuse in Cleveland*, London, HMSO.

Bynner, J., Elias, P., McKnight, A., Pan, H. and Pierre, G. (2002) *Young People's Changing Routes to Independence*, York, Joseph Rowntree Foundation.

Cawson, P., Berridge, D., Barter, C. and Renold, E. (2001) *Physical and Sexual Violence Between Children Living in Residential Settings: exploring perspectives and experiences*, Swindon, Economic and Social Research Council.

Cawson, P., Wattam, C., Brooker, S. and Kelly, G. (2000) *Child Maltreatment in the United Kingdom*, London, NSPCC.

Chapman, J. (2002) *System Failure: why government must learn to think differently*, London, Demos.

Colton, M. (2002) 'Factors associated with abuse in residential child care institutions', *Children and Society* 16, 33–44.

Corby, B. (2000) *Child Abuse: towards a knowledge base*, Buckingham, Open University Press.

DfES (Department for Education and Skills) (2003) *Every Child Matters*, Cm. 5860, London, The Stationery Office.

DoH (Department of Health) (1995) *Child Protection: messages from research*, London, HMSO.

DoH (1996) *Focus on Teenagers: research into practice*, London, HMSO.

DoH (1998a) *Caring for Children Away From Home: messages from research*, Chichester, John Wiley & Sons.

DoH (1998b) *Quality Protects*, London, Department of Health.

DoH (2001) *The Children Act Now: messages from research*, London, Department of Health.

DoH (2002) *The Children Act Report 2001*, London, Department of Health.

DHSS (Department of Health and Social Security) (1985) *Social Work Decisions in Child Care: recent research findings and their implications*, London, HMSO.

Farmer, E. and Owen, M. (1995) *Child Protection Practice: private risks and public remedies*, London, HMSO.

Furedi, F. (2001) *Paranoid Parenting: abandon your anxieties and be a good parent*, London, Penguin Press.

Gibbons, J., Conroy, S. and Bell, C. (1995) *Operating the Child Protection System*, London, HMSO.

Gilbert, N. (2002) *Transformation of the Welfare State*, Oxford, Oxford University Press.

Hill, M., Lambert, L. and Triseliotis, J. (1989) *Achieving Adoption with Love and Money*, London, National Children's Bureau.

House of Commons (2000) *Report of the Tribunal of Inquiry into the Abuse of Children in Care in the Former County Council Areas of Gwynedd and Clwyd Since 1974*, London, Stationery Office.

Hutton, W. (2002) 'So many targets, so many misses', *The Observer*, 22 December.

Jordan, B. and Jordan, C. (2000) *Social Work and the Third Way: tough love as social policy*, London, Sage.

Kurtz, Z. and James, C. (2002) *What's New? Learning from the CAMHS Innovation Projects*, London, Department of Health.

Lambert, R., Millham, S. and Bullock, R. (1970) *A Manual to the Sociology of the School*, London, Weidenfeld & Nicolson.

Laming, H. (2003) *The Victoria Climbié Report*, London, Stationery Office.

Layder, D. (1994) *Understanding Social Theory*, London, Sage.

Levy, A. and Kahan, B. (1991) *The Pindown Experience and the Protection of Children*, Stafford, Staffordshire County Council.

Millham, S., Bullock, R. and Cherrett, P. (1975) *After Grace – Teeth*, Brighton, Human Context Books.

Millham, S., Bullock, R. and Hosie, K. (1978) *Locking Up Children*, Farnborough, Saxon House.

Millham, S., Bullock, R., Hosie, K. and Haak, M. (1986) *Lost in Care*, Aldershot, Gower.

Owen, M. and Farmer, E. (1996) 'Child protection in a multi-racial context', *Policy and Politics*, 24 (3), 299–313.

Packman, J. and Jordan, B. (1991) 'The *Children Act*: looking forward, looking back', *Children and Society* 21 (4), 315–327.

Parton, C. and Parton, N. (1989) 'Women, the family and child protection', *Critical Social Policy* 24, 38–49.

Parton, N., Thorpe, D. and Wattam, C. (1997) *Child Protection, Risk and the Moral Order*, London, Macmillan.

Payne, H. and Butler, I. (2003) *Promoting the Mental Health of Children in Need. Quality Protects Research Briefing*, London, Department for Education and Skills.

Reder, P., Duncan, C. and Gray, M. (1993) 'A new look at child abuse tragedies', *Child Abuse Review* 2, 89–100.

Shain, F. and Ozga, J. (2001) 'Identity crisis? Problems and issues in the sociology of education', *British Journal of Sociology of Education* 22 (1), 109–120.

Taylor, L. and Taylor, M. (2003) *What Are Children For?*, London, Short Books.

Trinder, L. (1996) 'Social work research: the state of the art (or science)', *Child and Family Social Work* 1, 233–242.

Utting, W. (1991) *Children in the Public Care*, London, HMSO.

Utting, W. (1997) *People Like Us: the report of the review of the safeguards for children living away from home*, London, Department of Health/Welsh Office.

Wardaugh, J. and Wilding, P. (1993) 'Towards an explanation for the corruption of care', *Critical Social Policy* 37, 4–31.

Warner, N. (1992) *Choosing With Care*, London, HMSO.

Wolmar, C. (2000) *Forgotten Children: the scandal in Britain's children's homes*, London, Vision.

10

THE EVOLUTION OF FAMILY SUPPORT

HISTORY AND PROSPECTS

Michael Little and Ruth Sinclair

INTRODUCTION

When Roger Bullock began his research career in 1963, 'family support' was a term little used. Today it has become a part of day-to-day conversation for researchers, policy-makers and practitioners looking to support children in need. It is used in a variety of ways but with little clarity about the range of services it encompasses or what those interventions are seeking to achieve. Common to all usages, however, is the idea of services being provided to families where children are living at home and with the general purpose of relieving family stress and promoting the welfare of children.

This chapter seeks to summarise some of the research on family support over the last 40 years. It starts by setting out the particular English and Welsh policy context to family support. Next it discusses research on system dynamics that has led to the English and Welsh understanding of the concept. The chapter then deals with some of the emerging evidence from various countries on the needs of children and evaluations of what works in the family support arena. This evidence is used to suggest new ways of thinking about family support in the future.

THE POLICY CONTEXT

While the term 'family support' may not have had wide currency in the early days of Roger's career, the concept of support from social services departments to families at home has been the subject of fluctuating backing since that time and before (Gibbons 1992). Today family support has become part of the general shift of provision towards broad-based preventative services delivered by a wide range of agencies, including those in the

Forty Years of Research, Policy and Practice in Children's Services.
Edited by N. Axford, V. Berry, M. Little and L. Morpeth.
© 2005 John Wiley & Sons, Ltd. ISBN 0-470-01219-6.

voluntary and community sector. The Audit Commission (1994) report *Seen But Not Heard* refers to:

> Any activity or facility provided either by statutory agencies or by community groups or individuals, aimed at providing advice and support to parents to help them in bringing up their children. (p. 39)

In England and Wales, the term is closely bound up with the development of services offered, mainly by social services departments, under Part III and specifically Section 17 of the *Children Act* 1989. For example, Gibbons and her colleagues (1995) define family support as:

> The type of services which local authorities have a duty to provide or purchase for the purposes of promoting the welfare of children in need, wherever possible within their own homes. (p. 151)

Used in this way, family support is placed within what has been called a 'child welfare approach', with an emphasis on helping parents and working with them in the community in a supportive way (Parton 1997).

For many social workers, and for some of their managers, this form of family support came to be seen as an alternative to what they viewed as child protection services, or interventions directed specifically at children at risk of maltreatment. This view of family support was reinforced, with unintended consequences, by provisions under Section 47 of the *Children Act* 1989 that gave local authorities duties to act in cases where the child is at risk of maltreatment. The tensions between social workers' desire to protect on the one hand and support on the other have been well documented in research in the 1990s. The overview of research into the impact of the *Children Act* 1989 (DoH 2001) concluded that:

> Safeguarding children has always, rightly, been at the forefront of child welfare policy and practice, but it has not always been intertwined with promoting welfare. (p. 43)

Roger Bullock had led jointly an earlier review of research into child protection that sought to resolve these tensions by demonstrating that, in fact, family support was one of the primary mechanisms for protecting children from maltreatment (DoH 1995). It was noticeable from the research that families identified as having children in need, but where there were no protection issues, looked for the most part remarkably similar to those labelled as child protection cases. Rather ironically, the former label – children in need – resulted in rapid assessments and the provision of family support services, whereas the latter label – child protection – could result in protracted discussions about whether or not the child had been abused and little intervention. Of course, the contrasting labels of 'child protection' and 'children in need' were always misleading since both categories comprised children who were 'children in need' as defined by the *Children Act* 1989 in that their development was actually impaired or, in the absence of any change in circumstances, likely to become so.

Recognition of this imbalance and the need to change professional understanding and practice was articulated by the Department of Health in a clear statement of the principles and priorities for child care services – commonly referred to as the 'refocusing of services'

(Rose 1994). Essentially this called for a refocusing of priorities away from investigative child protection services and towards an investment in family support services as a way of protecting children. The goal was an integrated child care system that encompassed both family support and treatment services and that rebalanced child welfare and child protection issues.

For some commentators, acknowledging the increasingly ideological aspects of these discussions, family support came to characterise a policy direction subject to changing political whims rather than a description of a service. Katz and Pinkerton (2003), for example, remark that:

> Despite its deep roots in child welfare, family support as a coherent policy and practice perspective is still at a relatively early stage in its development. (p. 4)

Since 1997, when the Labour government took office, the policy agenda has been dominated by attempts to increase the range and type of preventative services for children in need. However, questions of effective child protection have remained, as evidenced by the Climbié Inquiry (Laming 2003), the subsequent Green Paper, *Every Child Matters* (DfES 2003), and the *Children Act* 2004. The government's vision for children's services, *Every Child Matters*, gives clear backing to family support, although the nature of that support differs from previous incarnations in at least three important respects. First, there is a focus on improved child outcomes, which should be measured in terms of children's health, safety, economic well-being, enjoyment, and achievement and contribution to society. Second, family support will be an integrated service, not something organised by social services alone. Health, education, the police and youth justice all have a role to play, not to mention various national and local voluntary and private providers. Third, it is intended to integrate universal, preventative, targeted and specialist services: in each of these spheres family support plays its part, for example, in the provision of a wide range of services in 'extended schools' and through widely available parenting education for all families.

This brief overview of the recent history of family support policy in England and Wales indicates some of the opportunities and constraints connected to service development. Whether opportunities will exceed constraints in the future will be determined largely by the ability of policy-makers and practitioners to find new ways of tackling old problems, not least in identifying what is being prevented, the ethics of supporting parents to support children and the integration of activity to promote well-being and protect children from maltreatment. The remainder of this chapter sets out the research evidence relevant to these challenges, dealing with system dynamics, the needs of children and evaluations of what works.

SYSTEM DYNAMICS

As with physical health, the social needs of children greatly exceed the services, family support included, that exist to meet those needs (Friedman 2001). This fact, together with the historical tendency to separate services for the deserving and undeserving poor (Parker 1990), has required that resources be rationed, so creating what are called 'system dynamics'. These dynamics strongly predict who will get help and the nature and duration of that help

(Wulczyn *et al.* 2000). For example, residential and foster care services tend to be supply led, meaning that take-up reflects the places available rather than the need for those places (Little *et al.* 1996). As a result, length of stay in a residential home or foster family becomes an important mechanism for controlling the dynamics of this part of the system and influencing the numbers of children in need who use these services.

Research on system dynamics reveals much about how children's services are used. We outline below seven points that illustrate how this bears upon our understanding of family support.

First, although data sources remain limited, the number of referrals to children's services is much greater than is generally recognised. Research in one English district found that about one in three children are referred to health, education, social care, youth justice or police services each year because of a social need (Little and Madge 1998). It seems reasonable to project that a much higher proportion of children will come to the notice of services over a 5-year period.

Second, most referrals for help are initiated by the parents of children in need (Axford *et al.* 2003). Where professional concerns arise, they are most likely to originate with general practitioners, health visitors and teachers (Gibbons *et al.* 1995). The majority of parents (about 57 per cent) turn first to their doctor, health visitor or their child's teacher when looking for help with a social need (Little and Madge 1998). These patterns imply that parents and other carers tend to be reasonably good at assessing their own children's social well-being and that they are looking for practical, targeted support for the problems they identify. The limited response that they tend to receive suggests that demand far exceeds the available supply.

Third, and potentially a consequence of the high imbalance between supply and demand, there are inefficiencies in the processing of referrals, with far more effort going into deciding which children should receive support than into actually offering that support (Farmer and Owen 1995). Generally speaking, the longer the case remains within the children's services process, and the more complicated are the social needs, the more likely it is that social care professionals – as opposed to those from other agencies – will assume responsibility for the case (Little and Madge 1998). The implication for children's services is that service users tend to wait a long time for a full assessment and that most requests for help are rejected or rewarded with a minimal response.

Fourth, the previously described distinction between child protection cases (which require investigation for maltreatment and may require compulsory powers to supervise the child at home or accommodate him or her away from home) and what have been called 'other children in need' is based as much on 'operational factors' – professional and organisa-tional procedures – as on the objective assessment of children's needs (Little and Gibbons 1993). Considerable resources are consumed in the processing of referrals, so restricting opportunities for family support and producing geographical (national and international) variations in service provision.

Fifth, for children allocated to the child protection pile of referrals, much more effort is invested in finding out if the child has been maltreated than in responding to identified social needs (Farmer and Owen 1995). As a consequence, children allocated to the 'other children in need' category are much more likely than the child protection cases to get support, and to get it rapidly (DoH 1995). This is in direct opposition to professionals' perception of the pattern, namely that the child protection label is needed to secure resources (Schuerman *et al.* 1994; Hallett 1995). Moreover, when there is an intervention at the end of a child protection inquiry, it tends to be of a process nature (monitoring the child or placing the child's name on a register of concern) or, in a minority of cases, it may result in the child being removed from his or her parents. Historically, less family support (or any other intervention that might logically reduce social need) has been offered to child protection cases than to some other groups of children in need (DoH 1995).

Sixth, whatever the administrative classification of the case, services offered tend to be 'thin' in the sense that they are short in duration and intensity (Little *et al.* 2003). (They contrast with 'thick' interventions, which are generally intensive and long term.) Typically, 'thin' interventions can be placed under a family support label and include advice and information, mediating access to other agencies or providing of small amounts of money and other material assistance. As will be seen, there has been little evaluation of the effects of these thin style interventions and there is scant evidence to suggest that delivered in isolation they have any marked effect on children's social needs (Sinclair *et al.* 1997). However, there is some evidence that, where delivered, they create a reasonable amount of user satisfaction (SSI/Audit Commission 1999, 2002; Ghate and Hazel 2002).

Seventh, many 'thick' interventions to address the social needs of children tend to involve periods of separation in residential and/or family foster care settings. These separations are subject to their own set of system dynamics described elsewhere in this book (especially Chapters 4 and 8). As a consequence, 'thin' family support has been viewed as an alternative to 'thick' separation in the same unhelpful way that so-called 'child protection' and 'other children in need' categories have been contrasted.

It is clear from the foregoing discussion that system dynamics have had a major influence on the way in which children's services function, particularly in relation to family support. It seems reasonable to hypothesise that the amount of family support provided by social services is a function of the amount of child protection activity taking place and of the number of children in state care. Changes in one part of the system will produce changes in other parts. Further, despite their predictive power, these system dynamics have been under-used as an instrument to improve the development of children's services. For example, tools exist (e.g. Bullock *et al.* 2002) to reduce the number of separations, shorten the length of stay and increase the number of returns of separated children – all of which should *de facto* increase the amount and quality of family support – but their take-up is low and their impact on child development as yet unknown.

THE NEEDS OF CHILDREN AND FAMILIES

One perspective on understanding and developing family support has been to research the way it interacts with other parts of the system of children's services. Another has been to study the needs of children and families and to reflect on how different forms of family support might meet or reduce those needs. At least three contrasting approaches have been taken to understanding the social needs of children and families, each of which has implications for understanding the role of family support type activity.

Developmental Psychology

Developmental psychologists are primarily interested in identifying the chains of effect that lead to abnormal (significantly different from the mean) patterns of child development. The search is for the causes of children behaving badly, having difficulties at school, being depressed and so on. The evidence is highly dependent on longitudinal representative studies of the general population and on evaluation studies of interventions designed to improve child development (Maughan 2001). This evidence is relevant to the understanding of family support in three ways.

First, nearly all social and psychological problems represent a combination of genetic and environmental risks, including influences from the family (e.g. domestic violence – McKeown and Kidd 2002), school (e.g. bullying – Olweus 1994, 2001) and community (e.g. lack of stimulation – Duncan and Brooks-Gunn 1994). There is an increasing understanding of the relative contribution to psychosocial difficulties of genetic and environmental risks (Ashbury et al. 2003) and the way in which the latter can multiply the effects of the former (Stevenson 2001). The implications for children's services are that interventions that deal with only one aspect of environmental risk are unlikely to be successful and that there will always be limitations to the effectiveness of combined approaches.

Second, environmental risks are best understood as a chain of negative effects that can be offset by protective factors (Morton and Frith 1995). For example, one route to antisocial behaviour is overcrowded accommodation that leads to maternal depression, which in turn reduces the quality of parenting and the amount of supervision given to the child (Rutter et al. 1998). Parents in these contexts who have themselves been well parented (a potential protective factor) are less likely to have children who display antisocial behaviour (Quinton and Rutter 1988). By definition, risks accumulate over time and the more enduring the risk the greater the likelihood of social and psychological problems. The implications of this research are that interventions targeted on specific risks in a chain of negative effects are more likely to be effective than general supports and that long-term interventions will be needed for problems that have been long in gestation.

Third, most children exposed to environmental stressors do not develop social or psychological problems (Haggerty 1994). This highlights the importance of good assessment, which helps to identify and balance the risk and protective factors in a child's life and thereby reduces the proportion of false positives. The application of good assessment tools is a prerequisite for the effective use of scarce resources in children's services.

Historically – with a few notable exceptions, such as the creation of various early years support programmes in the USA and more recently in some European states (Schweinhart et al. 1993) – family support services have not been subject to rigorous evaluation and hence child development research has had a relatively weak impact on social policy for children and hardly any impact on family support. Far more important have been sociological pressures.

Sociology and Social Policy

There has been an enduring interest among the general population in supporting what have been termed the 'deserving poor'; that is, children who, through no fault of their own, suffer restricted opportunities for healthy development (Pinchbeck and Hewitt 1969, 1973). Typically, a distinction has been made between these deprived children and the 'depraved' or 'feckless poor' – usually those exhibiting criminal behaviour (Hood 1965). In jurisdictions that reflect British historical patterns, the concept of 'less eligibility' has loomed large – the notion that state-funded interventions should not leave those children who receive them better off than children who are not eligible for such support (Parker 1990). The implications of this legacy for children's services have been profound and are seen particularly in the separation of services for poor children and in the creation of a so-called 'safety net' to capture those children who fall from grace with mainstream services. Family support services in England and Wales, such as the Social Fund or Supported Day Care, have historically been a part of this safety net.

Alongside the safety net there have been policies designed to reduce inequalities in child well-being, beginning with the work of Rowntree in Britain in the nineteenth century. In the last 30 years, the concept of poverty has been sharpened to include relative deprivation (Townsend 1979) and the inability to afford what the majority of people consider are necessities for participating in customary living patterns (Gordon *et al.* 2000). Inequality is generally tackled through fiscal policy and represents the greatest part of government's family support programmes in most western developed nations (OECD 1998). The introduction of community redevelopment programmes in Europe in the 1950s onwards is also closely associated with the drive to reduce inequalities in opportunity and the well-being of children (e.g. Halsey 1972; SEU 1998). Family support fits with this movement.

Service User Perspective

Partly prompted by an increased awareness of human rights, there has been greater attention in recent years to the views of the people who use children's services. Evidence on user views points towards potential disconnections between needs and services. On the whole, the parents of children in need are looking for practical, child-centred and time-limited interventions focused on the specific difficulties that they are experiencing at a particular moment in their child's development (Little *et al.* 2003). Parents recognise that problems come and go across the lifespan: a child may be antisocial at 5 years but well-behaved at 7; an adolescent may be depressed at 14 years but have reasonable mental health by 15 years. Parents do not see a distinction between the development of poor children and others; all children are potentially children in need at some point in their development. This points to a considerable mismatch in children's services between what is offered and what consumers want, or need.

This mismatch between the services offered and what is wanted is equally true for children and young people, who are increasingly being asked their views on matters that affect them personally as well as on those that relate to children as a group (Kirby *et al.* 2003). While the principle of ascertaining the views of young service users is now fairly well established, there are still issues to be addressed in making this effective – not least in including the views of younger children, who are most often the recipients of family support services (Sinclair 2004).

A recent research review on the impact of involving children in promoting change and enhancing the quality of social care services concludes that despite great increases in the amount of participation by children in decision-making and service planning, there is little evidence that this has had a significant impact on the provision or design of services (Danso *et al.* 2003; SCIE 2004). Although there are research findings that can help to inform the process of participation, there is a dearth of sound evaluations of the impact of involving children and ascertaining their views.

Summary

The state supports families in order to meet children's social needs, reduce inequalities in opportunity and improve child well-being. Progress towards the reduction of inequalities in the UK has been unsteady (Bradshaw 2002). Moreover, user satisfaction fluctuates and the level of social and psychological need among children continues to increase in the UK (e.g. Collishaw *et al.* 2004). A different approach to these problems has come from those working in the child development field who have attempted to design family support services (or by rigorous evaluation have contributed to the design of such supports) that might logically be expected to break the chains of negative effects operating in children's lives, thereby improving outcomes and so reversing some of the negative trends in child well-being. The following section summarises evidence of this type.

EFFECTIVENESS OF FAMILY SUPPORT ACTIVITY

As has been mentioned, there is little or no evidence that 'thin' family support is or could be effective in reducing social needs, although user satisfaction with this kind of intervention tends to be high. In recent years, there has been a trend in many European and North American states towards 'thick' family supports that are informed by an identifiable logic that sets out why the intervention might be expected to improve child development outcomes. The Head Start programmes in the USA, Sure Start in the UK and the Springboard programmes in Ireland illustrate the approach well (McKeown *et al.* 2001). These types of programmes are more likely to be subject to rigorous evaluation and so give a better indication of effectiveness (Little *et al.* forthcoming). What lessons can be drawn from this evidence? Six have been drawn out for the purposes of this review.

First, there remain few experimental studies in this area. Brenda Molloy (1996) undertook one of the earliest evaluations by random allocation of a family support model called Community Mothers in a disadvantaged area of Dublin in 1988. Local mothers were trained and employed to carry out structured visits to first- and second-time mothers with a focus on parenting skills, parent self-development, health care, nutrition and other aspects of child development. Compared to the control group, children receiving the intervention were more likely to receive all of their immunisations, to be read to daily, to be breast-fed for longer and later to receive a more nutritious diet. There was evidence of improved psychological health for the mothers. Similar models have been tested internationally, producing equally good outcomes (e.g. Barker and Anderson 1988; Barker 1991) but few reveal *why* the intervention leads to improved outcomes.

Second, the self-esteem and confidence of parents can be important target variables, as well as the practical aspects of child-rearing in the early years. The logic is that improving how parents feel about themselves and their ability to raise their children well will enhance their skills in parenting and negotiating (for services), both of which might be expected to contribute to enhanced child development. Van der Eyken (1990) describes the aims of Homestart as restoring mothers' control over their own lives and so creating a healthy environment for children. Newpin, which like Community Mothers has parents training one another, aims to reduce emotional stress and depression in mothers, boost their self-esteem and improve the quality of parent–child relationships (Cox 1996). PIPPIN, also based on a parent self-esteem model, aims to increase the level of engagement between parent and child in the first months of life (PIPPIN 2004). Each of these programmes has demonstrated some success in meeting its goals, although only Newpin has been evaluated rigorously. Several other problems have also hampered these approaches, including difficulties in replicating the programme consistently and problems with targeting interventions accurately at those who can benefit most (Cox 1996).

Third, some experiments have concentrated on the quality of the parent–child relationship as the child grows beyond infancy. The projects Instapje (for children less than 18 months) and Opstapje (for 4- to 6-year-olds) in The Netherlands are designed to help the parent to provide better quality support to the child and to increase parental and child participation in school. 'Instap' means finding an entrance and 'Opstap' means getting a better vantage point (the additional 'je' refers to the young age of the children being supported). Results of the evaluation are mixed. They suggest that the programmes result in better support for children and slight improvements in their development but have negligible benefits in terms of parent–child relationships (Bakker *et al.* 1997). A variety of parenting models designed to focus on more specific parenting practices and evaluated with more encouraging results have emerged from the Oregon Social Learning Center in the USA (Patterson *et al.* 1992), with promising replications in Europe (e.g. Sylva and Scott 2004).

Fourth, arguably the most positive results for improvement in child development come from offering the parent support but having relatively little direct involvement with the children. Two programmes tried-and-tested in several US states and now being tested in Europe illustrate this point. PATHS focuses on emotional recognition and self-regulation for the parents and produces significant improvements in their behaviour and problem-solving skills as well as a reduction in the need for special education placements for their children (PATHS 2004). Fast Track is focused more on education outcomes (CPPRG 1992; Dodge 1993). Generacion Diez extends these ideas to migrant populations and includes a focus on English as a second language, improving parent–teacher involvement and the child's social skills (Prevention Research Center 2004). These programmes appear to replicate well across different geographical locations.

Fifth, there have been disappointingly few rigorous evaluations of the type of family support offered by social services departments. Schuerman and his colleagues (1994) have evaluated the effectiveness of family preservation programmes (akin to family support in

England – Little 2000) aimed at reducing the use of out-of-home care in the USA. The nature of the intervention (aimed at changing system dynamics with child development as an unmeasured by-product) means that relatively little is known about outcomes. That said, the studies do indicate that programmes can reduce the use of substitute care (although not in cases of cocaine-exposed infants) and may reduce the risk of maltreatment in families where the primary need is parenting skills. There is also some evidence that family preservation services help families with housing difficulties and that they may reduce risks to development associated with such difficulties.

The only English evaluation of broadly drawn family support was undertaken by Gibbons and her colleagues (1990) when they contrasted family centres developed by several agencies and the voluntary sector in a part of a local authority called 'Newpath' with more orthodox provision in 'Oldweigh'. In 'Newpath' social workers operated from the family centres and alongside specialists offering community and family support. The study found modest positive effects on children's well-being (using parent self-report and a standardised measure of emotional distress) and concluded that the support of family, friends and neighbours – very often produced by family support services – is as important to families as professional help.

Sixth, when programmes go to scale, for example Head Start, Sure Start and Springboard, or home visiting for new mothers in England, their universal nature, high professional content and high user approval make evaluation results more difficult to read. In the USA, Olds and Kitzman (1990) have designed and evaluated 'home visitation' programmes in at least seven states, beginning in Elmira, New York, in the 1970s. The goal has been to enhance support to mothers during pregnancy in order to improve child outcomes and maternal development. Measured outcomes have been the maltreatment of children, hospitalisation and employment opportunities for mothers (which improve the economic well-being of the child). Significant effects have been found for mothers who receive additional services co-ordinated by a nurse visiting the home; the provision of the services alone brings no identifiable effect. Effect sizes vary from 15 points for maltreatment to 33 for hospitalisation.

As can be seen, results concerning the efficacy of these various examples of 'thick' family support are mixed. The approach taken in these models is quite distinct from the majority of family support offered by social services departments, with much greater potential for improved child outcomes and learning about what works and why in the 'thick' models. However, Cox (1996) has set out some of the weaknesses of these programmes, including the poor sensitivity and specificity of risk assessments with the consequences that many families who cannot benefit from the support get help, and many who could benefit miss out. Further, apart from the exceptions described above, few of these interventions have become mainstream and most lie outside the ordinary education and health services to which families normally turn first for help.

PROSPECTS FOR THE FUTURE

This chapter has set out some of the constraints and opportunities concerning family support over the 40 years of Roger Bullock's career. The starting point was an area of Roger's expertise, namely the way in which system dynamics promote or hold back service development. The end point has been evidence from studies specifically intended to evaluate the impact of fulsome family support on children's development. In the light of this analysis, what are the common themes and what is the pattern of emerging solutions in relation to family support?

First, the legacy of the notion of the deserving poor remains strong and continues to hinder the development of children's services – family support programmes in particular. Despite the introduction of large-scale prevention programmes like Sure Start, most new initiatives in England and Wales such as Children's Centres and the Children's Fund are only available in selected areas and for particular groups of children, hence continuing some separation between services for poor children and services for better-off children (DfES 2004). These trends are counter-productive; there is reasonable evidence to suggest that all children are children in need at some point in their development, so it makes no sense to differentiate on the basis of social status.

Second, prevention has been understood for too long as preventing the use of services thought to be potentially harmful. For example, some jurisdictions use foster care to prevent the use of residential care, and family support has tended to be offered as an alternative to child protection (Little and Mount 1999). This is illogical: if a service is viewed as unhelpful or harmful it should not be offered in the first place. Increasingly, children's services are being designed to reduce risks to child development and their effectiveness is being measured by a reduction in the level of impairment to health and development (using a range of simple measures) (DfES 2003). With shared objectives, children's services will require a healthy balance of prevention, early intervention, treatment and social prevention activity and a mixed economy of responses, family support included (DSRU 2004).

Third, inter-agency co-operation in most European and Australasian countries has improved radically in recent years (Hallett and Birchall 1992). Children's needs are not confined to single domains that can be adequately dealt with by a single discipline or agency. Much of the improvement has stemmed from a requirement for the effective sharing of information so that one part of children's services is aware of the child protection concerns known to another. There remains relatively little inter-agency co-operation at the point of service delivery, meaning that once a course of intervention is agreed, a single professional generally holds responsibility for implementing the plan. In England and Wales the creation of children's services – together with shared budgets, common assessment procedures, training modules and outcome targets – is increasingly being tried as a solution to these emerging problems.

Fourth, scandal – generally concerning some aspect of children's safety – continues to be a feature of children's services and is thought to explain the slow progress towards improving prevention services such as family support. Rather ironically, the child mortality rate attributable to maltreatment when the child is known to children's services is extremely small (less than one per 100,000 children) and dwarfed by accident rates and avoidable deaths from medical procedures (Sinclair and Bullock 2002; Sloper and Quilgars 2002). Increasingly, children's services leaders (politicians, policy-makers and managers) are becoming aware of their responsibility to acknowledge that not all deaths and injuries to children through abuse are avoidable or preventable by professionals and that sometimes an element of managed risk has to be taken by professionals with the goal of a greater common good.

Fifth, most jurisdictions now acknowledge the requirement for radically improved management information regarding needs, service-use and outcomes for the children and families they seek to serve (Ben-Arieh *et al.* 2001; Little *et al.* 2002). Without the rigorous collection of such information, there is a danger that some children with serious needs will not receive help while others with less serious difficulties will, and also that ineffective interventions are not identified and adjusted or decommissioned. Yet most countries devote less than half of 1 per cent of expenditure on children's services to research and evaluation, compared to at least 1 per cent in medical care (and 5 per cent in most industrial contexts). On the whole, children's services agencies have collected too much information and done too little with it. Emerging solutions stress the benefits of doing more with less by connecting clinical and management data, focusing on variables known from the child development literature to be useful, encouraging skills of diagnosis and prognosis and improving the use of information technology. Elsewhere we have suggested how the development of a taxonomy of children in need could provide a useful framework to take this forward (Sinclair and Little 2002).

Sixth, as the costs of children's services have generally grown year-on-year above the level of inflation, without any appreciable benefit to child well-being, there has been a consequent rise in interest in the cost-effectiveness of children's services and in rigorous evaluation techniques – especially those that randomly allocate potential programme recipients to treatment and control groups (Sheldon 1986; Farrington 2003). Unfortunately, most well-designed cost–benefit evaluations have concentrated on new interventions, including some family support programmes; such evaluations have not extended to traditional services. While this may be because much orthodox provision is not 'evaluable' (Rutman 1984), it means the new has to prove its value but the existing does not.

Seventh, the generally accepted principles that underpin children's services favour family support solutions. The requirement to look at all aspects of a child's development and not just in the area of pressing concern is one illustration (Parker *et al.* 1991). The growing recognition that intervention should build on a careful process of diagnosis and prognosis is another (Christakis 1999; Little 2002). Increasingly, children's services professionals will work on evidence about strengths as well as weaknesses in the child's development and seek to build on inherent resilience (Rutter 1979, 1987; Garmezy 1985; Gilligan 2001; Luthar 2003). The historical tension between services for children and services for family members is being replaced with an understanding that meeting children's needs frequently requires addressing the needs of other family members (Millham *et al.* 1986). These principles all support the development of family support interventions.

Finally, a clearer pattern of service development, implementation and evaluation is emerging, leading to the gradual improvement of children's services with a more solid place for family support activities at its heart. Cross-agency commitment to change is seen as a prerequisite to success. Finding a common language to facilitate communication and using evidence about the needs of children locally is another essential ingredient – concepts that symbolise so much of the work of Roger Bullock over his many years in research.

REFERENCES

Ashbury, K., Dunn, J., Pike, A. and Plomin, R. (2003) 'Nonshared environmental influences on individual differences in early behavioural development: a monozygotic twin differences study', *Child Development* 743, 933–943.

Audit Commission (1994) *Seen But Not Heard: co-ordinating community health and social services for children in need*, London, HMSO.

Axford, N., Little, M. and Morpeth, L. (2003) *Children Supported and Unsupported in the Community*, Report submitted to the UK Department of Health, Dartington Social Research Unit.

Bakker, I., Bakker, K., van Dijke, A. and Terpstra, L. (1997) *0 + 0 = 02*, Utrecht, Nederlands Instituut vor Zorg en Welzijn.

Barker, W.E. (1991) 'Empowering parents: the evolution, expansion and evaluation of a program', *Zero to Three* April, 8–15 National Center for Clinical Infant Programs, Arlington, USA. See also http://web.ukonline.co.uk/oaw/publications.htm

Barker, W.E. and Anderson, R.A. (1988) *The Child Development Programme: an evaluation of process and outcomes – a detailed statistical analysis of the programme outcomes*, Early Childhood Development Unit, Department of Social Work, University of Bristol.

Ben-Arieh, A., Kaufman, N., Andrews, A., Goerge, R., Lee, B. and Aber, L. (2001) *Measuring and Monitoring Children's Well-Being*, Dordrecht, Kluwer.

Bradshaw, J. (2002) 'Children and poor children', in Bradshaw, J. (ed.) *The Well-Being of Children in the UK*, London, Save the Children.

Bullock, R., Little, M. and Taylor, K. (2002) *Going Home? Findings and Guidance to Help Professionals Make Good Judgements About the Reunification of Families*, Dartington, Warren House Press.

Christakis, N. (1999) *Death Foretold: prophecy and prognosis in medical care*, Chicago, University of Chicago Press.

Collishaw, S., Maughan, B., Goodman, R. and Pickles, A. (2004) 'Time trends in adolescent mental health', *Journal of Child Psychology and Psychiatry* 45(8), 1350–1362.

Cox, A. (1996) *Child Abuse: a review of community based projects*, Paper presented to 11th International Congress on Child Abuse and Neglect, Dublin, 18–21 August.

CPPRG (Conduct Problems Prevention Research Group) (1992) 'A developmental and clinical model for the prevention of conduct disorders: the FAST Track Program', *Development and Psychopathology* 4, 509–527.

Danso, C., Greaves, H., Howell, S., Ryan, M., Sinclair, R. and Tunnard, J. (2003) *The Involvement of Children and Young People in Promoting Change and Enhancing the Quality of Services: a research review for SCIE*, London, National Children's Bureau.

DfES (Department for Education and Skills) (2003) *Every Child Matters*, Cm. 5860, London, The Stationery Office.

DfES (2004) *Towards Understanding Sure Start Local Programmes: summary of findings from the national evaluation*. Available at http://www.surestart.gov.uk/_doc/0-319D30.pdf

Dodge, K. (1993) 'The future of research on the treatment of conduct disorder', *Development and Psychopathology* 5, 309–317.

DoH (Department of Health) (1995) *Child Protection: messages from research*, London, HMSO.

DoH (2001) *The Children Act Now: messages from research*, London, The Stationery Office.

DSRU (Dartington Social Research Unit) (2004) *Refocusing Children's Services Towards Prevention: lessons from the literature*, Research Report 510, Nottingham, DfES Publications.

Duncan, G. and Brooks-Gunn, J. (eds) (1997) *Consequences of Growing Up Poor*, New York, Russell Sage.

Farmer, E. and Owen, M. (1995) *Child Protection Practice: private risks and public remedies*, London, HMSO.

Farrington, D. (2003) 'A short history of randomised experiments in criminology: a meager feast', *Evaluation Review* 273, 218–227.

Friedman, M. (2001) 'How to cure health care', *Public Interest*, Winter, 3–30.

Garmezy, N. (1985) 'Stress-resistant children: the search for protective factors', in Stevenson, J. (ed.) *Research in Psychopathology*, Tarrytown, Pergamon.

Ghate, D. and Hazel, N. (2002) *Parenting in Poor Environments: stress, support and coping*, London, Jessica Kingsley.

Gibbons, J. (ed.) (1992*) The Children Act 1989 and Family Support: principles and practice*, London, HMSO.

Gibbons, J., Conroy, S. and Bell, C. (1995) *Operating the Child Protection System*, London, HMSO.

Gibbons, J, Thorpe, S. and Wilkinson, P. (1990) *Family Support and Prevention: studies in local areas*, London, HMSO.

Gilligan, R. (2001) *Promoting Resilience*, London, BAAF.

Gordon, D., Adelman, L., Ashworth, K., Bradshaw, J., Levitas, R., Middleton, S., Pantazis, C., Patsios, D., Payne, S., Townsend, P. and Williams, J. (2000) *Poverty and Social Exclusion in Britain*, York, Joseph Rowntree Foundation.

Haggerty, R. (1994) 'Stress and coping: a unifying theme', in Haggerty, R., Sherrod, N., Garmezy, N. and Rutter, M. (eds) *Stress, Risk and Resilience in Children and Adolescents: processes, mechanisms and intervention*, Cambridge, Cambridge University Press.

Hallett, C. (1995) *Inter-Agency Co-operation and Child Protection*, London, HMSO.

Hallett, C. and Birchnall, E. (1992) *Co-ordination and Child Protection*, London, HMSO.

Halsey, A.H. (1972) *Educational Priority Volume 1: EPA Problems and Policies*, London, HMSO.

Hood, R. (1965) *Borstal Re-assessed*, Cambridge, Heinemann.

Katz, I. and Pinkerton, J. (2003) 'Perspective through international comparison in the evaluation of family support', in Katz, I. and Pinkerton, J. (eds) *Evaluating Family Support: thinking internationally, thinking critically*, Chichester, John Wiley & Sons.

Kirby, P., Lanyon, C., Cronin, K. and Sinclair, R. (2003) *Building a Culture of Participation: involving children and young people in policy, service planning, development and evaluation*, London, Department for Education and Skills.

Laming, H. (2003) *The Victoria Climbié Inquiry*, Cm. 5730, London, The Stationery Office.

Little, M. (2000) 'Family support', in Davies, M. (ed.) *The Blackwell Encyclopaedia of Social Work*, Oxford, Blackwell.

Little, M. (2002) *Prediction: perspectives on diagnosis, prognosis and interventions for children in need*, Dartington, Warren House Press.

Little, M. and Gibbons, J. (1993) 'Predicting the rate of children on the child protection register', *Research, Policy and Planning* 10, 15–18.

Little, M. and Madge, J. (1998) *Inter-Agency Assessment of Need in Child Protection*, Report submitted to the NHS South West Research and Development Directorate.

Little, M. and Mount, K. (1999) *Prevention and Early Intervention with Children in Need*, Aldershot, Ashgate.

Little, M., Axford, N. and Morpeth, L. (2002) *Aggregating Data: better management information and planning in children's services*, Dartington, Warren House Press.

Little, M., Axford, N. and Morpeth, L. (2003) 'Children's services in the UK 1997–2003: problems, developments and challenges for the future', *Children and Society* 17 (3), 205–214.

Little, M., Axford, N., Morpeth, L. and Weyts, A. (forthcoming) 'Evaluating children's services: recent conceptual and methodological developments', *British Journal of Social Work*.

Little, M., Bullock, R. and Mount, K. (1996) *Matching Needs and Services for Children Looked After*, Dartington, Dartington Social Research Unit.

Luthar, S.S. (ed.) (2003) *Resilience and Vulnerability: adaptation in the context of childhood adversities*, Cambridge, Cambridge University Press.

Maughan, B. (2001) 'Prospect and retrospect: lessons from longitudinal research', in Green, J. and Yule, W. (eds) *Research and Innovation on the Road to Modern Child Psychiatry: Volume 1, Festschrift for Professor Sir Michael Rutter*, London, Gaskell.

McKeown, K. and Kidd, P. (2002) *Men and Domestic Violence: what the research tells us*, Report for the Department of Health and Children. Available at www.doh.ie

McKeown, K., Haase, T. and Pratschke, J. (2001) *Springboard: promoting family well-being through family support services*, Dublin Stationery Office. Available at www.doh.ie

Millham, S., Bullock, R., Hosie, K. and Haak, M. (1986) *Lost in Care: the problems of maintaining links between children in care and their families*, Aldershot, Gower.

Molloy, B. (1996) *Building Protective Systems – from Small Beginnings*, Paper presented to 11th International Congress on Child Abuse and Neglect, Dublin, 18–21 August.

Morton, J. and Frith, U. (1995) 'Causal modeling: a structural approach to developmental psychopathology', in Cicchetti, D. and Cohen, D. (eds) *Developmental Psychopathology*, New York, John Wiley & Sons.

OECD (Organisation for Economic Cooperation and Development) (1998) *Children and Families at Risk: new issues in integrating services*, Paris, OECD.

Olds, D. and Kitzman, H. (1990) 'Can home visitation improve the health of women and children at environmental risk?', *Pediatrics* 86, 108–115.

Olweus, D. (1994) 'Annotation: bullying at school: basic facts and effects of a school based intervention program', *Journal of Child Psychology and Psychiatry* 357, 1171–1190.

Olweus, D. (2001) 'Peer harassment: a critical analysis and some important issues', in Juvonen, J. and Graham, D. (eds) *Peer Harassment in School: the plight of the vulnerable and victimized*, New York, Guilford Press.

Parker, R. (1990) *Away from Home: a history of child care*, Barkingside, Barnardos.

Parker, R., Ward, H., Jackson, S., Aldgate, J. and Wedge, P. (1991) *Looking After Children: assessing outcomes in child care*, London, HMSO.

Parton, N. (ed.) (1997) *Child Protection and Family Support: tensions, contradictions and possibilities*, London, Routledge.

PATHS (2004) *PATHS – Promoting Alternative Thinking Strategies*. http://www.colorado.edu/cspv/blueprints/model/programs/PATHS.html [accessed 13 August 2004].

Patterson, G., Reid, J. and Dishion, T. (1992) *Anti-social Boys: a social interactional approach*, Eugene, Castalia.

Pinchbeck, I. and Hewitt, M. (1969) *Children in English Society. Volume 1: From Tudor Times to the Eighteenth Century*, London, Routledge & Kegan Paul.

Pinchbeck, I. and Hewitt, M. (1973) *Children in English Society. Volume 2: From the Eighteenth Century to the Children Act 1948*, London, Routledge & Kegan Paul.

PIPPIN (2004) http://www.pippin.org.uk/ [accessed 13 August 2004].

Prevention Research Center (2004) *Generacion Diez*. http://www.prevention.psu.edu/projects/middle.html [accessed 13 August 2004].

Quinton, D. and Rutter, M. (1988) *Parenting Breakdown: the making and breaking of intergenerational links*, Aldershot, Avebury.

Rose, W. (1994) *An Overview of the Developments of Services: the relationship between protection and family support and the intentions of the* Children Act 1989, Paper presented at the Sieff Conference, September.

Rutman, L. (1984) 'Evaluability assessment', in Rutman, L. (ed.) *Evaluation Research Methods: a basic guide*, Beverly Hills, Sage.

Rutter, M. (1979) 'Protective factors in children's responses to stress and disadvantage', in Bruner, J. and Garten, A. (eds) *Primary Prevention of Psychopathology*, Hanover, NH, University Press of New England.

Rutter, M. (1987) 'Psychosocial resilience and protective mechanisms', *American Journal of Orthopsychiatry* 57, 316–331.

Rutter, M., Giller, H. and Hagell, A. (1998) *Anti-Social Behaviour by Young People*, Cambridge, Cambridge University Press.

Schuerman, J., Rzepnicki, T. and Littell, J. (1994) *Putting Families First: an experiment in family preservation*, New York, Aldine de Gruyter.

SCIE (Social Care Institute of Excellence) (2004) *Has Service User Participation Made a Difference to Social Care Services?* http://www.scie.org.uk/publications/positionpapers/pp03.pdf [accessed 3 September 2004].

Schweinhart, L., Barnes, H. and Weikart, D. (1993) *The High/Scope Perry Preschool Study Through Age 27*, Ypsilanti, High/Scope Educational Foundation.

SEU (Social Exclusion Unit) (1998) *Bringing Britain Together: a national strategy for neighbourhood renewal*, Cm. 4045, London, The Stationery Office.

Sheldon, B. (1986) 'Social work effectiveness experiments: review and implications', *British Journal of Social Work* 16 (2), 223–242.

Sinclair, R. and Bullock, R. (2002) *Learning from Past Experience: a review of serious case reviews*, London, Department of Health.

Sinclair, R. (2004) 'Participation in practice: making it meaningful, effective and sustainable', *Children and Society* 18, 106–118.

Sinclair, R. and Little, M. (2002) 'Developing a taxonomy for children in need', in Ward, H. and Rose, W. (eds) *Approaches to the Assessment of Need in Children's Services,* London, Jessica Kingsley.

Sinclair, R., Hearn, B. and Pugh, G. (1997) *Preventive Work with Families: the role of mainstream services*, London, National Children's Bureau.

Sloper, P. and Quilgars, D. (2002) 'Mortality', in Bradshaw, J. (ed.) *The Well-Being of Children in the UK*, London, Save the Children.

SSI (Social Services Inspectorate)/Audit Commission (1999) *Getting the Best from Children's Services: findings from joint reviews of social services 1998/9*, Abingdon, Audit Commission Publications.

SSI/Audit Commission (2002) *Tracking the Changes in Social Services in England: joint review team, sixth annual report 2001/2*, Wetherby, Audit Commission Publications.

Stevenson, J. (2001) 'The significance of genetic variation for abnormal behavioural development', in Green, J. and Yule, W. (eds) *Research and Innovation on the Road to Modern Child Psychiatry: Volume 1, Festschrift for Professor Sir Michael Rutter*, London, Gaskell.

Sylva, K. and Scott, S. (2004) *Enabling Parents: supporting specific parenting skills with a community programme*. http://www.edstud.ox.ac.uk/FELL/spokes.html[accessed 13 August 2004].

Townsend, P. (1979) *Poverty in the United Kingdom: a survey of household resources and standards of living*, Harmondsworth, Penguin.

Van der Eyken, W. (1990) *Homestart: a four-year evaluation*, Leicester, Homestart Consultancy.

Wulczyn, F., Bruner-Hislop, K. and Goerge, R. (2000) *An Update from the Multi-State Foster Care Data Archive: foster care dynamics 1983–1998*, Chicago, Chapin Hall Center for Children.

11

RESEARCH INTO THE FAMILY JUSTICE SYSTEM

RETROSPECT AND PROSPECT

Mervyn Murch and Douglas Hooper

INTRODUCTION

This chapter is in two parts. In the first we consider the climate of the times, 40 or so years ago, when social research began to be harnessed to the process of family law reform and to child care social policy in England and Wales. In doing so we refer to some of our own research concerning the family justice system – illustrating in particular three contemporary issues that we have studied periodically over a 30-year period of rapid social change. Throughout this time we have had regular links with Roger Bullock and colleagues in Dartington through symposia, conferences and numerous informal consultations. For these and other reasons, Dartington has come to have a special place in the developing world of interdisciplinary family justice studies. In the second part of the chapter we set our respective researches in the context of the far-reaching cultural shift that has taken place over the last 30 or so years from late modernity to post-modernity with its accompanying social fragmentation and individualism.

THE AGE OF REFORM

Dartington is now used regularly as a venue for family law conferences, but it may not be generally realised that the first of these occurred over 30 years ago. This was convened in 1971 by Sir Leslie Scarman, first chairman of the Law Commission. By the end of the 1960s, English family law had become a jungle of ad hoc rules, procedures and remedies exercisable or obtainable in a wide variety of courts with different, and sometimes over-lapping, jurisdictions. This, together with a steadily rising divorce rate accompanied by the greater availability of civil legal aid, placed the existing machinery under strain and forced a fundamental reappraisal of its purpose, methods and use of resources. Given the general

Forty Years of Research, Policy and Practice in Children's Services.
Edited by N. Axford, V. Berry, M. Little and L. Morpeth.
© 2005 John Wiley & Sons, Ltd. ISBN 0-470-01219-6.

idealism of the age and the advance of socio-legal research as a tool by which to better high-light social realities and deficiencies in the law, it was not surprising that reformers should begin to think that what was needed was a major rethink of the law's whole approach to the family. This included ideas about specialist family courts already in existence in certain parts of the USA.

An influential pamphlet, *Proposal for a Family Court* by Judge Jean Graham-Hall (1970), seeking to combine the family justice work of County Court and Magistrates' Courts, was followed in 1971 by the establishment of the Joint Law Commission/Home Office Family Court's Working Party chaired by Scarman. He then conducted a series of regional residential interdisciplinary consultations on the matter, including a visit to Dartington. Subsequently, the Law Commission's family court initiative was overtaken by the *Finer Committee on One Parent Families* (DHSS 1974), which examined the matter in detail (see below).

One of Scarman's early objectives was that the Law Commission should harness the findings of social research to the process of law reform – a view that did not find favour, at least initially, in the corridors of the Lord Chancellor's Department (LCD) (1983). A conversation between Scarman and Mervyn Murch at the initial Dartington Family Courts Conference in 1971, combined with the earlier arrival at Bristol University of Roy Parker, provided the vital impetus for Mervyn to launch his own family law research career, beginning with a Social Science Research Council study of the circumstances of families in divorce proceedings, with Douglas Hooper on the advisory committee. This investigation, which used a combination of court observation and 'consumer' interviews with parents, although intended as a study of the impact of divorce on families, also focused on the operation of the so-called welfare check in uncontested divorce proceedings and the work of the court welfare service (Elston *et al.* 1975; Murch 1980). That first empirical Bristol family justice research proved a springboard for a whole series of further family law studies by the Family Law Research Group, which developed first at Bristol University and more recently at the Cardiff Law School.

Socio-Legal Family Law Research – The Bristol/Cardiff/Dartington Contribution

Although the Conservative governments under Margaret Thatcher and John Major (1979–1997) generally pursued social and economic policies of retrenchment aimed at 'rolling back the frontiers of the State', they were not averse to family law reform, being particularly responsive to public concern about high divorce rates, the fragmentation of family life and growing concern about child abuse, connected to a series of child death scandals.

Consequently, the Law Commission was required to carry out a comprehensive review of child care law. This was preceded by a wide-ranging research programme, in which Bristol and Dartington played a part, funded mainly by the Department of Health. This prepared the ground for the *Children Act* 1989. Later, as part of its rolling programme of family law reform, the government turned its attention to the promotion of mediation, the updating of adoption law and reform of the grounds of divorce. On the latter, the Law Commission was influenced by research (Davis and Murch 1988) revealing serious shortcomings in the substantive law of divorce following the *Divorce Law Reform Act* 1969 and advocating no-fault divorce based on a period of separation (see *The Grounds for Divorce*, Law Comm. No. 192 1990), although the reforms proposed in the *Family Law Act* 1996 were subsequently not implemented by the new Labour administration (see Cretney 2003).

It must also be emphasised that the family law research undertaken at Bristol and Cardiff has been a relatively small part of a much wider research effort in this field, variously funded by the Economic and Social Research Council (ESRC), the Department of Health, the LCD and charitable foundations, notably the Joseph Rowntree Foundation and Nuffield. This should be seen as part of the community's response to the rapid social, economic and demographic changes concerning family life and to the emergence of new social constructions of childhood (see James and Prout 1990). Law and social policy have had to adapt and find solutions in the face of these changes, which have generated much public anxiety – sometimes verging on moral panic. Social research has come to be seen as a vital tool to describe and sometimes quantify the extent of these changes and to investigate the social problems (however defined) that appear to accompany them.

We turn now to three Bristol/Cardiff studies of family justice issues that have been conducted over the last 30 years. These illustrate the complex way in which socio-legal research has been drip-fed into the often protracted policy-making and law reform process.

Issue 1: Should the State Investigate the Welfare of Children in Undefended Divorce Proceedings? If so, How?

Ever since the end of the Second World War, which was followed by an increase in the availability of divorce, parliamentary concern has periodically been expressed about the position of children. Indeed, there is now a considerable body of social research suggesting that, although the majority of children who experience parental separation and re-partnering do *not* experience long-term harm, a significant minority do face an increased risk of detrimental outcomes. Whether this is caused by the separation itself or by the way parents handle family conflict is open to question (Rogers and Pryor 1998). We currently lack research evidence to identify those children who are most at risk (Hawthorne *et al.* 2003, p. 71).

As far as the law of England and Wales is concerned, since 1958 a petitioning parent has been required to inform the court of the proposed arrangements for the care and upbringing of any dependent children of the family. This so-called welfare check has never been regarded as an entirely satisfactory procedure because of the large numbers of children so affected and the consequent impracticalities of doing anything more than a cursory check. Also reformers are not agreed in principle as to whether the State should intervene to investigate the children's situation, especially since no such check is made in the increasing numbers of cases where unmarried cohabitant parents separate.

Since its inception, this judicial checking mechanism has undergone several important changes. Progressively its character has altered from: (a) a procedure applied in open court hearings of undefended divorce petitions; to (b) a 'special procedure' whereby circuit judges, before granting the divorce decree, interviewed petitioner parents privately in chambers about the content of their Statement of Arrangements before declaring that these arrangements were satisfactory or the best that could be devised in the circumstances; and to (c) the present quasi-administrative exercise whereby a district judge scrutinises the Statement of Arrangements along with the divorce petition before granting the decree absolute.

Under Section 41 of the *Matrimonial Causes Act* 1973 as amended by the *Children Act* 1989, the duty of the court now is to consider the proposed arrangements for children of the family with a view to deciding whether the courts should exercise any of its powers under the *Children Act* 1989 before granting the decree. In practice this rarely happens. It should further be noted that, since the *Children Act* 1989, the court's attention has shifted away from having to be satisfied that the divorce may proceed in the interests of the children (part of the symbolic exit from marriage, which in reality was what divorce proceedings had become) to finding some exceptional reason why the divorce should not go ahead. The assumption that lay behind this emphasis was that parents could be trusted in most cases to plan what is best for their children and that where they are in agreement it is unnecessary and potentially damaging for the State to intervene.

Between the early 1970s and late 1990s Murch and his colleagues conducted three major studies of the welfare check in undefended divorce at each stage in the procedure's development (Elston *et al.* 1975; Davis *et al.* 1983; Murch *et al.* 1999). These showed the procedure to be of little more than symbolic value. The private judicial interview introduced by the special procedure was a considerable improvement on the previous perfunctory judicial interrogation in open court. Nevertheless, although parents were often agreeably surprised by the judges' concern and interest, little by way of ongoing support could be offered by the court and the drafters of the *Children Act* 1989 therefore considered that the procedure could be dispensed with. As for the most recent study, which included the views of district judges and family solicitors as well as parents, again the overwhelming opinion was that it failed as a welfare check and was essentially symbolic. Moreover, the timing of the mechanism is misplaced, since children suffer most when parents first separate and not when a parent initiates divorce proceedings months or even years later. Further, some consider a major weakness of the whole approach is that, in what is now a paper-based system, information comes from the parents alone and they have every incentive to ensure that the court and the welfare authorities are not alarmed.

Following the latest research on Section 41, a further review of the procedure is under way in order to 'improve information about children available to the court, to encourage earlier identification of issues of concern and to place greater emphasis on mediation and conciliation at an earlier stage' (LCD 2002). No doubt prompted by the high-profile campaign by various groups of disgruntled and separated fathers who have difficulty in maintaining contact with their children, the review is now also part of government efforts to improve support services for family relationships (see DCA/DfES 2004, p. 30).

Issue 2: Should Children Participate in Family Law Proceedings? If So, How Should They Be Given an Effective Voice?

As has been pointed out elsewhere (Lowe and Murch 2001), the great shift in English law governing parents and children was the move from the position 'where children were of no concern at all to one where their welfare was regarded as the court's paramount concern' (p. 137), yet 'notwithstanding the entrenchment of the welfare principle, traditionally under English law children's futures have been decided on the views of adults, that is parents and professionals' (p. 137).

Even so, in the last few decades an equally important and far-reaching cultural shift has been taking place in the way that western democracies view the competence of children and define the nature of childhood. This new approach sees children less as passive victims of family breakdown and more as participant actors in the family justice process. Article 12 of the United Nations *Convention on the Rights of the Child* 1989 states that children have the right to an opportunity to be heard in all judicial and administrative proceedings affecting them and that children capable of forming views should be able to express them.

The *Human Rights Act* 1998, which gives effect in British courts to the *European Convention on Human Rights*, provides (under Article 6) for fair trial for children as well as for adults. Some argue that this vests a right in children to have separate representation in proceedings brought by or concerning them (Fortin 1999). However, particularly concerning private family law cases, such as might arise in child-related divorce proceedings, the courts of England and Wales have been cautious about giving children a direct voice in proceedings. This contrasts with the law of adoption where, since 1925, it has always been incumbent on the court to consider the wishes and feelings of the children having regard to their age and understanding, doing so through the agency of a guardian *ad litem* or reporter.

In public law care proceedings, the power to order that children should be separately represented from their parents followed on from the Maria Colwell Inquiry in 1974. Accordingly, Section 64 of the *Children Act* 1975 empowered the court to order that parents should not be treated as representing their children where there appeared to be a conflict of interest between parents and child. Although it took some years to implement this provision fully, by 1984 adequate legal aid had been obtained to enable almost all children involved in care proceedings to be represented separately and for specialist panels of suitably qualified guardians *ad litem*, independent of the local authority although administered by them, to be created – a pragmatic managerial solution that was always problematic.

In the early years of the guardian *ad litem* scheme, the Bristol family law group carried out several studies concerning the representation of children in child care proceedings and the development of the guardian *ad litem* service (Murch and Bader 1984; Hunt and Murch 1990). Various research monographs arising from this work helped the Department of Health in its preparation for the *Children Act* 1989 (Murch *et al.* 1990). These included an important study of the length of care proceedings that highlighted the problem of delays in cases involving very young children (see Murch and Mills 1987; Murch and Thomas 1993). But it was not until Masson and Winn-Oakley's (1999) study that the views of children on the receiving end of these services were sampled. As far as court services are concerned, this approach has since been developed by a number of other investigators (Lyon *et al.* 1998; Buchanan *et al.* 2001; Smart *et al.* 2001).

In Cardiff, Mervyn Murch has co-directed two such studies. The first was linked to a study of older children adopted out of care (Lowe *et al.* 1999; Thomas *et al.* 1999); the second examined children's experience of their parents' divorce (Butler *et al.* 2003). These investigations exposed children's need for information and support when they face critical change in their lives, and revealed that they often feel excluded from and bewildered by the decision-making process. Children's ignorance and fear of the courts was particularly marked. Both studies showed that while professionals work hard *for* children they do not necessarily work *with* them. Training and skill development in this area for professionals – social workers and lawyers alike – is woefully deficient.

Findings such as these are fuelling pressure for further reform. There is now a strong argument that in child-related disputes arising from a breakdown in parental relationships courts should make more use of the power to order that children be separately represented by a guardian under Rule 9.5 of the *Family Proceedings Rules* 1991 instead of relying simply on a welfare officer's report as the means by which to convey the children's wishes and feelings to the court – a principle now included in Section 122 of the *Adoption and Children Act* 2002. When this comes into force we may well see an increase in the use of this provision in private family law cases, particularly if the administration, resources and training of staff in CAFCASS (Children and Family Court Advisory and Support Service) can be substantially improved as recommended in 2003 in the *Third Report of the House of Commons Select Committee on the Lord Chancellor's Department*.

Issue 3: The Evolving Family Justice System – How Well Does Its Organisation, Structure and Processes Meet the Needs of Children and Families?

This chapter is not an appropriate place to detail how social research in general has informed the ongoing policy debates concerning the structure of the emerging family justice system and its support services. Suffice to say that two particular studies conducted at Bristol addressed certain aspects of the matter.

1. THE OVERLAPPING FAMILY JURISDICTION OF MAGISTRATES' COURTS AND COUNTY COURTS (1984–1987)

Although the initiative came from Bristol, the research was undertaken primarily for the benefit of the then *Inter-Departmental Review of Family and Domestic Jurisdictions* – termed the *Family Court Review*. This was the government's response to ongoing pressure from the Family Courts' Campaign led in the House of Lords by the late Professor Lord MacGregor of Durris, who had served on the Finer Committee on One Parent Families. As Cretney (2003) observes, Finer 'drew attention not only to the inadequacies of the contemporary court system as a framework for resolving family matters but also indicated the need for a more co-ordinated relationship between the legal framework and the needs of families' (p. 702). The Finer Committee had been particularly critical of the Magistrates' jurisdiction, wishing to see it abolished because of its association with local criminal courts. Finer's suggestion for local family courts (published in a year of acute financial crisis) was repeatedly frustrated by opposition from the Magistrates' Courts interests.

It was against this background that the Bristol overlapping jurisdiction study took place (Murch *et al.* 1987). Where there was a choice of jurisdiction between County Courts and

Magistrates' Courts, and where they offered identical or similar remedies, the study sought to ascertain what factors influenced solicitors' choice of court. It also surveyed courts in order to provide quantitative data on the volume of work in each category of case. It sampled the views of solicitors and litigants about the procedural advantages and disadvantages of the two kinds of court (i.e. professional judge or bench of lay magistrates) and explored litigants' reactions to the process of adjudication in each court. The study revealed that there was major variation in workload and speed of throughput between courts of similar type; that in general County Courts were favoured by solicitors; and that litigant parents wanted major improvements in courts' administration to avoid delay and unnecessary expense. They also wanted less intimidating procedures and in some places better reception and waiting facilities. The idea of family courts was favoured as offering a chance to establish a non-stigmatic and more responsive institution, employing conciliatory rather than adversarial procedures.

On reflection, from the point of view of using research to effect change, it was a pity that this study was not more widely published; it was distributed to a few academics and advisers in the LCD and Home Office, the authors perhaps underestimating the reluctance of some of the more senior officials to undertake any major reform of the family jurisdiction. Nevertheless, once Lord Mackay of Clashfern arrived in the LCD the government began a rolling programme of family law reform. From then on, a number of improvements recommended by the study began – for example, in some Magistrates' Courts a new building scheme to provide special rooms to hear family matters. Moreover, as preparations for child care law reform began, steps were taken to rationalise and restructure the two court systems. These involved creating specialist family proceeding courts at the Magistrates' Court level and introducing a system of child care and family hearing centres at the County Court level with provision for transferring cases between them according to complexity and urgency. Lord Mackay also appreciated the need to bring the administration of Magistrates' Courts within the ambit of his department. But major improvements in linking the management information systems of the two types of courts, which had been called for in the research as a means of addressing the problems of delay in certain kinds of proceedings and in certain courts, did not follow. Indeed, some years after the *Children Act* 1989, a study showed that, if anything, the problem of delay was getting worse (Hunt and Macleod 1999).

Although a unified system of local family courts as envisaged by the Finer Committee did not emerge, the Law Commission's review of child care law served to concentrate official and professional thinking about the need to rationalise the court structure to give effect to the principles of the new Act. It also heightened awareness that family law was a distinctive interdisciplinary branch of civil jurisprudence, a point fully appreciated by Lord Mackay (1991), who commented that, in family work, knowledge of the 'black letters of the law' did not take one very far, urging all those involved (judges, social workers, lawyers and specialist medical experts) to develop common perspectives and a mutual understanding of each other's disciplines.

2. THE INQUIRY INTO SUPPORT SERVICES FOR COURTS WITH A FAMILY JURISDICTION (1987–1990)

It was at this critical period of reappraisal, new thinking and reform in the late 1980s that we studied the support services for the family jurisdictions – services which in a variety of ways provide the infrastructure for what we saw as the emerging family justice system (Murch and Hooper 1992). We wanted to explore how the various professional groupings (judges, court administrators, court welfare officers, guardians *ad litem* as well as official and relevant non-governmental organisations) viewed the parameters and nature of the system, which was in the process of being reorganised following the *Children Act* 1989.

This particular inquiry had more impact than we expected. First, it set out a conceptual analysis of the family justice system as a whole – including not only its court machinery but its supporting legal services, welfare machinery and the place of mediation services. From this point onwards it was noticeable that the term 'the family justice system' became more widely used. Second, the inquiry found that there was widespread support for the Finer Committee's idea of unifying the three separate services that, at the time, provided welfare reports and child representation in the family courts. This study and others may well have helped to clear the ground for what became CAFCASS, introduced by the *Criminal Justice and Court Services Act* 2000. Third, the inquiry emphasised the interdisciplinary character of the system and proposed that the President of the Family Division should establish a co-ordinating policy-making committee for the administration of the jurisdictions – a meeting ground for the relevant professional organisations, the judiciary and government officials who had a direct interest in operational matters. Fourth, it stressed the importance of continuing professional education and development run on interdisciplinary lines.

Following a Dartington conference, these ideas were carried forward by the then President of the Family Division, Sir Stephen Brown. He asked Lord Justice Thorpe to establish and chair what was termed the President's Interdisciplinary Committee. Meeting regularly, this has served a vital role in keeping the essential interdisciplinarity of family justice work firmly on the agenda of a number of constituent specialist professional groupings – doing so at a time when the initial enthusiasm for interdisciplinary work engendered by the *Children Act* 1989 had begun to falter (see Thorpe and Clarke 1998, 2000). It has also helped to support and foster local court liaison around the country and, through its specialist Education and Training Sub-Committee, promoted the concept of interdisciplinary continuing professional education. During the last few years this has seen the development of a core curriculum for those whose work brings them within the ambit of the family justice system. In 2004 the government established a national Family Justice Council to put the interdisciplinary work of the family justice system on a much firmer official basis. In time the intention is that this will incorporate the President's Interdisciplinary Committee and the work of its Education and Training Sub-Committee.

FROM HIGH MODERNITY TO POST-MODERNITY

Our contention is that the work of social research and family law over the past 40 years, such as we have illustrated above, has been construed essentially in what is now recognised as the late modernist period of social and psychological thought. Moreover, many of those still involved in law reform and research have been imbued with the social values of this period – a period that prized ideas of coherence and stability – notwithstanding the staggering changes in intimate human behaviour to which we refer later in this chapter. But now the new era of post-modernism is developing around a quite different set of social values.

The core ideas that make up post-modern concepts revolve around the idea of relative rather than absolute truth (as revealed by rational scientific means, which is a mark of modernism). In addition, a sceptical questioning of social authority, whether in the form of parent, teacher or doctor, is a mark of the social aspects of relativism together with the often market-inspired emergence of what has come to be called consumerism.

In a series of penetrating sociological commentaries, Zygmunt Bauman (1987, 1993, 1995) sets out a developing analysis of this all-pervading cultural shift that is transforming the economic and social context of life in western societies. One of the ideas he advances is that, in the more confident and stable world of late modernity life, strategies – at least for educated middle-class males – were constructed around the idea of the career as a job for life, particularly in the various professions and trades. This arose, he suggests, from a Protestant work ethic in the industrial and technical society of late modernity. The notion of vocation was often linked in people's minds with a concept of career progression as part of their 'identity-building' process. Bauman (1995, pp. 85–86) suggests that often such progress took on the characteristic of a pilgrimage through life but that 'the world is not hospitable to pilgrims anymore'. The point that Bauman makes is particularly challenging to those in the now decreasing generation of academics and practitioners whose formative years were in the 1950s and 1960s – people who might still very well regard themselves in part, at least, as pilgrims in the figurative sense.

In contrast to the more confident, predictable world of late modernist social reform, which may well have largely run its course in the UK by the end of the twentieth century, we now inhabit a world in which the rules of the life game in consumerist post-modern society keep changing during the course of the game itself. In this fragmentary, episodic post-modern world, people are constrained to live more in the present and to adopt flexible lifestyles more in keeping with the rapidity of social change where they can avoid the hazards of becoming trapped or fixed in long-term commitments. People who have adapted to post-modernity approach life with nothing 'remotely reminiscent of the sense of purpose and rugged determination of the pilgrimage'. All this amounts in post-modern human beings to a life strategy to deal with what is seen as the horror of being bound and fixed. In Bauman's view, 'the hub of post-modern life strategy is not identity building (i.e. trade, profession, calling, etc.), but the avoidance of being fixed'. He then goes on to develop a critique of what he sees as several common lifestyles, which, as it were, are replacing the middle-class centrality of the modernist pilgrim. These he terms 'the stroller', 'the vagabond', 'the tourist' and 'the games player', all of whom eschew lasting commitment to the enterprise and offer a joint metaphor for the world of post-modernism (Bauman 1995, pp. 92–99).

Implications for Family Justice

If we apply these concepts to observed family structural change over the last 30 years or so, then we argue that the new modes of living in personal and family life have altered how family structures are defined and socially constructed – developments to which the legal system and family law in particular have struggled to adapt. The curious thing here is that perhaps the research and social policy communities have been struggling to find causes and cures for these fundamental shifts of family patterning using the ordered and rationalistic modes of modernistic thinking that were probably more appropriate to former modes of personal well-being.

The broad outlines of these changes that have occurred over a single generation and in a very changed working and leisure world (Dex 2003) reflect the fluidity and flux that seem to characterise post-modernism. They include: the enhanced longevity of both sexes and especially women; the rise of serial monogamy as a mode of continuing intimate relationships; for a significant and large minority the process of family break-up and reforming; the psychological discontinuities in children's formative years of experience; and the substantial proportion of women in employment outside the home and the hiatus in their personal trajectory when they have children.

Clearly a number of these changes have led to a degree of personal turbulence that for many has been hard to manage. Rates of mental ill health, for instance, are significantly higher for separated or divorced men and women (Hooper 2004), and children are substantially more likely to suffer significant psychosocial problems when they have experienced serious parental conflict and family break-up (Pryor and Rodgers 2001). In turn, rapid problem-solving and an enhanced degree of personal satisfaction and gratification may be sought in order to balance the uncomfortable experience of change.

Yet despite this search for personal satisfaction, people also yearn for stability – providing there is not too much of it! One example of this is the relatively rapid rate at which divorced and separated individuals seek another long-term intimate relationship, often by marrying again. Certainly all the evidence from children's responses to family break-up is that they seek to know what is happening and then try to achieve a regularity in their daily lives that gives them a sense of control and stability (see Butler *et al.* 2003). Here the whole apparatus of the legal system plays an increasingly important role. Legal structures give some credibility to the ideas of continuity and coherence that are lacking in the whirl of post-modern life. Like hospitals, courts have fascinated people (witness the popularity of many television programmes), perhaps because the dramas enacted there enable the watcher to identify and empathise with the disordered lives portrayed.

Implications for Socio-Legal Research

Individualistic, episodic and fragmentary aspects of the post-modern era (including employment and economic uncertainty allied to shifting consumerist values) not only affect family stability profoundly but also, increasingly, permeate the attitudes and values of those involved in government policy-making and law reform. As far as socio-legal research is concerned, two aspects of this worry us: first, the effect on government's research commissioning and funding processes; and second, the impact on those who might wish to pursue long-term research careers in the child care and family justice fields.

Government departments have always been ambivalent about any research that might expose ineffective policies and malfunctioning administration. Nevertheless, in the relatively liberal era of late modernity that followed the Second World War, the ethos of the civil service, cautious though it might well have been, was clearly committed to providing Ministers with 'independent' advice – independent in the sense that it was not heavily or overtly influenced by the political shade of the government of the day; hence units such as Dartington and Thomas Coram; hence, too, substantial government funding for the social and medical research councils.

But from the Thatcher years onwards this approach began to change, influenced in part, we would argue, by the underlying cultural shift to post-modernity that had begun to take place. One sign of this was the increased use by government departments of competitive tendering for academic research projects linked more and more to short-term problem-solving initiatives. Another was the abandonment of the response mode to academics wishing to undertake policy-related research. Throughout this period there was a steady reduction in the number of government-supported research units. The ESRC was also encouraged to focus less on research that was theoretical and more on studies with direct relevance to government and community purposes. In higher education increasing student numbers and mounting staff workloads restricted academic opportunities for major long-term research, even though the introduction of the recurrent research assessment exercise (RAE) in the 1980s increased individual research competitiveness among established academics and between universities and their departments. This had the effect of encouraging staff to move to the better endowed departments.

All of this had important consequences. First, government increasingly controlled the social policy and law reform agenda. Second, life for experienced contract researchers became more hazardous. These days few but the most confident and entrepreneurial would wish to build careers on the basis of contract research, particularly if it was likely to produce uncomfortable messages for government. Moreover, the structuring of the RAE with its emphasis on individual achievement encourages short-term outputs and a safety-first attitude. Third, academics who might wish to develop their own research initiatives increasingly have to turn for funding to the research councils and to the charitable foundations, whose limited resources are often linked to fluctuations in the stock market.

Paradoxically, this new cultural era and altered research environment increases, in our opinion, the importance of maintaining a strong, competent and interdisciplinary research infrastructure in the child care and family justice fields. The very rapidity of social and economic change produces stresses and strains on family life that need to be charted and evaluated if family law and social policy are to be responsive and relevant to people's lives. There is much more that we need to know about the interactions between changing family life patterns and educational, health, legal and social welfare systems. Also, given globalisation and European integration, research increasingly needs to take account of international comparisons and perspectives. Furthermore, in recent years there has been growing recognition that legal and social welfare practice in child care and family justice work needs to be soundly research-based. Indeed, in child care, Dartington has long taken major initiatives in this respect; for example, the long-term work on problems that children experience when they return from residential care. In doing so, it has sought to respond to another feature of post-modernism, namely the development of a risk-averse culture which, as Ulrich Beck (1986), Anthony Giddens (1990, 1991) and others have pointed out, gives rise 'to an increasingly risk-producing, risk-monitoring and risk-managing society' (Bauman 1995, p. 279).

CONCLUSION

What does this shift from high modernity to post-modernity imply for independent social research centres like the Dartington Social Research Unit? Until recently they have usually been able to adapt swiftly to emerging research fields because they are small enough and governed non-hierarchically. In Dartington's case, the Unit has shared the positive image of 'Dartington': this is high status but also liberal and often challenging to the received wisdoms of the day, so that the Zeitgeist has actually been post-modern before its time! Unlike a university, independent research units often present no hostages to the fortune of the single disciplinary academic ghettos, since they invariably recruit people who are able to answer the appropriate research question without regard to discipline but with considerable regard for scholarly work.

But this very productive tradition, which has been fostered at Dartington by Roger Bullock and his colleagues, depends on securing reasonably long-term funding. More fundamentally, it also relies on a coherent underlying framework that gives security to the individual researchers, in terms of both personal development and methodological advances. Without these factors, it is arguable that promising researchers will no longer want to gain career experience in what can be seen as fairly idiosyncratic institutions (some might prefer it, of course). While independence of thought and practice is vital, therefore, our concern is that any isolated unit dependent on soft money is vulnerable in current circumstances, however worthy its purpose and competent its staff. Whether and how they will survive in post-modern conditions remains to be seen.

REFERENCES

Bauman, Z. (1987) *Legislators and Interpreters*, Cambridge, Polity Press.
Bauman, Z. (1993) *Post-modern Ethics,* Oxford, Blackwell.
Bauman, Z. (1995) *Life in Fragments: essays in post-modern ethics*, Oxford, Blackwell.
Beck, U. (1986) *Risikogesellshaft: auf dem Weg in eine andere Modern*, Frankfurt Suhramp. [*Risk Society Towards a New Modernity.*]
Buchanan, A., Hunt, J., Bretherton, H. and Bream, V. (2001) *Families in Conflict*, Bristol, Policy Press.
Butler, I., Scanlan, L., Robinson, M., Douglas, G. and Murch, M. (2003) *Divorcing Children: children's experiences of their parents' divorce*, London, Jessica Kingsley.
Cretney, S. (2003) *Family Law in the Twentieth Century: a history*, Oxford, Oxford University Press.
Davis, G. and Murch, M. (1988) *Grounds for Divorce*, Oxford, Oxford University Press.
Davis, G., MacLeod, A. and Murch, M. (1983) 'Undefended divorce: should s. 41 of the *Matrimonial Causes Act* 1971 be repealed?', *Modern Law Review* 46, 121.
Dex, S. (2003) *Families and Work in the Twenty First Century*, York, Joseph Rowntree Foundation.
DCA/DfES (Department for Constitutional Affairs/Department for Education and Skills) (2004) *The Government's Response to CASC Report 'Making Contact Count'* at page 30, March 2004.
DHSS (Department of Health and Social Security) (1974) *Report of the Committee on One Parent Families* (The Finer Report), Cmnd. 5629, London, HMSO.
Elston, L., Fuller, J. and Murch, M. (1975) 'Judicial hearings of undefended divorce petitions', *Modern Law Review* 38, 632.
Fortin, J. (1999) 'The Human Rights Act's impact on litigation involving children and their families', *Child and Family Law Quarterly* 11, 224.
Giddens, A. (1990) *The Consequences of Modernity*, Cambridge, Polity Press.

Giddens, A. (1991) *Modernity and Self Identity: self and society in the late modern age*, Cambridge, Polity Press.

Graham-Hall, J. (1970) *Proposal for a Family Court*, London, National Council for One Parent Families.

Hawthorne, J., Jessop, J., Pryor, J. and Richards, M. (2003) *Supporting Children Through Family Change*, York, Joseph Rowntree Foundation.

Hooper, D. (2004) 'Relationship difficulties: causes and cures', in Feltham, C. (ed.) *What's the Good of Counselling and Psychotherapy?*, London, Sage Publications.

Hunt, J. and Murch, M. (1990) *Speaking Out for Children: findings from the voluntary sector's first specialist guardian ad litem team*, London, The Children Society.

Hunt, J. and Macleod, A. (1999) *The Last Resort*, London, The Stationery Office.

James, A. and Prout, A. (eds) (1990) *Constructing and Reconstructing Childhood: contemporary issues in the sociological study of childhood*, London, The Falmer Press.

LCD (Lord Chancellor's Department) (1983) *33rd Legal Aid Annual Reports (1982–1983)*, pp.165–174, HC 137 London, HMSO.

LCD (2002) *Promoting Inter-Agency Working in the Family Justice System*, London, Lord Chancellor's Department.

Lord Mackay of Clashfern (1991) *The Upjohn Lecture*.

Lowe, N. and Murch, M. (2001) 'Children's participation in the family justice system: translating principles into practice', *Child and Family Law Quarterly* 13 (2), 137–150. [Reprinted in revised form in Dewar, J. and Parker, S. (eds) (2003) *Family Law: processes, practices, pressures*, Oxford, Hart Publishing.]

Lowe, N., Murch, M., Borkowski, M., Weaver, A., Beckford, V. and Thomas, C. (1999) *Supporting Adoption: reframing the approach*, London, BAAF.

Lyon, C.M., Surrey, E. and Timms, J. (1998) *Effective Support Services for Children and Young People when Parental Relationships Break Down: a child centred approach*, London, Gulbenkian Foundation.

Masson, J. and Winn-Oakley, M. (1999) *Out of Hearing*, Chichester, John Wiley & Sons.

Murch, M. (1980) *Justice and Welfare in Divorce*, London, Sweet & Maxwell.

Murch, M. and Bader, K. (1984) *Separate Representation for Parents and Children: an examination of the initial phase*, London/Bristol, Department of Health and the University of Bristol.

Murch, M. and Hooper, D. (1992) *The Family Justice System*, Bristol, Jordan's Family Law.

Murch, M. and Mills, L. (1987) *The Duration of Care Proceedings: a report to the Department of Health and the Review of Child Care Law*, Bristol, Socio-Legal Centre for Family Studies, University of Bristol.

Murch, M. and Thomas, C. (1993) *The Duration of Care Proceedings*, London, HMSO.

Murch, M., Borkowski, M., Copner, R. and Griew, K. (1987) *The Overlapping Family Jurisdiction of Magistrates' Courts and County Courts: a study for the inter-departmental review of family and domestic jurisdiction*, Bristol, Socio-Legal Centre for Family Studies, University of Bristol.

Murch, M., Hunt, J. and McLeod, A. (1990) *Representation of the Child in Civil Proceedings: summary of conclusions and recommendations for the Department of Health*, Bristol, Socio-Legal Centre for Family Studies, University of Bristol.

Murch, M., Douglas, G. et al. (1999) *Safeguarding Children's Welfare in Uncontentious Divorce: a study of s. 41 of the Matrimonial Causes Act 1973*, Lord Chancellor's Department Series 7/99.

Pryor, J. and Rodgers, B. (2001) *Children in Changing Families: life after parental separation*, Oxford, Blackwell Publishing.

Rogers, B. and Pryor, J. (1998) *Divorce and Separation: the outcomes for children*, York, Joseph Rowntree Foundation.

Smart, C., Neale, B. and Wade, A. (2001) *The Changing Experience of Childhood: families and divorce*, Cambridge, Polity Press.

Thomas, C., Beckford, V. with Lowe, N. and Murch, M. (1999) *Adopted Children Speaking*, London, BAAF.

Thorpe, the Right Honourable Lord Justice and Clarke, E. (1998) *Divided Duties: care planning for children within the family justice system*, Bristol, Jordan's/Family Law.

Thorpe, the Right Honourable Lord Justice and Clarke, E. (2000) *No Fault or Flaw: the future of the Family Law Act 1996*, Bristol, Jordan's/Family Law.

Part III

LOOKING FORWARDS

12

EUROPEAN DEVELOPMENTS IN JUVENILE DELINQUENCY AND JUVENILE JUSTICE

Peter van der Laan and Monika Smit

INTRODUCTION

In September 2003 the Committee of Ministers of the Council of Europe (CoE) adopted a recommendation drafted by a committee of experts on new ways of dealing with juvenile delinquency (Recommendation Rec(2003)20, 2003). There were two main reasons for drafting this recommendation. First, there were concerns about levels of juvenile crime and increased levels of violent crime in particular, requiring new policies and strategies. Second, the CoE has grown rapidly over the last decade and now has 45 member states, the new members all coming from central and eastern Europe. They are confronted with problems similar to those facing western European countries but also have to deal with specific economic and social constraints related to their own domestic situation. The previous recommendation concerning social reactions to juvenile delinquency was believed not to cover sufficiently the specific situations of the new member states.

In this chapter, the major issues of the CoE recommendation are presented. Against the background of trends in delinquency and developments in juvenile justice similarities and differences between countries and groups of countries are described. Remarkably, two European countries – England and Wales and the Netherlands – seem to follow a different track.

At first sight, the whole process of drafting, discussing and finally adopting such an international recommendation has little to do with the activities of the Dartington Social Research Unit in general and those of Roger Bullock in particular. At times it is a rather tedious job in which civil servants and lawyers often play a more decisive role than social scientists, and where diplomacy seems to be more important than creativity. On the other hand, a transnational approach in which there is a sincere willingness to look over one's own hedge, and where there is an open mind to take stock of what is going on elsewhere,

Forty Years of Research, Policy and Practice in Children's Services.
Edited by N. Axford, V. Berry, M. Little and L. Morpeth.
© 2005 John Wiley & Sons, Ltd. ISBN 0-470-01219-6.

seems to fit perfectly well in the Dartington tradition. Also, the issues that are addressed by the recommendation – juvenile delinquency and juvenile justice – have long been at the centre of Dartington's – and Roger Bullock's – interests and activities (Millham *et al.* 1978; Bullock *et al.* 1990; Little 1990; Bullock *et al.* 1992). The Dartington team knows very well that making international comparisons brings along a whole range of conceptual and methodological difficulties (Bullock 1992).

NEW WAYS OF DEALING WITH JUVENILE DELINQUENCY

The CoE's Recommendation on new ways of dealing with juvenile delinquency reads as follows (p. 2):

> That governments of member states
> – be guided in legislation and policies and practice by the principles and measures laid down in this recommendation;
> – bring this recommendation and its explanatory memorandum to the attention of all relevant agencies, the media and the public; and
> – acknowledge the need for separate and distinct European rules on community sanctions and measures and European prison rules for juveniles.

The Explanatory Memorandum of the Recommendation reiterates many of the principles contained in the recommendation from 1987 on social reactions to juvenile delinquency (Recommendation No. R(87)20), including (p. 3):

> – that the juvenile justice system is only part of the overall response to juvenile crime;
> – that the juvenile justice system should avoid repressive approaches and focus on education and reintegration;
> – that juveniles should at least receive the same level of procedural safeguards as adults; and
> – that depriving juveniles of their liberty should only be used as a last resort and that, as far as possible, interventions should be carried out in the juvenile's home environment.

However, new responses are also needed, and a broad range of suggestions are included, a few of which will be mentioned here. To start with, and similar to the state of affairs for adults, the CoE should develop for minors European Prison Rules and European Rules for Community Sanctions and Measures. The execution of such far-reaching sanctions should be governed by sets of rules that are more specific than guidelines from the United Nations. Unfortunately, the existing European Prison Rules implicitly, and the European Rules on Community Sanctions and Measures explicitly, exclude minors. Both in central and eastern European countries and in western European countries, Prison Rules may help to reduce the negative side-effects of the use of secure accommodation. Young people in custody are highly vulnerable, with high rates of suicide and suicide attempts, other forms of self-harm and bullying indicating that custody can be a traumatic experience (Goldson 2002; Graham and Newburn 2003; Kowalzyck 2003; Ruchkin *et al.* 2003).

In the same vein, it is believed that limits should be set on the period of time spent in a police station or in pre-trial detention. It is widely accepted that young people should be kept separate from adults. This should also be the case for limiting the time spent in such provisions. Therefore, bail schemes and other alternatives should be developed and promoted.

Furthermore, countries are advised to use interventions that have been proved to work. An evidence-based approach is still far from common. England and Wales and Sweden have introduced the formal accreditation of programmes that meet certain standards, with other countries considering following suit. Today, there is ample evidence that interventions can be effective if they meet certain conditions. The Explanatory Memorandum states that parents have a role to play in reducing the risk of their children offending and reoffending. Parents are, to a greater or lesser extent, responsible for the behaviour of their children and should, therefore, accept responsibility and take certain actions not only with regard to their child but also to themselves. That is why initiatives are supported that explicitly address and possibly change parents' behaviour concerning their children by means of parenting courses and the like.

Another substantial issue is restorative justice. Developments in New Zealand and Australia, in which victims and close relatives of the young offender meet to discuss the behaviour and the possible solutions, including reconciliation and compensation, are followed in an increasing number of European countries and deserve broad support (Braithwaite 2002).

It is also recognised increasingly that dealing with young offenders requires greater collaboration between different stakeholders. Alongside the police and justice-related organisations, those who should play a role in interventions include local authorities, the education and health system, volunteers and victim support schemes. The aim is to create a multiagency approach at a local level. This is not easy to accomplish for countries that are accustomed to a highly centralised way of governing the country, with the police and the judiciary dominating criminal policies.

Finally, in the light of an increasing involvement in crime of young people from minority ethnic groups, and the need to respond to this phenomenon in a non-discriminatory way, the idea of so-called 'race impact statements' – currently used in England and Wales – should be explored. Such statements set out explicitly how the needs of minority ethnic groups have been taken into consideration in the administration of justice and in policy more generally, and state the procedures and safeguards that have been implemented to ensure that reforms do not inadvertently discriminate against them.

EUROPEAN TRENDS IN JUVENILE DELINQUENCY

The actual situation with respect to juvenile delinquency in most of the current 45 member states of the CoE is largely unknown, so it is difficult to discern trends over the years. Many European countries lack the infrastructure and means to produce reliable crime data over longer periods (Krajewski 2003). Available data are based on recorded crime known to the police and other authorities. As we know, official data do not automatically reflect the actual state of affairs since they depend strongly on police efforts and on the willingness of victims to report crime. They are also affected by political and police priorities and policy changes. Countries in central and eastern Europe are no different from western European countries in this respect. That said, certain differences may be explained by a differential emphasis on the principles of legality or discretion. This may lead to different numbers of young people questioned and subsequently arrested or diverted and, therefore, either included in or omitted from statistics (Neubacher *et al.* 1999) (Table 12.1). It is believed that differences exist between former communist countries and some western European countries where diversionary practices have been strongly developed. In Germany, for instance, 836 juveniles per 100,000 inhabitants are arrested for a crime but only 100 per 100,000 are convicted. In Russia, by contrast, 121 juveniles per 100,000 inhabitants are arrested and almost the same number (101) are convicted.

Table 12.1   Number of juveniles suspected (arrested), convicted and imprisoned in 2000 (per 100,000 inhabitants)

Country	Suspected	Convicted	Admitted to prison
Azerbaijan	6.92	3.90	1.02
Bulgaria	70.65	41.53	0.14
Czech Republic	172.85	41.28	1.07
Germany	836.85	100.29*	9.00
Russia	121.82	101.75	11.63

*1999 figures.
Source: United Nations Surveys on Crime Trends and the Operations of Criminal Justice Systems.

Self-report studies, in which young people are interviewed about their delinquent and anti-social behaviour irrespective of police detection and arrest, are helpful in providing additional information (Junger-Tas and Haen-Marshall 1999). However, they are available in only a few, predominantly western European, countries, are often a one-time-only event and do not always cover the whole country (Junger-Tas *et al.* 1994).

As a result, reliable and valid comparisons of levels of juvenile delinquency between countries on the basis of official police or court data or self-report data cannot be made. It is not possible to calculate precisely differences in levels of juvenile crime between two or more countries (Walgrave and Mehlbye 1998). Consequently, it is impossible to conclude that there is more juvenile delinquency in, for instance, the Netherlands than in England and Wales or in western Europe compared with eastern Europe.

Difficulties in assessing exact levels of crime, however, leave open the possibility of identifying major crime *trends*, especially when lengthier time periods are examined and major societal or administrative changes are taken into account. Pfeiffer (1998) published an overview of juvenile crime and violence in 10 European countries (all Scandinavian and western European apart from Poland). On the basis of police statistics and, where available, self-report studies, Pfeiffer painted a picture of overall stable and sometimes even declining levels of juvenile crime. However, in many countries, police data also showed a sometimes small but nevertheless ongoing increase in violent crime. Robberies, minor and more serious assaults and threats with bodily harm had become more common and more young people were carrying weapons (mainly pocket knives and stilettos).

Self-report studies are less reliable with regard to more controversial types of criminal behaviour, such as serious violent offending or sexual offending (Junger-Tas and Haen-Marshall 1999). Nevertheless, those that are available corroborate the analyses of police data. Numbers are small compared to the involvement of young people in other types of crime but more young people reported participation in bullying, fighting, harassment and so on. Furthermore, young people reported that they are carrying weapons more often, for instance when they are going out at weekends. Even though they do not intend to use these weapons – they are to help the young person 'to feel safe' – the risk of doing so is undoubtedly greater (Van der Laan and Nijboer 2000).

Estrada (2001), using the same kind of data as Pfeiffer, came to slightly different conclusions. Estrada argues that the increase in violent crimes committed by minors as shown by police data is largely the result of increased awareness and societal concerns regarding young people. The actual increase is less marked and results from changes in the way certain actions by young people are perceived and judged by the public, the police and the judiciary. In the Netherlands, for example, handbag-snatching was occasionally considered so-called 'simple theft' 10 to 15 years ago (Freeling 1993); today, it is always regarded as theft under threat of violence or with the actual use of violence (robbery). The former falls into the category of property offences whereas the latter no doubt is seen as a violent crime. Yet the act itself has not changed. This 'inflation of violence' is reported for other types of behaviour (Egelkamp 2002).

Occasional country reports from western Europe (Mehlbye and Walgrave 1998) and some central and eastern European countries (Dünkel and Drenkhahn 2003) subscribe to the trend of overall stability combined with increased violent crime.

The Explanatory Memorandum to the Recommendation concludes that, on the basis of available data and reports in combination with anecdotal evidence from country delegates, absolute levels of juvenile delinquency and violent crime in some central and eastern European countries are seemingly lower than in western Europe. But it also supposes that, especially with regard to property crime, central and eastern European countries are catching up. Recent data from the Russian Federation and several other former communist countries suggest that violent crime committed by young people has increased quite dramatically (Pridemore 2002; Babachinaite 2003; Filipčič 2003; Krajewski 2003; Markina 2003; Šakić et al. 2003; Tarbagaev 2003; Válková et al. 2003).

The explanation for such trends lies in the changing lives of young people. Particularly in central and eastern Europe, societies have changed rapidly over the last 10 to 15 years (Pridemore 2002). The following relevant changes can be identified (Explanatory Memorandum, p. 3):

- the rise in child poverty and income inequality;
- the greater incidence of divorce and family breakdown and its impact on parenting;
- the growing experimenting at an increasingly young age with drugs and alcohol;
- the decline of the youth labour market and the rise in unemployment among young adults;
- the increasing concentration of social and economic problems and related crime and violence in specific areas like inner cities and/or housing estates;

- the mass migration of ethnic minorities into and within Europe;
- the increased risk of psycho-social disorders among young people.

Changes in societies may have led not only to increasing levels of juvenile crime and violence, but also to concerns about the possible involvement in delinquency of specific groups of young people, notably girls, young children and members of minority ethnic groups. Owing to a lack of reliable data and surveys it is difficult to establish if more girls are involved in delinquency today than in the past or if children are increasingly younger when they commit their first offence, although there seems to be some increase with regard to the former (Rutter *et al.* 1998). The situation concerning young members of minority ethnic groups is different. In some western European countries ad hoc studies clearly show higher levels of delinquency among young people from these groups (Tonry 1997). In some countries, young Moroccans or young people from the Caribbean or Somalia are over-represented in police statistics; in others, young Turks or young immigrants from eastern Europe. Some central European countries report – although without robust statistical support – a disproportional involvement in crime of Roma and Sinti youngsters. Selection mechanisms in the processing of cases by the police and the judiciary may account partially for such patterns.

Another trend, also requiring more reliable data, concerns the sometimes serious and violent crimes committed by young offenders in groups or gangs and their alleged links to serious, sometimes transnational, organised crime (Klein *et al.* 2001). The vulnerability of certain groups of young people due to their ethnic and/or socio-economic status makes them an interesting target for adults involved in organised crime.

It is possible that the trends and changing trends in juvenile delinquency described above are relatively recent. As far as western Europe is concerned, there are no signs that particular changes started before the 1980s and 1990s. The first few decades after the Second World War may have been relatively quiet and stable. In central and eastern Europe documentation on juvenile delinquency before the end of the Soviet regime is scarce. The rapid social and economic changes that followed the fall of the Iron Curtain also affected juvenile behaviour. Therefore, in central and eastern Europe, too, juvenile delinquency has changed in nature and frequency mainly during the last one or two decades.

DEVELOPMENTS IN JUVENILE JUSTICE

In the same way that juvenile delinquency has changed over the years, so have the ways in which juvenile delinquents are dealt with by society. Since the mid-1980s, many European countries have also revised their legislation. New penal laws, separate from those for adults, have been introduced or are under consideration (Courakis 2000), especially in central and eastern Europe where many countries have decided to change laws that date back to the former communist regimes (Válková 2001; Stańdo-Kawecka 2003). Legislation in some of these new democracies is therefore relatively modern compared to those in many western countries.

As with juvenile crime it is difficult to show the kind of developments and changes that have taken place in juvenile justice. Few countries produce reliable statistics on police and public prosecutor decisions, on punishments imposed by the courts or on the use of prison and other measures. A further complication is that in several countries reactions to delinquent behaviour stem from civil or administrative law. Such decisions are not included in official penal statistics. Also, the fact that certain approaches find their way into legislation is no guarantee that they are actually put into practice. Many countries – in central and eastern Europe in particular – find it difficult to go ahead with the new structures and programmes because they lack the resources for vital infrastructure, professional organisations and trained staff.

Nevertheless, it seems fair to say that diversionary measures and punishments that are executed in the community instead of in secure residential settings are imposed more frequently and in more countries than in the past. In at least 29 member states legislative and/or pragmatic provisions are made for community sanctions. These are taken seriously in numerous European countries, not only by practitioners and policy-makers but also by judicial authorities, politicians and governments (Recommendation Rec(2000)22, 2000). The best-known and most frequently imposed community sanction is *community service*. This implies doing unpaid work for the benefit of the community, for a specified number of hours, within a fixed period of time, preferably during leisure time (Van der Laan 2000). Community service is often regarded as an opportunity for the offenders to repair the damage they caused. In some countries the use of community service is still in an experimental stage, reflecting the relatively small numbers of young people involved, while in others the annual number of community service orders imposed is impressive and increasing.

Among the very recent alternatives to custody are electronically monitored curfew orders (Whitfield 1997). In essence, these require an offender to remain at a specified place, for a certain number of hours during a certain period of time. The curfew is monitored electronically using a bracelet – or tag – fitted to the offender's ankle. The method can be used as surveillance only and as an addition to intensive supervision. The latter may include weekly home visits by a probation officer and a requirement for the offender to participate in specified activities, such as training courses, community service and drug and alcohol tests. In Europe, trials for adults started in England and Wales in 1989, following a little later in Sweden (1994) and the Netherlands in (1995) (Van der Laan, 2002). In England and Wales and the Netherlands experiments with minors started in 1998 and 2000 respectively. In England and Wales the scheme was rolled out nationally in 2002 after a 2-year experiment in two pilot areas (Elliott *et al.* 2000). The Dutch experiment was held in one court district and was officially halted in Spring 2002 due to a lack of eligible candidates (Terlouw and Kamphorst 2002).

A further important development in juvenile justice in Europe concerns the role of the victim (Walgrave and Mehlbye 1998). Interventions and punishments that pay respect to victims, and try to incorporate their needs and interests materially or otherwise by encouraging mediation and reconciliation between victim and offender, have gained popularity and are given serious governmental support in several countries in both the west and the east (Miers 2001). Data on the numbers involved remain difficult to collect, however. Under the umbrella of restorative justice an increasing number of countries are also introducing family group conferences (Bazemore and Walgrave 1999; Johnstone 2002).

Other noticeable changes in juvenile justice during the recent past concern the age of criminal responsibility. The minimum age of criminal responsibility ranges from 7 years in Switzerland to 18 in Belgium (Courakis 2000) (Table 12.2). In several countries the minimum age has been raised or will be raised in the near future. A number of central European countries seem to have followed the German legislation and opted for 14 years. The situation in Germany is also closely observed with respect to the upper age limit, with the majority of young adult offenders there aged 18 to 21 dealt with under juvenile penal law. Austria has already followed this example. Applying adult penal law to juveniles is exceptional. The Netherlands seems to be the only country where the possibility of dealing with 16- and 17-year-olds under adult law has been extended. The process for referring a young person to an adult court has been made easier and is practised more often.

Table 12.2   Age of criminal responsibility

Austria	14	Lithuania*	16
Belgium	18	Luxembourg*	18
Bulgaria	14	Macedonia*	16
Croatia	14	Moldova*	16
Cyprus	10	The Netherlands	12
Czech Republic	15	Norway	15
Denmark	15	Poland	13
England and Wales	10	Portugal	12
Estonia*	15	Romania	14
Finland	15	Russian Federation*	16
France*	13	Scotland	8
Germany	14	Slovak Republic	15
Greece	12	Slovenia*	16
Hungary	14	Spain	14
Iceland	15	Sweden	15
Ireland	12	Switzerland	7
Italy	14	Turkey	12
Latvia	14	Ukraine*	16
Liechtenstein	12		

*Exceptions possible.
Source: Courakis (2000) (revised).

Developments in the opposite direction are also noticeable. In particular, England and Wales and the Netherlands are concerned about the involvement in crime of children below the age of criminal responsibility. Lowering that age-limit has not been considered seriously but specific measures for these children and their parents have been introduced or are under study (Bol 2002).

The idea of paying attention to parents and other important people in the immediate vicinity of young offenders is not new. Over a century ago, juvenile crime was often considered to be the result of parental neglect and poor parenting. It led to the notion of *parens patriae* – the state assuming the role of the parents in bringing up children at risk. Today, young people are held more and more responsible for their own acts but at the same time the role and influence of parents and other adults is increasingly acknowledged. In some countries this has led to specific measures aimed primarily at the parents. The best-known example is the introduction in England and Wales in 1998 of the Parenting Order and the Child Safety Order. These require parents to supervise and look after their child properly. This may include taking a parenting course, arranging supervision by another responsible adult when the parents themselves are not at home, keeping their child at home in the evening and at night and ensuring that their child attends school (Bottoms and Dignan 2001). In the Netherlands, the possibility of and the necessity for such orders are being studied.

Despite the many innovations in juvenile justice and the ever-increasing popularity of community sanctions and measures, custodial sentences form the backbone of juvenile justice systems in many, if not all, European countries. Little is known, however, about the use of custodial sentences. For most countries exact numbers of custodial sentences and other forms of detention are not available. Neither is it possible to be specific about the actual length of custodial sentences. The circumstances in which young people are held in detention are also largely unknown, although reports from the European Committee for the Prevention of Torture and Inhuman or Degrading Punishment (2003) give reason for concern. Even more problematic is the situation with regard to pre-trial detention. Proper registration is lacking, leaving us with little or no information. Based largely, again, on anecdotal evidence it seems that after years of reduction in some western European countries the use of detention for young offenders is increasing due to repressive tendencies in society (Graham and Newburn 2003; Van der Laan 2003). In central and eastern Europe an opposite trend is apparent: fewer and shorter custodial sentences, although numbers are still high and sentences are relatively long.

Two other, partly related, developments are also important to mention. First are the notions of early onset, early detection and early intervention. Longitudinal research suggests that antisocial or unruly behaviour at a young age should be seen as an indicator of the possible emergence at a later stage of a serious and sometimes violent criminal career (Loeber and Farrington 2001). These signs should therefore be taken seriously and the need for preventive measures early in the child's life should be considered. A second development is the increased knowledge about the kind of interventions that may lead to an actual reduction of (re-)offending (Andrews et al. 1990; Andrews 1995; McGuire and Priestley 1995; Lipsey and Wilson 1998). Large meta-analyses show that certain interventions with certain offenders and in certain circumstances can indeed make a difference. The reduction of reoffending by 5 per cent and up to 40 per cent is no longer beyond reach, provided that so-called 'What Works' principles are applied. The aforementioned publications identify the following characteristics as making interventions more effective:

- addressing the criminogenic factors that caused or directly contributed to the offending behaviour (e.g. antisocial attitudes, drug misuse, poor cognitive skills, educational failure and poor parenting);
- ensuring a close match between the risk of reoffending and the nature, intensity and duration of the intervention;
- employing practitioners whose teaching approach best matches the learning potential of the offender (i.e. structured participatory styles rather than unstructured didactic styles) and that uses material specifically tailored to the offender's needs and abilities;
- using community-based interventions that are closely connected to the offender's home environment rather than based in institutions;

- drawing on a range of methods (e.g. social skills training, anger management, problem-solving) often referred to as a cognitive behavioural approach (which addresses perceptions, thinking, feeling and behaviour).

DIFFERENCES AND SIMILARITIES BETWEEN COUNTRIES AND REGIONS

Based on the above, what are the most important transnational similarities and differences in juvenile crime and justice, and how might they be explained? With regard to juvenile crime, the following regional differences seem to exist:

- Juvenile crime levels in central and eastern Europe are not (yet) as high as in western Europe.
- Violent juvenile crime is stable in Scandinavia but increasing elsewhere.
- Violent juvenile crime has increased more strongly in western European countries than in central and southern European countries.
- Alcohol- and drug-related crime is on the increase, but more strongly in central and eastern Europe.
- Property crime is increasing in central and eastern Europe but is stable elsewhere.
- Girls are increasingly involved in crime in western Europe; however, their involvement is limited compared to that of boys.
- All over Europe young people from minority ethnic groups are increasingly involved in crime, but ethnicity differs between countries and regions.
- Young people seldom commit crime on their own but almost always in groups; the degree of organisation of such groups varies between countries and regions.

Differences between regions are very much related to the economic and social development of countries and the difficulties they have. The economic, social and often isolated position of minority ethnic groups also plays a role, although countries differ from each other in the variety of ethnic groups that are present, and some groups are more strongly over-represented in crime statistics than others. The relatively low level of violent juvenile crime in Scandinavian countries may be explained by the well-developed social welfare system in those countries as well as by the relatively high integration of migrants (Bol 2002).

Juvenile justice systems are often described in terms of two extremes: the *welfare model* and the *justice model* (Dünkel 1991; Courakis 2000; Junger-Tas 2001). The welfare model focuses on the offender rather than on the offence or the victim. The young offender is deemed to need treatment, re-education and rehabilitation. Measures are taken in the best interests of the child. If needed, long treatment-oriented sentences can be imposed in order to deal properly with the personality of the young person. If treatment outside of the judicial system is preferred, cases can be diverted. Proportionality is of little relevance in the welfare model.

In the justice model it is the offence that matters and not the offender and his or her personality. Proportionality is crucial in that the length or severity of the sentence is linked to the offence committed. In both the welfare and the justice models alternative types of sanctions are welcomed: in the welfare model because they are believed to be (more) effective in terms of special prevention; and in the justice model because some sanctions, such as community service, acknowledge the young person's own responsibility for his or her behaviour and for making good what has gone wrong. The justice model more than the welfare model acknowledges the importance of rights and safeguards: young people should enjoy the same protection in the justice system as adults.

Some scholars propose *restorative justice* as a third model (Marshall 1996; Walgrave 2001). Here, a central role is given to the victims and their interests. Solving the conflict between offender and victim, both in material and immaterial ways, is considered more important than imposing a sentence without any reference to the victim.

The characteristics and developments of European juvenile justice systems show a varied geographical pattern, as we have seen for crime trends:

* Southern and eastern Europe juvenile justice systems are more welfare-oriented, whereas certain northern European countries have shifted into the direction of the justice model.
* A few countries have seriously introduced restorative justice kind of approaches.
* The idea that custodial sentences should be used as a last resort only is widespread, but in many countries – in all regions except Scandinavia – the numbers of custodial sentences are still high.
* Several, mainly western and northern European, countries have successfully introduced diversionary measures and alternative sanctions.
* The minimum age of criminal responsibility shows an upward trend in most central and eastern European countries.
* Rights and safeguards for young people have been strengthened in most countries.

Overall, one can say that differences between states are becoming smaller. Countries are moving towards a 'balanced' justice model (Courakis 2000). The idea that education or rehabilitation is to be preferred over punishment prevails and goes hand-in-hand with an increasing emphasis on restoring the harm or damage caused. At the same time, juveniles are given more rights and safeguards.

ENGLAND AND WALES AND THE NETHERLANDS

England and Wales and the Netherlands seem to develop in a different direction from other countries with regard to juvenile justice (Graham 2002; Van der Laan 2003). Although societies across Europe are becoming less tolerant and more repressive in their reactions towards juvenile delinquents, this seems strongest in England and Wales and the Netherlands. Here, the number of custodial sentences seems to rise more rapidly, and increasingly young people are taken into pre-trial detention. They are also the only two countries in Europe to introduce electronically monitored curfews for minors. The countries also share a certain sympathy for 'scared straight' programmes and interventions that resemble US boot camps. The former take young offenders or juveniles at risk of offending to prisons for adults where they have often confrontational discussions with inmates. The idea is that the experience will dissuade them from offending in the future. In the boot camp style programmes, military-like discipline and order play a pivotal role. New laws and official guidelines that restrict the use of diversionary measures to first-offenders have also been introduced in both countries.

Neither England and Wales nor the Netherlands has formally lowered the minimum age of criminal responsibility, but England and Wales has abolished the principle of *doli incapax* (the principle that for children aged 10 to 13 years who have committed an offence the prosecution has to prove that it was the juvenile's intention to do so and also that the juvenile knew that what he or she was doing was wrong) and both countries focus increasingly in their crime prevention policies on younger children. Interventions have been introduced that are formally not of a penal nature but that much resemble some of the penal measures for young people. The English Child Safety Order is aimed at children under the age of 10 displaying antisocial or unruly behaviour and the Dutch Stop is for children under 12 years who have committed minor offences, such as vandalism and shoplifting. Both are civil measures but can have penal consequences. As for the upper limit of juvenile penal law the Netherlands has widened the possibility of referring minors to adult court.

Elements of restorative justice are noticeable in both England and Wales and the Netherlands. Family group conferences are included in the English Intensive Supervision and Surveillance Programmes (ISSP) for repeat offenders (Little *et al.* 2004) and the recently introduced Reparation Order stresses the importance of compensating for the damage caused. In the Netherlands, restorative justice is practised mainly by the intensive use of community service orders, but lately mediation and conferencing are gaining more support.

The two countries also share an increased interest in the effectiveness of interventions. Much attention is given to the so-called 'What Works' approach, stressing the importance of using intervention programmes that meet theoretical, methodological and intrinsic standards (McGuire and Priestley 1995). In line with this approach an accreditation system of (potentially) effective interventions has been established in England and Wales, so that only accredited programmes can be applied and funded. The Netherlands is preparing for such a system.

CONCLUSION

Juvenile delinquency and juvenile justice in Europe do not take a uniform shape. Trends and ideas differ between countries and regions. However, there are also many similarities and groups of countries are moving more closely to each other. Why England and Wales and the Netherlands are developing in a different, somewhat more repressive direction is a matter for speculation. No doubt, both countries' strong orientation towards the other side of the Atlantic Ocean – the USA in particular – is part of the explanation.

Unfortunately, detailed information on both delinquency trends and juvenile justice developments in Europe is lacking. We do not know precisely what is happening. In order to understand and explain similarities and differences, and to take appropriate policy measures, more effort should be put into collecting and analysing the same kind of data from every country (Bala and Bromwich 2002). The CoE's first *European Sourcebook of Crime and Criminal Justice Statistics* (Kilias and Rau 2000), although useful, concentrates on adults; extending it to juveniles or developing a separate sourcebook on minors would help with understanding cross-national patterns and trends.

A final point concerns the relationship between research, policy and practice, a longstanding interest of Roger and the Dartington Unit, particularly at the national and local levels (see Bullock *et al.* 1998). But what impact do *supranational* law and guidance have on national policies for children, and to what extent are they evidence-based?

The impact of a recommendation by the CoE on policies and practices concerning juvenile delinquency and juvenile justice is unknown. As 'soft law', CoE recommendations do not have statutory force (Nijboer 2001), so we should not expect immediate changes in national approaches towards juvenile delinquency and juvenile justice. At best, a recommendation can work as a leverage to introduce new policies and practices, to amend existing ones, and to put pressure on government politics. In central and eastern European countries, some of which are working very hard to change penal legislation for juveniles and bring it more in line with that in western Europe, recommendations from the CoE are welcomed because they point the directions in which new legislation and practical provisions should move. In addition, the very recent expansion of the European Union and the increasing importance in the so-called 'Third Pillar' of a shared approach to crime and justice matters mean that any common statement on specific topics may increasingly influence national policies.

It is also important to note that, traditionally, the CoE depends heavily on research when drafting recommendations and rules. In Recommendation Rec(2003)20 we can see this in the prominent position of accumulated knowledge concerning the causes and correlates of juvenile delinquency and the nature of effective crime prevention methods. For instance, the calls to pay attention to the early onset of problem behaviour, and to actively involve parents when dealing with juvenile delinquents, originate from developmental and life-course criminological research that has shown the importance of family factors. Similarly, the promotion of programmes that meet so-called 'What Works' principles rests on large meta-evaluations and meta-analyses. CoE recommendations are more evidence-driven today than they were in the past.

Ultimately, recommendations are important but not enough. A strong relationship between research, policy and practice cannot be enhanced only by conventions, rules and regulations from international bodies such as the Council of Europe, the United Nations or the European Union. It also requires international co-operation at a more practical level. This can be done by means of international seminars and, more importantly, through joint initiatives regarding comparative and cross-national research and the development of instruments, policy and practice tools that can be used in several countries – and these are, therefore, exactly the kinds of activities for which the Dartington Unit and its staff stand. Such an approach, in combination with the open-mindedness and willingness to look over one's own national boundaries that characterise Roger Bullock and his colleagues, may turn 'soft law' into 'hard practice'.

REFERENCES

Andrews, D.A. (1995) 'The psychology of criminal conduct and effective treatment', in McGuire, J. (ed.) *What Works: reducing re-offending – guidelines from research and practice*, Chichester, John Wiley & Sons.

Andrews, D.A., Zinger, I., Hoge, R.D., Bonta, J., Gendreau, P. and Cullen, F.T. (1990) 'Does correctional treatment work? A clinically relevant and psychologically informed meta-analysis', *Criminology* 28, 369–404.

Babachinaitė, G. (2003) 'Youth violence and its causes in Lithuania', in Dünkel, F. and Drenkhahn, K. (eds) *Youth Violence: new patterns and local responses – experiences in East and West*, Mönchengladbach, Forum Verlag Godesberg.

Bala, N. and Bromwich, R.J. (2002) 'Introduction: an international perspective on youth justice', in Bala, N., Hornick, J.P., Snyder, H.N. and Paetsch, J.J. (eds) *Juvenile Justice Systems: an international comparison of problems and solutions*, Toronto, Thompson Educational Publishing.

Bazemore, G. and Walgrave, L. (eds) (1999) *Restorative Juvenile Justice: repairing the harm by youth crime*, Monsey, Criminal Justice Press.

Bol, M.W. (2002) *Jeugdcriminaliteit over de grens*, Den Haag, WODC (2002/4).

Bottoms, A. and Dignan, J. (2001) *Youth Justice in Great Britain*, Paper presented at the conference 'Crime and Justice', Cambridge, England (18–20 October).

Braithwaite, J. (2002) *Restorative Justice and Responsive Regulation*, Oxford, Oxford University Press.

Bullock, R. (1992) 'A framework for making international comparisons of services for adolescents', in Bullock, R. (ed.) *Problem Adolescents: an international view*, London, Whiting & Birch.

Bullock, R., Gooch, D., Little, M. and Mount, K. (1998) *Research in Practice: experiments in development and information design*, Aldershot, Ashgate.

Bullock, R., Hosie, K., Little, M. and Millham, S. (1990) 'The characteristics of young people in Youth Treatment Centres', *The Journal of Forensic Psychiatry* 1, 329–350.

Bullock, R., Little, M. and Millham, S. (1992) 'Applying restitutive justice to young offenders: observations from the United Kingdom', in Messmer, H. and Otto, H.-U. (eds) *Restorative Justice on Trial*, Dordrecht, Kluwer Academic Publishers.

Courakis, N. (2000) *A Typology of Juvenile Justice Systems in Europe*, Strasbourg, Council of Europe (PC-JU (2000) 28 REV 5).

Dünkel, F. (1991) 'Legal differences in juvenile criminology in Europe', in Booth, T. (ed.) *Juvenile Justice in the New Europe*, Sheffield, Joint Unit for Social Services Research.

Dünkel, F. and Drenkhahn, K. (eds) (2003) *Youth Violence: new patterns and local responses – experiences in East and West*, Mönchengladbach, Forum Verlag Godesberg.

Egelkamp, M.M. (2002) *Inflation von Gewalt? Strafrechtliche und kriminologische Analysen von Qualifikationsentscheidungen in den Niederlanden und Deutschland*, Groningen, Universiteit Groningen.

Elliott, R., Airs, J., Easton, C. and Lilly, J.R. (2000) *Electronically Monitored Curfew for 10- to 15-year-olds: report of the pilot*, London, Home Office Research and Statistics Directorate.

Estrada, F. (2001) 'Juvenile violence as a social problem', *British Journal of Criminology* 41, 639–655.

European Committee for the Prevention of Torture and Inhuman or Degrading Treatment or Punishment (2003) *The CPT Standards*, Strasbourg, Council of Europe (CPT/Inf/E (2003) 1).

Filipčič, K. (2003) 'Different forms of youth violence in Slovenia', in Dünkel, F. and Drenkhahn, K. (eds) *Youth Violence: new patterns and local responses – experiences in East and West*, Mönchengladbach, Forum Verlag Godesberg.

Freeling, W. (1993) 'De straf op tasjesroof. Hoe het strafklimaat strenger werd', *Proces* 72, 76–82.

Goldson, B. (2002) *Vulnerable Inside: children in secure and penal settings*, London, The Children's Society.

Graham, J. (2002) 'Juvenile crime and justice in England and Wales', in Bala, N., Hornick, J.P., Snyder, H.N. and Paetsch, J.J. (eds) *Juvenile Justice Systems: an international comparison of problems and solutions*, Toronto, Thompson Educational Publishing.

Graham, J. and Newburn, T. (2003) 'Het vuur aan de schenen van jonge veelplegers in Engeland en Wales: recente ontwikkelingen', *Tijdschrift voor Criminologie* 45 (2), 193–203.

Johnstone, G. (2002) *Restorative Justice: ideas, values, debates*, Cullompton, Willan Publishing.

Junger-Tas, J. (2001) *The Juvenile Justice System: past and present trends in western society*, Paper presented at the DVJJ conference 'Juvenile Justice', Luxembourg.

Junger-Tas, J., Terlouw, G.J. and Klein, M.W. (eds) (1994) *Delinquent Behavior among Young People in the Western World: first results of the international self-report delinquency study*, Amsterdam, Kugler Publications.

Junger-Tas, J. and Haen-Marshall, I. (1999) 'The self-report methodology in crime research', in Tonry, M. (ed.) *Crime and Justice: a review of research* 25, 291–367.

Kilias, M. and Rau, W. (2000) '*The European Sourcebook of Crime and Criminal Justice Statistics*: a new tool in assessing crime and policy issues in comparative and empirical perspective', *European Journal on Criminal Policy and Research* 8, 3–12.

Klein, M.W., Kerner, H.J., Maxson, C.L. and Weitekamp, E.G.M. (eds) (2001) *The Eurogang Paradox*, Dordrecht, Kluwer Academic Publishers.

Kowalzyck, M. (2003) 'Youth violence in prison: the practice and situation of juvenile pre-trial detention in the German federal state Mecklenburg–Western Pomerania', in Dünkel, F. and Drenkhahn, K. (eds) *Youth Violence: new patterns and local responses – experiences in East and West*, Mönchengladbach, Forum Verlag Godesberg.

Krajewski, K. (2003) 'Patterns of juvenile delinquency and juvenile violence in Poland', in Dünkel, F. and Drenkhahn, K. (eds) *Youth Violence: new patterns and local responses – experiences in East and West*, Mönchengladbach, Forum Verlag Godesberg.

Lipsey, M.W. and Wilson, D.B. (1998) 'Effective interventions for serious juvenile offenders', in Loeber, R. and Farrington, D.P. (eds) *Serious and Violent Juvenile Offenders*, London, Sage.

Little, M. (1990) *Young Men in Prison*, Aldershot, Dartmouth.

Little, M., Kogan, J., Bullock, R. and Van der Laan, P. (2004) 'ISSP: an experiment in multi-systemic responses to persistent young offenders known to children's services', *British Journal of Criminology* 44 (2), 225–240.

Loeber, R. and Farrington, D.P. (2001) 'The significance of child delinquency', in Loeber, R. and Farrington, D.P. (eds) *Child Delinquents*, London, Sage.

Markina, A. (2003) 'Juvenile crime prevention strategies in Estonia', in Dünkel, F. and Drenkhahn, K. (eds) *Youth Violence: new patterns and local responses – experiences in East and West*, Mönchengladbach, Forum Verlag Godesberg.

Marshall, T. F. (1996) 'The evolution of restorative justice in Britain', *European Journal on Criminal Policy and Research* 4, 21–43.

McGuire, J. and Priestley, P. (1995) 'Reviewing "What Works": past, present and future', in McGuire, J. (ed.) *What Works: reducing re-offending – guidelines from research and practice*, Chichester, John Wiley & Sons.

Mehlbye, J. and Walgrave, L. (eds) (1998) *Confronting Youth in Europe*, Copenhagen, AFK.

Miers, D. (2001) *An International Review of Restorative Justice*, Crime Reduction Research Series Paper 10, London, Home Office.

Millham, S., Bullock, R. and Hosie, K. (1978) *Locking Up Children*, Aldershot, Saxon House.

Neubacher, F., Walter, M., Válková, H. and Krajewski, K. (1999) 'Juvenile delinquency in Central European cities: a comparison of registration and processing structures', *European Journal on Criminal Policy and Research* 7 (4), 533–557.

Nijboer, J.F. (2001) 'Recommendations. Over het "zachte"recht van de Raad van Europa', *Justitiële Verkenningen* 27, 81–87.

Pfeiffer, C. (1998) 'Juvenile crime and violence in Europe', *Crime and Justice: a review of research* 23, 255–328.

Pridemore, W.A. (2002) 'Social problems and patterns of juvenile delinquency in transitional Russia', *Journal of Research in Crime and Delinquency* 39, 187–213.

Recommendation No. R(87)20 (1987) *Social Reactions to Juvenile Delinquency*, Strasbourg, Council of Europe.

Recommendation Rec(2000)22 (2000) *Improving the Implementation of the European Rules on Community Sanctions and Measures*, Strasbourg, Council of Europe.

Recommendation Rec(2003)20 (2003) *New Ways of Dealing with Juvenile Delinquency and the Role of Juvenile Justice*, Strasbourg, Council of Europe.

Ruchkin, V.V., Schwab-Stone, M., Koposov, R.A., Vermeiren, R. and King, R.A. (2003) 'Suicidal ideations and attempts in juvenile delinquents', *Journal of Child Psychology and Psychiatry* 44 (7), 1058–1066.

Rutter, M., Giller, H. and Hagell, A (1998) *Antisocial Behaviour by Young People*, Cambridge, Cambridge University Press.

Šakić, V., Ivčič, I. and Franc, R. (2003) 'Self-reported substance use and delinquent behaviour among Croatian youth', in Dünkel, F. and Drenkhahn, K. (eds) *Youth Violence: new patterns and local responses – experiences in East and West*, Mönchengladbach, Forum Verlag Godesberg.

Stańdo-Kawecka, B. (2003) 'New local strategies in individual countries: Poland', in Dünkel, F. and Drenkhahn, K. (eds) *Youth Violence: new patterns and local responses – experiences in East and West*, Mönchengladbach, Forum Verlag Godesberg.

Tarbagaev, A. (2003) 'Criminal youth violence and its prevention in the Russian Federation and in the Krasnoyarsk Territory', in Dünkel, F. and Drenkhahn, K. (eds) *Youth Violence: new patterns and local responses – experiences in East and West*, Mönchengladbach, Forum Verlag Godesberg.

Terlouw, G.J. and Kamphorst, P.A. (2002) *Van vast naar mobiel*, Den Haag, WODC (Onderzoek en beleid 95).

Tonry, M. (ed.) (1997) *Ethnicity, Crime, and Immigration*, Chicago, The University of Chicago Press.

Válková, H. (2001) 'Jugendstrafrechtreform in Tschechien in Sicht?', *Monatschrift Kriminologie* 84 (5), 396–409.

Válková, H., Thomová, J. and Stočesová, S. (2003) 'First results from a survey on violence among students in Pilsen in the Czech Republic', in Dünkel, F. and Drenkhahn, K. (eds) *Youth Violence: new patterns and local responses – experiences in East and West*, Mönchengladbach, Forum Verlag Godesberg.

Van der Laan, P.H. (2000) *Evaluation Research concerning Community Sanctions and Measures in Europe*, Strasbourg, Council of Europe (PC-ER (2000) 5).

Van der Laan, P.H. (2002) *Juveniles and Electronic Monitoring: recent experiences in England and Wales and the Netherlands*, Strasbourg, Council of Europe (PC-JU (2002) 21).

Van der Laan, P.H. (2003) 'Police and judicial reactions to youth crime: the situation in the Netherlands', in Dünkel, F. and Drenkhahn, K. (eds) *Youth Violence: new patterns and local responses – experiences in East and West*, Mönchengladbach, Forum Verlag Godesberg.

Van der Laan, P.H. and Nijboer, J. A. (2000) 'Van zakmes tot pistool', *Tijdschrift voor Criminologie* 42 (2), 104–117.

Walgrave, L. and Mehlbye, J. (1998) 'An overview: comparative comments on juvenile offending and its treatment in Europe', in Mehlbye, J. and Walgrave, L. (eds) *Confronting Youth in Europe*, Copenhagen, AKF.

Walgrave, L. (2001) *Met het oog op herstel*, Leuven, Acco.

Whitfield, D. (1997) *Tackling the Tag: the electronic monitoring of offenders*, Winchester, Waterside Press.

13

CREATIVE ARTS AND SOCIAL RESEARCH
SIX LESSONS

Roger Bullock

INTRODUCTION

In this chapter, I have been asked to discuss the influence on my social research activities of a life-long interest in the performing and creative arts. In these terms, I include two other passions of mine, music hall and football, as well as the more familiar music, literature, art and architecture.

My initial thought on being set this task was to compete for inclusion in *Private Eye*'s Pseuds' Corner. I have heard many pretentious claims in my lifetime, from an amateur theatricals producer who dictated that his *Hamlet* set should combine 'rich Titian contrasts with Monet transparencies' to musicologists who have compared 'the dainty footwork of soccer stars to the delicate movement of ballet'. Whatever the merits and inspiration of such parallels, they seem to me parasitic in that neither takes forward the contribution of the other; in other words, images are borrowed to illustrate rather than develop ideas.

Of course, we are all inspired and fulfilled by some aspect of the arts, whether it be a cathartic wind-down at the end of the day or delight at a phrase or story. Nearly every schoolchild of my generation was introduced to poetry by two compositions: Keats's *On First Looking into Chapman's Homer* and Shelley's *Ozymandias*. I suspect that post-war austerity meant that only one book of poetry was in use. I, like thousands of others, learned these by heart and both have come regularly to mind ever since.

The youthful Keats expresses elation at reading the new Homer translation, and his words 'Much have I travell'd in the realms of gold . . . yet did I never breathe its pure serene / Till I heard Chapman speak out loud and bold . . .' sprang to mind when I first encountered texts I still hold dear: Robert Merton (1949) on social theory; Hall, Land, Parker and Webb (1975) on social change; Michael Rutter (1979) on adolescent transitions; and so on. Similarly,

Forty Years of Research, Policy and Practice in Children's Services.
Edited by N. Axford, V. Berry, M. Little and L. Morpeth.
© 2005 John Wiley & Sons, Ltd. ISBN 0-470-01219-6.

when publications once sweated over are long forgotten, the fate of the once great Egyptian emperor whose worn statue the desert traveller meets – '"My name is Ozymandias, king of kings: / Look on my works, ye Mighty, and despair!" Nothing beside remains. Round the decay / Of that colossal wreck, boundless and bare, / The lone and level sands stretch far away' – beautifully sums up the situation.

There are also portrayals of situations that stay in one's memory. The 'old believers' in Moussorgsky's opera *Khovanshchina* are a case in point. They prepare for death rather than compromise their faith and are happy for all that they know and cherish to go up in smoke. Although I have always been rather partial to their conservatism, I also sympathise with those trying to change their views with the latest evidence. Similarly, one would have given one's right arm to come up with phrases as pithy and witty as Oscar Wilde's description of fox hunting as 'the unspeakable in pursuit of the uneatable' or Churchill's perception of the Royal Navy as 'rum, bum and the lash'. They seem to capture things exactly.

But, the important question is: Does the precision of these portrayals improve social research? Does Dickens have much to tell poverty researchers, can listening to *Fidelio* help us to understand empowerment? Does the music hall capture prevailing social mores or can watching West Bromwich Albion football club enlighten us about the dreams and escape routes of people in those massive working-class towns that interest me so much? The creative arts have been around for thousands of years and it is easy to select some part of them to illuminate aspects of what is a relatively new science.

At the most general level, I think the answer is 'not much' because a great deal of the action in literature and drama is geared to some dénouement or fate. Empirical truths about social conditions, no matter how sensitively portrayed, are somewhat secondary to the plot and the author's beliefs or 'agenda'. The need for climax and drama leads to exaggeration and unlikely coincidences. I recall watching an episode of the BBC television hospital drama 'Casualty' with a group of nurses in which a lot of exciting things happened. There was a case of Lassa fever (which meant isolating staff), an outbreak of anthrax (which meant the burning of all the equipment), a doctor got stabbed and a patient sold drugs to a young orderly. When I enquired whether this was typical of work in an Accident and Emergency department, the nurses said, 'these things might happen over a 40-year nursing career, but they don't occur on the same shift!' However, as I will try to explain, there are considerable benefits for more specific matters of drawing parallels between social research and the performing and creative arts.

This sense of awe of the creative arts probably derives from the fact that I have virtually no creative talent. Although a competent pianist, I have never composed anything. I cannot even improvise or play well without music and my art skills stalled in the first year of a secondary school curriculum dominated by maths and Latin. Despite my early organ-playing and wonder at remarkable hymn lines such as 'pavillioned with splendour and girded with praise', my writing style is frankly uninspired; indeed, my colleague Spencer Millham, a superb prose writer, once asked, 'where did you learn to write, in a quarry?' At school, I began an essay paragraph with the words 'Consequently, therefore, . . .' which so annoyed the English teacher that he called me 'Consequently, therefore Bullock' for the rest of term.

I can only admire those blessed with such gifts and seek satisfaction with tangential contacts – limited to once helping Dietrich Fischer-Dieskau push a car and being eased aside in a narrow corridor by a shuffling and aged E.M. Forster. My greatest respect is reserved for sculptors: How does one conceive a shape from a block of stone, how does one start and what if you make a mistake? When feeling unduly self-satisfied with my more modest social work research achievements, I always remember the advice of my mentors – Roy Parker's reminder that 40 years ago in child care research, you had only to read four books to be a world expert and Spencer Millham's quip that in physics we would all be lab techs.

In exploring these issues, I shall discuss six areas where I think there is a mutually beneficial relationship between artistic and research creativity. They are: the development of ideas; the temporal and eternal; form and content; seeking wholeness; the role of the artist/researcher in society; and presenting the truth.

THE DEVELOPMENT OF IDEAS

I have long been fascinated by the development of ideas, whether in the arts or social theory. Where do they come from? Is creativity more a question of reshaping what is known or are there 'quantum leaps' where a whole new approach erupts from nowhere?

My early sociological theory teaching from Norbert Elias and Anthony Giddens suggested that ideas develop in three ways. Some are products of a continuing dialectical process whereby a train of thought intrinsically produces challenges, leading to a synthesis of opposing ideas. Others are more akin to evolution where ideas are adapted, with the best ones being retained. A third view is that change occurs to correct imbalances in the functional relationships between the parts of a society.

Each of these models is probably extreme and social theorists who divide the process of change into clear stages are probably taking considerable artistic licence. Sometimes, developments seem circular, with 'what goes around comes around'. The current moves in child care social work to a children's service and a focus on prevention recall the debates when I first began work in the 1960s. In others, there is a time lag between innovation and implementation. I never cease to be amazed at the different architectural styles of the adjacent façades of St Pancras and Kings Cross railway stations in London, scarcely guessing that the more radical design predates the traditional one by at least a decade. Some creative people have needed imaginary enemies to fire their work. Schumann contrasted the gentle, poetic Florestan with the vehement Eusebius, the firebrand Caravaggio loathed the derivative works of Carracci and so on, just as the Marxists have dismissed the functionalists as contributors to social research.

Just as interesting as the development of ideas is the way that they emerge in particular social, economic and political contexts. I have seen such trends in nearly 40 years of social research: the great optimism of sociology in the 1960s, the resurgence of psychology in the more individualistic 1980s and the concern for cost theory economics as resources diminished in the 1990s.

It is not very original to suggest that social theories, like schools of art and music, reflect the societies in which they flourished, or to note how short so many of the so-called golden ages were. But, three points from the arts seem worth adding. First, much art, especially architecture and religious painting, is enhanced by its context and seems lifeless once removed. For other works, this seems less so, and greatness seems to emanate wherever they are placed. Second, technological improvements greatly aid implementation, so that the better design of stone arches – for example, with the replacement of the round Norman arch with the Gothic pointed arch – allowed more stained glass while iron technology enabled St Pancras station to be given a remarkably modern roof. Third, outside forces can shape not only the inspiration but also the progress. Hence, forces such as the need for improved defence, changes in religious belief or even abstract thinking, such as the essays of John Ruskin, can all be shown to have contributed to artistic and cultural development at different times. But once again, we could be falling into the trap of the dilettante and merely selecting bits and pieces to draw interesting parallels. Can these ideas be tested? How do they aid the pursuit of truth?

THE TEMPORAL AND THE ETERNAL

Having had a clergyman headmaster, I along with 666 other boys enjoyed seven years of daily religious assemblies. Occasionally, our attention was fixed on the proceedings and always in my mind has been St Paul's advice in II Corinthians, chapter 4, 'for the things which are seen are temporal, but the things which are not seen are eternal'. This seems to me to be a perennial tension in social research, particularly as its policy relevance changes from one year to the next.

Certainly, both the arts and social research display similar patterns of growth and decay. As a boy, I used to visit my local library, which housed a huge music collection. I was constantly surprised by how many of the works on the shelves are now unheard. There were dozens of competently composed choral works (e.g. Stanford's *Revenge*), piano pieces (e.g. Thomas Dunhill) and operatic scores (e.g. *The King's Henchmen*) that reflected once popular fashion but now never see the light of day. In my lifetime, 12-tone music, once a necessary item in any classical concert, has virtually disappeared.

Why is it that some works survive and others fall away? Quality is obviously important but so, also, may be the ability to say something 'eternal' rather than temporal. In social research, similar fads and fashions can be observed but a weakness compared with great art is that brilliant methods of investigation soon date. We still read *King Lear* but do not copy Benjamin Franklin and fly kites with keys attached to understand lightening. What happens, it seems to me, is that the work that survives, or enters the literature in research parlance, is that which, although based on scrutiny of the 'temporal', clarifies the 'eternal'. Current studies of Romanian orphans are yielding new information on the ability of children to overcome severe deprivation, findings that will be relevant to the issue of neglect and its aftermath long after the children originally scrutinised have grown up. Similarly, issues of children's separation and return, a longstanding interest of the Dartington Social Research Unit, will long outlive current legislation and guidance.

If we adopt the rather idealistic view that the purpose of research is the pursuit of truth and that to achieve this we need to explain rather than describe things, we can extend the exploration of the issues discussed so far.

The question that arises is: Can knowledge of the arts help with scientific explanation? It can certainly help us empathise. We can see and feel the agony in a Michelangelo Pietà or be aroused by the jealous ravings of Othello, and from these experiences hypotheses about human behaviour may be generated. But artistic endeavour is unlikely to produce a vaccine or build a safe bridge and as the social sciences have developed sophisticated methodologies to incorporate the feelings and perceptions of individuals they do not need to acknowledge models from the arts.

I suspect, however, that the relationship is more complex. I have noticed (though with little empirical evidence!) that many scientists become religious or right-wing in old age, perhaps in a search for the order they seek for society. But this is a limited view, continuing the long debate about the extent to which theories of the natural sciences apply to societies. A different stance is found in a quotation from Pascal that I hold dear. When discussing the relationship between religion and science and the assumption that the former must automatically give ground to the latter, he said: 'the opposite of science is not religion but poetry'. When it was suggested that surely the opposite of poetry is prose, he continued, 'no, the opposite of prose is metre'. While this elevates the status of poetry as an alternative to science, it also compounds the question that opened the previous paragraph. Are science and art fundamentally irreconcilable or are both means to the same end, namely the pursuit of truth?

FORM AND CONTENT

We all admire a good presentation and both artists and researchers seek the best means of communication. In Dartington publications, we have always tried to avoid the ramblings of Bruckner, the superficial flamboyance of Liszt and the unintelligible plots of many operas. But on occasions we have had to borrow their techniques. There is an uncanny similarity between Mahler's solution when uncertain where to go next – to bring in the brass – and a common response of social researchers facing a similar blockage – 'let's listen to what the users say'.

It is in the area of form and content that I think that artistic and research knowledge becomes mutually reinforcing because creative artists and social scientists face similar problems. This is especially manifest in the relationship between pattern and variation. Social surveys may establish patterns but also have to account for variations within them, phenomena that can be difficult to understand and that weaken any generalisations. Very few research reports have successfully combined findings about the national situation – for example, with regard to the characteristics and experiences of children looked after in substitute care – with a satisfactory analysis of variation, such as differences between the local authorities studied.

I have no easy solutions to this problem but, being an organist, have always admired Bach's attempt to resolve this. In his fugues and passacaglias, he is able to state a clear, simple and sometimes unpromising theme yet incorporate complex variations around this, almost exhausting all possibilities of expression. Thus, the variations become more interesting than the overall pattern. Obviously, we cannot ask Bach to set our research reports to music but there are lessons from how he handles this problem. I entertain similar ideas when I accompany psalms. In the Church of England, the same words are set to different chants, so the pattern is set. It is again the way that variations in this pattern are handled that mirrors the difficulties of social research. The same lessons might be derived from others adopting this approach, not least the metaphysical poets, who succeed in drawing everything possible from an initially limited idea.

A second problem of interest to me has been how to integrate formal and informal processes or cultures in the same presentation. The relationship between the official and unofficial in organisations has long fascinated me although, inevitably, some social scientists reject this model. But, having studied hundreds of residential establishments, I think it is still useful. I have long been intrigued by mediaeval paintings where the activities of the onlookers are as interesting as the main theme. This reaches its height in the work of Brueghel the Elder. The Kunsthistoriches Museum in Vienna is fortunate to display 14 Brueghels in one gallery. What is interesting is that while the official titles are phrases such as *Hunters in the Snow* or *Peasant Wedding*, the sub-text of lechery, drunkenness and gambling is equally informative. These paintings are masterly examples of ways that the informal can be integrated with the formal in the presentation of a single idea.

A third, more obvious source of looking at how the creative arts and social research benefit each other is by understanding 'process'. The sense of disintegration in Visconti's film of *Death in Venice*, the induction to the stepmother role in *The Sound of Music* or portrayals of love and hate found in films, books and plays all illuminate complex social processes, despite the tendency for exaggeration and coincidence mentioned earlier. Indeed, in a study of children returning to their families from out-of-home care, I found that the 22-verse parable of the Prodigal Son in St Luke's Gospel contained all the necessary ingredients to understand the process. The function of the 260-page book on the research was to add when, where, how often and with what effect.

SEEKING WHOLENESS

The establishment of truth in the social sciences relies on agreeing the threshold for the amount and quality of knowledge needed to reach a conclusion. Of course, this process never ends and risk and probability rather than absolute certainty will always be the order of the day. Again, I have always been impressed by Robert Merton's discussion of objectivity in the social sciences and his argument that it does not rest in an individual project, although we should always aim to minimise distortion. Rather, it is achieved by the institutional structure of science and the values of communism, organised scepticism, universalism and economic disinterest that underpin it. Thus, a scientific argument is rarely the work of one person but of separate initiatives by different people.

I have looked for other models to understand this process better and, once more, have found inspiration in the creative arts. Italian frescoes, for instance, are the work of numerous craftsmen. How can co-operative work produce such magnificent creations? Has this any relevance for research teams or social care agencies working together? The secret seems to be that they were carried out to a master plan, the technology was sound and the individuals were highly competent. I have never felt that too many cooks spoil the broth.

Sculpture also seems to me a unique form of expression in that one can view the product from all angles. David is instantly recognisable as David but can be viewed from different sides. Yet, somehow the different perspectives add up to the recognisable whole. In a famous sketch in which Les Dawson and Roy Barraclough dress up as two North Country women visiting a sculpture exhibition, Cissie, on seeing the well-endowed David, exclaimed, 'No wonder my Fred used to get undressed in the dark.' But other perspectives are possible.

Finally, I wish to challenge the stereotypical contrast of the artist as a passive recluse and the social scientist as a technocrat. I have seen great technological change in my time as a researcher. In the 1960s there were no computers or calculators and data were entered onto cards by clipping a V-shape against numbers round the edge. Analysis was undertaken by pushing knitting needles through each hole. If these were clipped, the card fell out of the pack and could be counted. Statistical calculations took ages, a Spearman rank correlation on a large sample taking a whole day. Now computers usable anywhere have transformed techniques. Neither have the creative arts stood still and their whole history is one of innovation and experiment, whether as a result of cinematic equipment or the invention of new musical instruments. Today whole films are created by computer animations, for example *Toy Story* and *Shrek*. Great artists have always welcomed technical innovation to provide new means of expression.

The extent to which technological advances have improved the product is a moot point. One of the dubious benefits of retirement is the opportunity to watch daytime television, surely the prime candidate for technology outrunning content with its beautifully presented but trite discussions and fatuous quiz games. Naturally, more sophisticated analysis means more robust results but whether the final presentation on Word documents and Powerpoint is better than before is questionable. Should we bemoan the loss of delightful prose to bullet points (73 in the conclusions of the last social work book I read) or is this just confirming my sympathy for the 'old believers'? I am inclined to think that the habit of getting material on computers at any cost can be a substitute for careful thought. Furthermore, features that might attract and intrigue a reader can be lost. I recall being moved by the sight of the simple wooden table on which Tolstoy wrote *War and Peace* and compared this with what would now be churned out so speedily. I once unintentionally titillated my colleagues by mentioning that I had purchased new writing equipment, which, much to their disappointment, turned out to be an expensive Mont Blanc pen. Interestingly, this was disallowed by the accountant as a legitimate professional expense whereas a far more costly computer gadget would almost certainly have passed his scrutiny.

Being interested in the music hall, I particularly appreciate humour as a mechanism to gain an audience's attention. Although it is a silly observation, for some reason modern computer technology seems dour and serious and any entertainment has to be obtained from seedy e-mails or practical jokes. It makes a good companion to social work which also noticeably lacks a gallows humour. Jokes are by their very nature aggressive and, as Freud suggested, may mask areas of tension in our lives. They therefore tend to be viewed as disrespectful to social services' clients, many of whom are disadvantaged and vulnerable. Yet, one of Shakespeare's contributions was to show that tragedy and humour can be the same thing: his greatest tragedy, *King Lear*, employs many devices previously used only in comedies, notably disguise and mistaken identity. Humour can have a positive effect even if some people find the butts of jokes distasteful. They can enshrine serious social criticism, as in the songs of Flanders and Swann or the comedy of Chaplin. One of my favourite examples was when Bob Hope was asked why his family emigrated to America. 'I guess they knew I wouldn't become King' came the reply. Interestingly, the real reason was that his father had got a job as a stonemason on a new cathedral.

I have also watched the techniques used by great comedians to communicate with their audience. Max Miller beckoned you into his confidence, as if offering privileged information, 'Here, let me tell you . . .' etc. Frankie Howerd was quite different. He rushed on stage all flustered and began by asking the audience where they came from. 'Anyone from Bristol?' he would ask. To those answering 'yes', he replied, 'My brother's in Bristol tonight – he's a burglar!'

Wholeness is about perfection and requires completeness in the perception, execution and delivery of the goods. We are all influenced by our training and the norms prevailing in the circles in which we move and these are what determines our comfort levels. Paradoxically, advances in technology that should make life easier have accompanied greater specialisation that makes communication more difficult. I believe that in social research we might benefit from the skills offered by those successful in other areas and with whom we may see ourselves as having little in common.

THE ROLE OF THE ARTIST/RESEARCHER IN SOCIETY

What then should be the role of creative artists and social researchers in society? I have noted for many years that patronage played a major part in commissioning works. How far do we have to accept this constraint? Is the alternative starvation in a lonely garret? 'Don't expect to save the world, all your aim can be is to leave things better than when you found them' was the parting advice of the eminent physician Lord Adrian at my graduation 40 years ago. But, interestingly, since that exhortation, artists seem to have become freer than their social research counterparts to pursue their interests within any bureaucratic post they might hold.

I was brought up with the music of Elgar and, living in the Midlands, heard talks by people such as Adrian Boult, and George Thalben-Ball who had worked with him. Elgar was something of a local hero, being self-taught and having faced immense struggles with the establishment and experienced anti-Catholic prejudice. He was a person I was taught to respect. One of the features of the upward social mobility produced by the 1944 *Education Act* was for successful pupils like me to move through a variety of settings that seriously challenged their cultural assumptions. First there was grammar school, then university. Imagine my shock, therefore, when I first started work at King's College, Cambridge, to hear a venerable don opine that 'Elgar was an awful man. He just wanted to be a country gentleman. He had no conception of the role of the artist in society.' Poor Elgar, and poor me!

Thanks to Ken Russell's film and Michael Kennedy's biography in the 1960s, we are now somewhat wiser. Elgar certainly did seek a squire's life but how he suffered for his art is deeply moving. His reported discussion with his wife, Alice, as to whether it was worth paying seven shillings and six pence to renew the American copyright on the *Dream of Gerontius* is especially sad, particularly as nowadays scholars earn a living writing about it. I think that creativity, whether in art, music or research, is inevitably painful in that the continual thought required isolates you from family and friends and the sheer task of writing, let alone the thinking, is exhausting. It may be true that every artist must be pilloried, but within this common experience and the aim to improve situations, artists and researchers alike have always kept a watchful eye on the box office. Richard Strauss made no bones about seeking commercial success for his operas and many social researchers have done quite well in terms of finance and status on the backs of the poor.

But in the struggle for perfection and novelty, with whom are creative people most in touch? It is sometimes claimed that Elgar was the last serious composer to reach the hearts of the people and that music lovers simply cannot whistle or sing much of modern music to themselves. Similarly, while I greatly enjoyed a recent Lucian Freud exhibition, I am left bewildered by much of the contemporary art I see, even though I do my best to appreciate it. In social research, who was the last great researcher and theorist to inspire a large audience – Engels, Rowntree, who? Those who are popular nowadays seem less profound, their performances almost outdoing their content. So, does the popularity of John Adams's music, the history of Simon Schama or the popular psychology and management manuals found on every railway station bookstall offer us lessons in successful dissemination? Or, will greatness always rise to the surface and stay there? In short, we face the familiar question: How are we to judge long-term consequences?

Dissemination has long been an interest of the Dartington Social Research Unit and we have tried to present research knowledge in different ways to different audiences. The research overviews on child protection and looking after children away from home presented complex arguments in a novel way and helped professionals to review their own work. In the study of the Caldecott Community, we juxtaposed the diary of a teenage pupil and our research findings (Little with Kelly 1995).

Whatever the success of these methods, and they have been evaluated, two things continue to concern me about the dissemination process. One is the way that traditionally presented academic reports, laying out the sample, methods and results, are singularly unattractive to social work managers and practitioners. They simply do not read academic journals, and there is no penalty for not doing so. This is reinforced by the attitude in academic circles that popularity equals vulgarity. Second, the media, which could play a useful role in this, seem not only to want 'news' but also rarely to step outside London to seek it. With the Metropolis as the centre of their world, it is unusual for the working-class conurbations I referred to earlier to get a mention unless something very dramatic happens. Moreover, the subject I find particularly informative, sociology, although obsessed by the working classes, has shown much less interest in life on large, dreary council estates than in more exotic communities, even though the former is the norm for millions of people. Why does the education of minority groups in Haringey get more attention from journalists than staff shortages in the Potteries?

What does this mean for the social sciences? Can it be that selectivity affects the emphasis in truth rather than the truth itself? I have long struggled to reconcile political rhetoric and sociological evidence. Should the artist and social scientist challenge the detail or nod with approving caution, provided the politician's heart is in the right place? One of my childhood shocks was seeing the proportion of children in different towns going to grammar schools. I could not believe that West Bromwich, the centre of my world, was near the bottom along with Bootle, Wigan and Merthyr Tydfil (London was not then presented by boroughs as it is now). Even at that age, it was apparent that there was something socially distinct about these unprepossessing industrial locations, even though their populations were not far short of big cities. Smethwick, just down the road, for example, bore the unlovely title of an 'urban district', an apt summary indeed.

It was equally clear that the scant provision of secondary education led to low expectations. Indeed, I found it difficult to match political talk of opportunity with what I saw. In my first primary school, no one had 'passed for the grammar' for the last eight years and in my second school, half of the 220 children in the top year never took, let alone failed, the 11+ exam. Later, I was to continually hear my headmaster praise the wide social mix admitted to the Direct Grant system when a furtive survey conducted with an equally sociologically curious third-former, who actually knew every road in Birmingham, showed that only six of the 666 boys lived in council houses. This was despite the fact that 60 per cent of Birmingham's population were so accommodated. A fitting epitaph for socially concerned artists and scientists could be, therefore, 'a friend of the unfashionable'.

PRESENTING THE TRUTH

If the establishment of truth is confounded by selectivity in areas of interest, there is a further risk of dilution in its presentation. One of Blake's Proverbs of Hell states: 'Truth can never be told so as to be understood, and not be believed in.' My final concern links several of the examples used so far. These are: the unlikely combinations of dramatic events in 'Casualty', Max Miller's ability to hold an audience and my headmaster believing only what he wanted to believe. Can we ever hope for success in all three areas?

It would be invidious to compare social research publications as if for an Oscar award. But the contrasts are sufficiently vivid to be worrying. Early on in my career, I noted that Stanley Cohen and Laurie Taylor's (1972) short and highly readable account of Durham maximum security prison completely dominated the more rigorous articles by their assistants published in journals some time later. About the same time, I was made aware that social work is predominantly a consensus discipline when a publisher rejected a script because it contained too many 'makes no difference' findings. Of course, we can make progress with popular and 'good news' research only for so long. As explained, much social research that has sought to describe rather than to explain has been very successful, simply because this brush-clearing was an essential beginning in a context where so little was known.

However, I think the difficulties of achieving social change and the frustrations increasingly faced by well-intentioned governments are raising questions that have to be answered by a different kind of research – on topics that are far more specific and that is tighter in its methodology, replicates other studies and tests hypotheses blind. In addition, more attention will have to be given to alternative explanations of findings and the use of methodologies that eliminate other possible causes of outcomes. These include: the placebo effect, where the style of the intervention is of more consequence than the intervention; problems of comparing 'like with like' – a difficulty that haunts the comparison of findings from different studies; and the cycles of remission and relapse characteristic of many social and psychological problems.

These hopes may be pie in the sky given the poor employment conditions of contract researchers but it is helpful to recall that, when I started work, child and adolescent psychiatry was in a similar position to child care now. Michael Rutter and colleagues initiated a different programme of research, which drew criticism from sceptics who highlighted the multiplicity of variables, the uniqueness of each individual and the importance of feelings. Nevertheless, they managed to transform knowledge (Le Couteur 2001). There is no child care equivalent of Rutter and Taylor's (2002) handbook *Child and Adolescent Psychiatry*, now in its fourth edition.

These suggestions would yield considerable benefit for children's services. They would encourage the features of a modern system of provision, highlighted as desirable by extensive research, namely: finding mechanisms to prioritise risk, setting out eligibility for services, ensuring that provision matches the needs of the child and identifying a single process leading to a continuum of interventions from prevention to intervention. All of these seem necessary not only to achieve optimal outcomes but also to justify ever-increasing expenditure and to counter litigation. They would undoubtedly help to nurture the informed and sensitive service to which we aspire.

To go further than this would be pretentious but I hope it shows how much of our work at Dartington has tried to take these ideas forward and to please Lord Adrian by leaving things better than we found them.

IN PARADISUM

At the retirement celebration for Roy Parker in 1992, Spencer Millham went through Roy's university colleagues and compared each one with a tree. One was like unto a cherry (lots of blossom but disintegrating at the first puff of wind), another a trumpet flower and a third a prickly pear. When it came to Roy, the audience waited with baited breath but the comparison turned out to be more gentle. The olive was proposed – a modest, unpretentious tree that produces a massive amount of fruit usable in many enriching ways. I leave it to the imagination to nominate the plant that would best describe me; a friend suggests a damson tree, not just because I adore the excellent jam made from its fruit but because it is a 'bitter fruit than can be sweet at times'. But, from what I have discussed in this chapter, there is one setting (not a tree) that I am likely to find especially satisfying.

Throughout my life I have always enjoyed watching cricket. I started watching West Bromwich Dartmouth in the Birmingham League as a boy and soon graduated to county games. I am not sure what it is that attracts me – perhaps the mathematical aspects of scores and players' averages, perhaps the ability to doze yet stay involved. Cricket is a fine game and, despite what critics say, can be extremely exciting when the initiative swings from one side to the other in a matter of minutes.

Visitors to Dartington will also know that the hour between four and five o'clock on Wednesday afternoon is very special for me. It is the weekly live broadcast of choral evensong on BBC Radio Three. I have always loved cathedrals and now I know why. Here is the wholeness so rarely encountered these days. In the beauty of architecture, the craft of carvers, the music, art and language, one can recall earlier functions of teaching, dissemination, libraries and healing and contemplation.

Where do these two pleasures come together? In my favourite place, the county cricket ground at Worcester. There, one can watch the game eating tea and cake accompanied by the cathedral chimes and views of the great west window. I often wish buildings could speak – what tales that sturdy tower and ornate pavilion could tell. If those eternal aspects can be combined with the temporal experience of hearing the cathedral choir or watching a flawless innings beneath those Victorian gables, I begin to have visions of what might be possible.

As social research is a fledgling discipline, these discussions can only open the debate on lessons from the creative arts for social research. To paraphrase Churchill's imagery again: they are not the end, they are not even the beginning of the end; but they are probably the end of the beginning. As Brecht pleads at the close of *The Good Woman of Setzuan*, 'There must be some end that would fit; ladies and gentlemen, help us to look for it.'

REFERENCES

Cohen, S. and Taylor, L. (1972) *Psychological Survival: the experience of long-term imprisonment*, London, Penguin Books.

Hall, P., Land, H., Parker, R. and Webb, A. (1975) *Change, Choice and Conflict in Social Policy*, London, Heinemann.

Le Couteur, A. (2001) 'Appreciation of Professor Sir Michael Rutter', In Green, J. and Yule, W. (eds) *Research and Innovation on the Road to Modern Child Psychiatry: Volume 1, Festschrift for Professor Sir Michael Rutter*, London, Gaskell.

Little, M. with Kelly, S. (1995) *A Life Without Problems? The achievements of a therapeutic community*, Aldershot, Arena.

Merton, R.K. (1949) *Social Theory and Social Structure*, Glencoe, IL, The Free Press.

Rutter, M. (1979) *Changing Youth in a Changing Society: patterns of adolescent development and disorder*, London, Nuffield Provincial Hospitals Trust.

Rutter, M. and Taylor, E. (eds) (2002) *Child and Adolescent Psychiatry*, 4th Edition, Oxford, Blackwell.

14

WHERE NEXT FOR SOCIAL RESEARCH AT DARTINGTON?

Nick Axford and Louise Morpeth

INTRODUCTION

Anyone who has read even a handful of the contributions in this volume will recognise the impressive legacy that Roger Bullock and his colleagues have bequeathed to those at Dartington who seek to follow in their footsteps. Building on 40 years of high-quality and often extremely influential research is both a privilege and daunting. This chapter sketches out how, as two of the people involved in setting the direction for the Dartington Unit, we intend to utilise and develop this endowment. As such it is necessarily – and hopefully forgivably – strong on references to Dartington's work.

A REFOCUSING OF STUDIES

The work of the Dartington Unit is best described as the study of child development in the context of children's services. When Royston Lambert, Spencer Millham and Roger (1970) studied boarding schools they took a sociological approach and wanted to understand what difference a boarding school made to children's lives compared to day education. The study was interested in outcomes, but not in the sense of child development; rather, the focus was on understanding children's aspirations, how they talked and their relationship to the institution. Unit research will continue to look at subgroups of the child population but with a focus on mapping the life trajectories of groups of children with similar needs rather than on defining those groups in terms of the services they receive. Further, with children's services increasingly defined as services organised but not necessarily provided by health, education, police and social services for children in need, our interest in services such as accommodation, family support and youth justice will continue but more attention will be paid to related professions, such as health visiting and educational psychology.

Forty Years of Research, Policy and Practice in Children's Services.
Edited by N. Axford, V. Berry, M. Little and L. Morpeth.
© 2005 John Wiley & Sons, Ltd. ISBN 0-470-01219-6.

A good example of what this aspect of refocusing the topics investigated means in practice is a series of studies in which we have gathered information about the needs, service take-up and coping strategies of children and families living in the community (e.g. Axford *et al.* 2003a). The studies examine data about the children's health and development (assessed using standardised questions and instruments) and analyse the input of children's services agencies. The approach is a hybrid of basic and applied research.

We have found ourselves drawing increasingly on the field of developmental psychopathology to inform this work, with its focus on the mechanisms by which risk and protective factors affect children's trajectories (e.g. Rutter 1989, 1999). Thus, as with most previous Unit work, studies continue to view children's lives holistically but in addition there is an intention to explore how children's needs change over time and how services affect these changes.

This aspiration is best reflected at present in a 5-year evaluation by the randomised controlled trial (RCT) of a programme for disaffected young people aged 15–18 years. The programme seeks to change the behaviour of participants by means of a week-long residential course with intensive follow-up by volunteers over a 9-month period. Following extensive work to enhance the evaluability of the programme, the study tracks over 12 months two groups of young people (150 in each) – one that receives the intervention and one that continues to receive orthodox provision – and measures aspects of their well-being and behaviour using standardised instruments. The aim is to chart the chains of risk that lead to antisocial behaviour with this group of young people and to assess if and how the intervention breaks those chains.

Underlying this general approach is the tension familiar to social researchers between theoretical and practical orientations. To help to resolve this, much energy has been invested over the past decade in developing a conceptual framework to assist with analysing the predicament of vulnerable children and also with building and testing interventions to improve outcomes measured in terms of health and development (Little 2001). This followed a Department of Health Chief Scientist's visit to Dartington in 1994, when it was suggested that the Unit should attempt to bring together the ideas, concepts and methods that underpin its work. Known as 'Common Language', the framework links together four core concepts – need, service, threshold and outcome – which encapsulate concepts from the literature on child psychopathology, such as risk and protective factors (Little *et al.* 2004a) and also incorporates the more sociological and phenomenological perspectives of 'life route' and 'process' (Bullock *et al.* 1998a, p. 7) (Box 14.1).

All work at Dartington is meant to be underpinned by, and contribute to, the evolution of this common conceptual framework. The scientific studies are all concerned to some extent with identifying the pattern and severity of the children's needs, and most examine what happens to children's health and development over time – in other words 'outcomes'. They also analyse the services that children receive and seek to understand the contribution that these services make to child outcomes. In relation to development work, the Unit and its sister activities have produced a set of clinical and planning practice tools aimed at helping practitioners and managers to undertake common tasks such as assessment, prognosis and service design (Box 14.2). The common language means that the tools link together.

Box 14.1 Core Common Language Concepts

Risk refers to the way in which certain attributes and circumstances render children particularly vulnerable to a range of social and psychosocial problems.

Protective factors work in certain contexts to reduce individual risks of social or psychological problems; they break the links in a chain of risk factors.

Need is a snapshot of risk and protective factors in a child's life; it translates aspects of child development into a picture of what a child needs for healthy development – better parenting, protection from bullying, and so on.

Threshold is a summary of the seriousness of children's needs in terms of impairment to health and development.

Outcome refers to the impact of a service on a child's well-being and is measured in terms of health and development (or the extent to which needs have been met).

Service captures the nature of the intervention by specifying what was provided, when, where, by whom, over what period, at what frequency, and why.

Life route describes the decisions made by children (or by families on the child's behalf) that affect life chances.

Process is defined as the decisions made by professionals and/or courts (in response to the life route) that affect the child's life chances.

Box 14.2 Dartington practice tools

Clinical decision-making:
Going Home? helps with managing the care careers of looked-after children.
Paperwork is a clinical assessment tool.
Prediction encourages practitioners to make and use prognoses.
Threshold offers a framework for determining the extent of impairment to children's development.

Management planning:
Aggregating Data helps with collecting and analysing management information.
Matching Needs and Services is a method for designing needs-led services.
Structure Culture Outcome is used to improve residential services for children.

For details on all practice tools see www.dartington-i.org/commonlanguage and www.warrenhousepress.com.

TIGHTENING RESEARCH METHODS

The Dartington Unit has a long tradition of exploiting secondary data on populations of children in receipt of services. This includes data held on files about children but also other administrative materials. In *After Grace – Teeth*, for example, such documents were used to better understand the goal priorities of schools and aspects of the control process (Millham *et al.* 1975). Anyone who has witnessed the pace at which Roger tears through an agency file balanced on his knee in some social services broom-cupboard will see the fruits of doing such work over 40 years.

The work allowed the development of skills in weighing and organising this information and in drawing from it incisive conclusions. It also contributed significantly to the understanding of service processes – what agencies do for children and why. But a recurring experience was the frustration of finding such accounts sparse or with sections left incomplete (Brown *et al*. 1998) and of needing to wade through bundles of loose papers occasionally to find some crucial piece of the jigsaw (Walker *et al*. 2003). And, of course, it meant that most of the Unit's work concerned children in contact with a children's services agency, be it a children's home, secure treatment centre or approved school. What about other children?

Current work at the Unit seeks to build on these experiences. Complementing initiatives elsewhere, efforts are being made to help to improve the quality of data recorded in case files. For example, Paperwork, a clinical practice tool, requires attention to risk and protective factors in all areas of a child's life and encourages the practitioners to set out systematically on paper their analyses of causal chains (Little and Mount 2003). It improves record-keeping by encouraging professionals to collect less information but to do more with it. An electronic version is being tested in various authorities and will allow the information to be aggregated routinely for planning and research purposes.

Another method rolled out in several areas attempts to look at *all* children and not just those known to agencies. One of the community studies referred to above looked at patterns of need and service-use for a cross-section of children ($N = 964$) living in two communities – one urban, one rural – in England. The results raise questions about existing estimates of the proportion of children in need and provide a picture of the type and volume of service activity in discrete neighbourhoods. They suggest that for every child in need receiving a service as many as 1.6 do not (Axford *et al*. 2003a). They also indicate that up to one in three (31 per cent) children receive assistance when they do not display actual or likely impairment to their health or development, while some of those whose needs are more pressing do not get a service (21 per cent of those who reach a threshold of significant impairment). The survey method is being written up into a practice tool that local authorities can use to assess reliably the needs of children living in their area (in line with the *Children Act* 1989).

Another traditional feature of Unit studies has been the mix of qualitative and quantitative techniques (Bullock *et al*. 1992). Roger occasionally regales an audience with tales of time spent living in boarding schools undertaking non-participant observation, and most Unit books contain sympathetic (and often amusing) pen-portraits of children in various quarters of the child care system – see especially *Lost in Care* (Millham *et al*. 1986). The purpose of these case studies is invariably to explain and illuminate rather than simply to illustrate. Studies such as *Secure Treatment Outcomes* (Bullock *et al*. 1998a) have also sought to use fairly sophisticated statistical techniques, such as cluster analysis and logistic regression, to analyse data, in particular to help with developing taxonomies and with predicting children's likely career-paths and outcomes.

Again, we are anxious that current and future work builds on these features. In terms of data-collection methods, the community studies referred to earlier involved gathering detailed first-hand accounts from carers but these are supplemented with data from standardised scales on topics ranging from social cohesion to self-esteem. Subsequent adjustments to the community or social epidemiology survey methodology include improving the sampling technique and gathering some data directly from children, including through the use of ACAPI (Audio-Computer-Assisted-Personal-Interviewing).

Some of the new work requires the development and testing of new measures (where none exist). The widely acknowledged weaknesses of common service descriptors such as 'family support' and 'foster care' have prompted attempts to reconceptualise services as 12 'technologies' – including advice, information, advocacy, treatment and practical assistance – and then to specify their discrete components – provider, duration, location and so on (e.g. Morpeth 2004). An alternative approach to recording children's ethnicity followed directly from realising the limitations of the census classification for studying a community in which over 60 different languages were spoken (Abunimah et al. 2002). It links to the acknowledged need to address the tendency to aggregate small ethnic groups to produce categories that bear quantitative analysis but have no logical unity. Finally, some of the PhD studies at Dartington explore different ways of measuring contested concepts such as childhood social exclusion, organisation and child maltreatment.

Experiments in using different techniques of analysis are also underway. In particular, considerable effort has been invested in testing approaches to classifying children according to their needs (Sinclair and Little 2002). The Matching Needs and Services practice tool involves practitioners and managers grouping together cases using a qualitative classification or 'shuffling' process (Little et al. 2001). Aggregating Data is similar but works with quantitative data and encourages agencies to group cases statistically using cluster analysis (Little et al. 2002a). Since the ultimate test of the resulting taxonomies is their predictive power and contribution to building effective services, a number of interventions developed using these approaches are being evaluated in the UK and elsewhere in Europe using experimental methods.

Most Unit studies over the years have had a longitudinal element. A handful are essentially evaluations, tracking what happens to children following an intervention such as a mentoring scheme (DSRU 1997) or the Catch 'em Young programme designed to prevent antisocial behaviour among adolescents (Cleaver 1991). A more frequent practice has been to take a retrospective look, and then to use that information to predict what will happen to children, and ultimately to test the accuracy of those predictions – as in *Children Going Home* (Bullock et al. 1998b).

The value of thinking prospectively for understanding patterns of child development and identifying potentially suitable interventions is easily underestimated. A theme that Roger drums into anyone who works at the Unit is the danger of assuming that because, say, a disproportionate number of young offenders have been abused, ergo most victims of maltreatment will commit crimes. Another mantra is the difference between risk and probability; the fact that, for instance, a smoker may be at high risk of developing heart disease compared with other people but still only have a small chance of dying from the condition. Also connected is the appreciation that protective factors are contextual: as Roger puts it, rubber boots are pretty useless if you are running to escape a burning building but they may be protective if you are struck by lightning. In other words, what might not seem particularly 'protective' at one moment may become so in the future. These observations might seem self-evident but they derive from prospective research and indicate the need for more such studies. Evaluations using randomly allocated groups are relatively rare in children's services, especially in social care (for an exception see Monck *et al*. 1996), but they are starting to be an important feature of the Unit's portfolio. For example, in addition to the one currently under way (see above) there was a study of ISSP (Intensive Supervision and Support programme) for persistent young offenders (Little *et al*. 2003b) and a planned study will examine outcomes for children in residential care. Much of the work to date in this vein has been around helping agencies to make interventions 'evaluable' and includes: the development of logic models or 'theories of change' setting out why and how a service should break causal chains; the use of data from agency files combined with clear target group criteria to ensure that the right candidates for the intervention are engaged; and specifying the service components to improve the consistency of delivery (Axford *et al*. 2003b). Where it proves difficult to create real control groups we have experimented with 'shadow controls' (Rossi *et al*. 1999) using structured social histories to help to predict best and worst case scenarios for what will happen in a case *without* help (Little 2002; Axford and Berry 2003).

CONTRIBUTING TO EVIDENCE OF 'WHAT WORKS'

What works for children in need? By any estimation the volume of research and knowledge in children's services has burgeoned over the last 40 years. Today it is difficult to keep up with the number of articles and reports being produced, particularly if work in health, education and youth justice is considered alongside social care, and even more so if an international perspective is taken. To make things manageable there are attempts to distil the research, with many excellent summaries now available; indeed, Roger has been involved with several such initiatives (see DHSS 1985; DoH 1991, 1995, 1998).

Even so, it is commonly acknowledged that there is much we do not know about children's development and how it is affected by services. With this in mind, scientific evaluations will make up a significant part of the Unit's programme for the foreseeable future. The random allocation studies that are under way were noted above. Work by Dartington in various local authorities in England involves collecting information about local needs, designing new, needs-led services and then evaluating those services using a range of methods (e.g. Little *et al*. 2002). Increasing use is made in these studies of techniques that enhance causal inference, for example exploring dose–effect and tracing how far links in the intervention's logic model are realised (Axford *et al*., 2005). Other projects involve training practitioners and managers to think more systematically about evaluation (see Dartington-i 2003).

Self-evidently, this work happens in a wider context and all research centres must adapt to the funding and commissioning climate of the times. The last 40 years have witnessed a shift from long-term programmes based around designated central government-sponsored units and conducted by career researchers – effectively the context for most of Roger's work – to a predilection for short-term problem-solving studies. It might be characterised as a move away from strategic studies concerned with problems of considerable generality that are likely to endure over a period of decades and towards tactical studies aimed at providing quick answers to the specific and immediate problems faced by policy-makers (notwithstanding recent initiatives by the Economic and Social Research Council and the Department of Health, for example on changing youth and parenting). Depending on one's perspective, this can present a dilemma, namely whether to follow the external agenda or to set and pursue an internal agenda that takes a different direction.

The Unit's aim has been to fashion a long-term programme of work and to take on work that fits within that programme. Roger is an architect of this approach; indeed for all his prudence he has always been an enthusiastic risk-taker. The common language referred to above is intended to give the approach continuity and coherence, while large-scale studies funded by central government, research councils and other bodies are supplemented with work for local authorities that is adapted in various ways so that it feeds into the wider programme while also meeting customers' needs. In its purest form the approach becomes a scientific development cycle, in which research studies produce instruments for policy-makers and practitioners, the application of which generates new findings, which in turn can be used to test and refine hypotheses.

That is the intent as regards the research programme but who should do the work? Again, the dilemmas that this poses will be familiar. What is the right balance in a research centre between specialists and generalists and between experienced and younger staff? How multidisciplinary should the team be? What mix of skills do people require to be a researcher in our field? And so on. Taking just one of these issues, Roger and colleagues at Dartington have demonstrated a strong commitment over the years to training a new generation of researchers in children's services. They have done this in the traditional way by supervising doctoral students – some based at the Unit (including us) – and by nurturing the careers of many others. There are other ways of addressing the same concern, for example the Nuffield Foundation's post-doctoral programme.

To take the Dartington approach forward we have developed a more structured curriculum for PhD students in the field of child development and children's services, with participants dividing their time between work on orthodox Unit research studies and writing their theses. Roger is one of the lecturers on the programme. The breadth of studies undertaken by students on the programme illustrates the potential of re-analysing existing data or of at least 'piggybacking' postgraduate research onto larger studies. To date they include a comparison of the education of children in care in four European countries (Weyts 2002), an examination of different ways of conceptualising child well-being and their implications for services (Axford 2003) and an exploration of the relationship between the organisation of children's services and the outcomes they achieve (Morpeth 2004). An ongoing study is looking at the differential effects on child development of exposure to child maltreatment and domestic violence (Berry, forthcoming).

EXPERIMENTING WITH SHAPING POLICY AND PRACTICE

The Dartington Unit has always tried to make research findings relevant to the process of policy-making and some modest claims can be made for its effectiveness over the years. For example, the 1978 study *Locking Up Children* (Millham *et al.* 1978) was an influence on government policy which limited the number of local authority secure beds for children to around 300. Often the impact was the product of relationships forged with influential individuals in central government (see Millham 1993). Partly as a result of this, Dartington studies were among those that informed the framing of the *Children Act* 1989, aud refocused efforts aimed at seeing family support as a means of protecting children (Cleaver and Freeman 1995; DoH 1995). This work was heavily focused on social services.

Since the Labour government took office in 1997 there have been important changes in children's services, with implications for how research feeds into policy-making. Although responsibility for children is now largely concentrated in the Children, Young People and Families Directorate, some of it lies elsewhere (for example, youth justice and mental health) and most family support is undertaken by providers working independently of social services – Sure Start, the Children's Fund, Connexions and so on (Little *et al.* 2003). In addition, and perhaps more so than before, policy-making is not so much a linear, top-down model in which an idea is translated effortlessly into practice as an incremental or interactive model in which ideas are continually reshaped at the coalface (Newman 2002). On several fronts in children's services central government is setting out a broad direction or framework and encouraging local flexibility in its implementation.

It is in this context that the Unit has consciously adjusted the way it seeks to influence policy and practice. As well as seeking to communicate effectively to *all* agencies and continuing to liaise with central government policy-makers, its attention has shifted since the mid-1990s towards service innovation at the local level with the intention of enabling effective practice to filter-up (from local to national) and out (from one place to another). This endeavour is embodied by numerous so-called 'test sites' in the UK, other European countries and the USA – partnerships with agencies eager to develop and test needs-led, evidence-based services. Significant gains from the approach are apparent in terms of inter-agency collaboration and service innovation but more work is needed to determine if they result in improved outcomes measured in terms of children's health and development (Little *et al.* 2002b; DSRU 2004).

Prior to this, in the 1990s, the Dartington Unit's longstanding commitment to effective dissemination took on other forms. Roger was instrumental in helping to establish Research in Practice to communicate research findings to front-line practitioners as well as a 'teaching-hospital' style partnership with a local social services department aimed at facilitating the understanding and application of research evidence in practice. A journalist with information design skills was recruited, initially mainly to improve the readability and appearance of the Unit's products. These ventures met with varying degrees of success (e.g. Thistlethwaite 2000; Randall 2002) and lessons were learned about harnessing the power of visual explanation to illuminate rather than merely to make things look attractive (Bullock *et al.* 1998c).

At about the same time, the Unit also started to develop 'practice tools' (see above). These now form the primary avenue for thc Unit's dissemination efforts to practitioners. They take the ideas, methods and to some extent the findings from full-scale research studies and translate the main components so that they can be used by people working with children. They help professionals to test the findings and discover if they hold true in the context of their own work, and, in the process, contribute to concrete improvements in children's services. For example, one early tool, Going Home?, aids decision-making in matters related to the return of children separated from their families (DSRU 1992); another, Structure Culture and Outcome, provides an opportunity for reflection on how children's homes can improve life for their residents (Bullock *et al*. 1999). Roger was a catalyst – with others – for these and the other initiatives, and is himself a master disseminator with his trademark mix of razor observation and witty aside – perhaps honed in the variety clubs to which his comedian brother took him as a youngster.

The practice tools are designed not so much to impart findings as to inculcate research-based ways of thinking (DSRU 2004). They encourage the development of 'made knowledge' – information that an individual re-analyses and works through until it is understood implicitly – as opposed to 'used knowledge', which involves a more superficial understanding (see Taylor and White 2000). Put another way, and drawing on the knowledge management literature, practice tools seem to adopt a 'soft' approach, often referred to as 'knowledge pull', in which the answer to the problem of improving research utilisation is to motivate colleagues to share relevant evidence, with knowledge seen as a *process* (Nutley *et al*. 2003). This contrasts with the 'hard' version, also known as 'knowledge push', in which the answer is to codify and transmit information, with knowledge viewed as an *object*. But do practice tools work?

It has never been the Dartington Unit's intention to argue that research knowledge should be the sole influence on practice with vulnerable children. There are at least four other concerns to be reckoned with, notably legal requirements, moral norms, pragmatic restrictions and consumer views. These influences are not necessarily complementary (Little 1997). For example, campaigners might welcome a ban on smacking but evidence for its value is scarce and since 9 out of 10 children will have been hit by their parents/carers (Smith *et al*. 1995) how would it be possible to enforce? There is also a danger of researchers and policy-makers colluding to design interventions that cannot be implemented for want of resources or because children and families refuse to use them. Indeed, the ship of state would have churned up much muddy water had its voyage ardently followed certain research ideas: there is a lot to be said for maintaining the status quo.

Even so, like other applied researchers, we want our research to have an impact. Unfortunately, measuring this is not quite so easy as injecting findings with a dye and tracing their journey through the capillaries of the policy-making process. But a scientific approach to dissemination should be possible; indeed, Roger and others have studied where practitioners obtain their information from, the extent to which it changes practice and its importance relative to other factors concerning research utilisation of the number of documents distributed (Bullock *et al*. 1998c; Weyts *et al*. 2000). Most new Unit publications are therefore evaluated against up to three measures: availability/use, effect on individual and agency practice and impact on children's health and development (see Knott and Wildavsky 1981). For example, the assessment tool Paperwork is being assessed for the proportion of forms completed, the quality of services fashioned and provided by those practitioners using the tool and outcomes for recipients of those services compared with children in a control group (Bullock *et al*. 2003).

Some of the lessons learned from these exercises and similar research by others will, hopefully, inform the mechanisms by which we seek to influence policy and practice. A good PhD topic would be to explore how our field can become more sophisticated at presenting research in the light of emerging knowledge from linguistics, anthropology and neuroscience concerning how people process information (see, e.g., Byrnes 2001). We are interested to see if training undergraduate and newly qualified practitioners in Common Language ideas would help to improve the quality of services provided and the ensuing outcomes for children. A more ambitious idea, never seriously considered, would be to develop a service-provider arm to the organisation and test evidence-based interventions close-at-hand; common in medicine and child psychiatry, this model is not so far from where the Unit began its life at Dartington in 1968. In a cross-cultural experiment, it invited children from the north of England to live with predominantly middle-class children in the private Dartington boarding school and, in return, sent Dartington boarders to live in the coal-mining communities of the Dearne valley (Kidel 1990).

RECONFIGURING THE ORGANISATION

Management gurus are forever at pains to stress that the structure and culture of an organisation should be driven by its aims: form follows function. For many years the Research Unit was a small organisation focusing almost exclusively on research. To realise the aspiration of disseminating robust scientific research effectively and of linking it to the development and evaluation of services, the Warren House Group was created. It shelters the five activities that have emerged from the Dartington Unit. Alongside the Unit, which continues to focus on scientific research studies, it comprises Dartington-i (devoted to service development), DeMo (the communication design studio that produces most Unit publications), Warren House Press (the in-house publisher) and the Centre for Social Policy (a network of senior and experienced experts and policy-makers from across children's services that supports the group's work).

Change in organisations is rarely pain-free, and the changes here have involved lengthy formal and informal discussions both about internal matters, such as working culture, use of building space and number of staff, and about external issues, such as relations with professional groups and universities. The organisation continues to evolve and it was fitting that when the group was established as an independent charity in July 2003 Roger became its first Chair of Trustees.

THINKING INTERNATIONALLY

The Dartington Unit's interest in cross-national work stretches back to the 1980s and an exchange between England and the Carolinas of researchers, practitioners and policy-makers interested in youth justice and welfare programmes. At a conference of participants, Roger noted some of the pitfalls of international relations: for example, how a 1910 phrase book for British travellers to Italy included under the section 'at the hotel' such indispensable phrases as 'Put the luggage there' and, should orders be unfulfilled, 'I shall inform the British Ambassador about this'; and how Spencer Millham, on the Unit's first visit to the USA, told an immigration official that he intended to stay for a 'fortnight' only to find his card stamped with the next day's date – a query and explanation led the officer to bellow, 'You said for t'night, man, and that ain't two weeks' (Bullock 1992).

Despite such misunderstandings, the Unit's international work continues to evolve. In addition to staff participating in conferences and networks of similar centres from other countries, various comparative pieces of work are under way or in the pipeline that should help with explaining childhood problems and their resolution in terms of wider social forces rather than local legislation and personalities. Thus, the community study in England has been replicated in rural Pennsylvania, inner-city Philadelphia and the Dublin conurbation and a book on the effects of movement on child development is being written, with contributors from different countries discussing topics such as Palestinians moving from Jordan to Chicago, Moroccan children migrating through Spain and France, and refugee and asylum-seeking families in a London community.

CONCLUSION

This chapter is an attempt to set out continuities and change at the Dartington Unit. We want to maintain the Unit's traditional strengths – the use of administrative data, viewing children's lives holistically, mixing quantitative and qualitative methods, the attempt to incorporate meaning, and so on – but we also have to look forward. We are very fortunate to have 40 years of history behind us as an organisation but, at the same time, it would feel wrong to use the resources at our disposal to repeat the work of the last four decades. At least six features will characterise the course we take.

First, we continue to be interested in children in need and services for them, but whereas previous work examined interventions and outcomes from a systems perspective we are increasingly interested in developmental trajectories and specifying the components of interventions more precisely.

Second, we intend to continue to try to develop theory, although the sociological perspective is being integrated into a common framework to help to explain how and why children's services impact on child development.

Third, we are interested in 'within-individual' change. Unit studies have always taken a longitudinal perspective but they have mostly been retrospective and often based on poor-quality data or single sources – weaknesses that we are seeking to address.

Fourth, we will invest in evaluating services rigorously. Although previous Unit work considered service populations it rarely focused on child development outcomes. New features are strategies to make services evaluable and the use of control groups. RCTs are by no means the only way to evaluate services but more studies of this type are needed.

Fifth, we are keen to see our research have an impact but whereas in the past this was primarily through influential individuals in central government increasingly we are doing it by way of local experiments in research-driven service innovation.

And sixth, we continue to be interested in different methods of disseminating research but we want to use scientific methods to develop a better understanding of how effective these efforts are both in terms of their take-up and their impact on children's lives.

The dilemmas facing Dartington and other independent research centres conducting work in children's services are, in many ways, perennial and there is much to be learned from those who have grappled with similar issues in the past. In this respect we were fascinated to read Barbara Tizard's (2003) frank and personal account of life at the Thomas Coram Research Unit in London in the period 1973–1990. The Coram Unit also specialises in the study of children's development and children's services, though with a stronger educational thrust than Dartington. Many of the problems addressed in its development resonate with those we have elaborated in this chapter. So too do some of the solutions attempted, for example: seeking to construct a strategic research programme; placing value on common spaces and birthday celebrations to mitigate the often lonely experience of research; deliberately recruiting staff from different disciplinary backgrounds; attempting various methods of reaching non-academic audiences; looking to train and retain younger staff via a PhD programme so that in time they acquire the depth of knowledge required for good research; and so on. It is fitting and perhaps unsurprising that the instigator of many of these developments at Thomas Coram, Jack Tizard, was a good friend of Roger's until his untimely death and that Barbara Tizard is a fellow of the Centre for Social Policy at Dartington.

The approach of the Dartington Unit as outlined in this chapter represents just one attempt to contribute to improved outcomes for children in need in a changing research and policy context. It has weaknesses and will continue to evolve. We will do well to achieve anything remotely approaching what has been done by Roger and others but we know that the climate in children's services in England and Wales is perhaps the most auspicious it has been for some time, with extensive and largely progressive reforms under way following the Laming (2003) Inquiry into the death of Victoria Climbié and the Green Paper *Every Child Matters* (DfES 2003). We also know that the Unit benefits from being built on the thinking, commitment and imagination of Roger Bullock: rather as a stick of rock is run through with the name of a seaside town – the kind of which Roger is so fond, with an end-of the-pier variety show and a dodgy chip shop.

REFERENCES

Abunimah, A., Axford, N., Little, M. and Morpeth, L. (2002) *Recording race and ethnicity for children in need*, Unpublished Paper, Dartington Social Research Unit / Chapin Hall Center for Children.

Axford, N. (2003) *Child Well-Being from Different Perspectives: defining, measuring and responding to need, violated rights, poverty, poor quality of life and social exclusion*, Unpublished PhD Thesis, University of Exeter.

Axford, N. and Berry, V. (2003) *Exploring the potential of shadow controls in the evaluation of children's services*, Working Paper 8, Dartington Social Research Unit.

Axford, N., Berry, V. and Little, M. (2003b) *Enhancing the evaluability of a programme for disaffected young people*, Working Paper 6, Dartington Social Research Unit.

Axford, N., Little, M. and Morpeth, L. (2003a) *Children Supported and Unsupported in the Community*, Report submitted to the Department of Health, Dartington Social Research Unit.

Axford, N., Little, M., Morpeth, L. and Weyts, A. (2005) 'Evaluating children's services: recent conceptual and methodological developments,' *British Journal of Social Work*, 35(1), 73–88.

Berry, V. (forthcoming) *The Differential Impact of Child Maltreatment and Exposure to Domestic Violence on Children's Outcomes*, Unpublished PhD Thesis, University of Bath.

Brown, E., Bullock, R., Hobson, C. and Little, M. (1998) *Making Residential Care Work: structure and culture in children's homes*, Aldershot, Ashgate.

Bullock, R. (1992) 'Introduction', in Bullock, R. (ed.) *Problem Adolescents: an international view*, London, Whiting & Birch.

Bullock, R., Little, M. and Millham, S. (1992) 'The relationship between quantitative and qualitative approaches to social policy research', in Brannen, J. (ed.) *Mixing Methods: qualitative and quantitative research*, Aldershot, Avebury.

Bullock, R., Little, M. and Millham, S. (1998a) *Secure Treatment Outcomes: the care careers of very difficult adolescents*, Aldershot, Ashgate.

Bullock, R., Gooch, D. and Little, M. (1998b) *Children Going Home: the re-unification of families*, Aldershot, Ashgate.

Bullock, R., Gooch, D., Little, M. and Mount, K. (1998c) *Research in Practice: experiments in development and information design*, Aldershot, Ashgate.

Bullock, R., Little, M., Ryan, M. and Tunnard, J. (1999) *Structure, Culture and Outcome: how to improve residential services for children*, Dartington, Dartington Social Research Unit.

Bullock, R., Axford, N., Little, M. and Morpeth, L. (2003) 'Predicting the likelihood of family reunification in the foster care system', *Diskurs* 2/2003, 26–33.

Byrnes, J. P. (2001) *Minds, Brains, and Learning: understanding the psychological and educational relevance of neuroscientific research*, New York, The Guilford Press.

Cleaver, H. (1991) *Vulnerable Children in Schools: a study of Catch 'em Young, a project aimed at helping 10 year olds transfer school*, Aldershot, Dartmouth;

Cleaver, H. and Freeman, P. (1995) *Parental Perspectives in Cases of Suspected Child Abuse*, London, HMSO.

Dartington-i (2003) *Evaluating Good Practice with Children and Families: a practitioners' primer*, Dartington, Warren House Press. www.dartington-i.org/evaluation.

DfES (Department for Education and Skills) (2003) *Every Child Matters*, Cm. 5860, Norwich, The Stationery Office.

DHSS (Department of Health and Social Security) (1985) *Social Work Decisions in Child Care: recent research findings and their implications*, London, HMSO.

DoH (Department of Health) (1991) *Patterns and Outcomes in Child Placement*, London, HMSO.

DoH (1995) *Child Protection: messages from research*, London, HMSO.

DoH (1998) *Caring for Children Away from Home: messages from research*, Chichester, John Wiley & Sons.

DSRU (Dartington Social Research Unit) (1992) *Going Home: key factors in the return process*, Dartington, Dartington Social Research Unit.

DSRU (1997) *A Friend in Need? The CSV 'Allies' Befriender Project for Children in Residential Care*, Dartington, Dartington Social Research Unit.

DSRU (2004) 'Experiments in using practice tools to disseminate research', in Klöckner, C. and Paetzel, U. (eds) *Kindheitsforschung und kommunale Praxis: Praxisnahe Erkenntnisse aus der aktuellen Kindhietsforschung*, Wiesbaden, VS-Verlag.

Kidel, M. (1990) *Beyond the Classroom: Dartington's experiments in education*, Bideford, Green Books.

Knott, J. and Wildavsky, A (1981) 'If dissemination is the solution, what is the problem?', in Rich, R. (ed.) *The Knowledge Cycle*, Beverly Hills, Sage.

Lambert, R., Millham, S. and Bullock, R. (1970) *Manual to the Sociology of the School*, London, Weidenfeld & Nicolson.

Laming, Lord (2003) *The Victoria Climbié Inquiry*, Cm. 5730, London, TSO.

Little, M. (1997) 'The re-focusing of children's services: the contribution of research', in Parton, N. (ed.) *Child Protection and Family Support: tensions, contradictions and possibilities*, London, Routledge.

Little, M. (2001) *Using a Common Language to Change the Pattern of Services for Children in Need*, Dartington Social Research Unit. http://www.whg.org.uk/commonlanguage/documents/lectures/1_CLforchildreninneed.pdf

Little, M. (2002) *Prediction: perspectives on diagnosis, prognosis and interventions for children in need*, Dartington, Warren House Press.

Little, M. and Mount, K. (2003) *Paperwork: the clinical assessment of children in need*, Dartington, Warren House Press.

Little, M., Madge, J., Mount, K., Ryan, M. and Tunnard, J. (2001) *Matching Needs and Services, 3rd Edition*, Dartington, Dartington Academic Press.

Little, M., Axford, N. and Morpeth, L. (2002a) *Aggregating Data: better management and planning information in children's services*, Dartington, Warren House Press.

Little, M., Axford, N. and Morpeth, L. (2003) 'Children's services in the UK 1997–2003: problems, developments and challenges for the future', *Children and Society* 17 (3), 205–214.

Little, M., Axford, N. and Morpeth, L. (2004a) 'Risk and protection in the context of services for children in need', *Child and Family Social Work* 9 (1), 105–118.

Little, M., Bullock, R., Madge, J. and Arruabarrena, I. (2002b) 'How to develop needs-led, evidence-based services', *MCC: Building Knowledge for Integrated Care* 10 (3), 28–32.

Little, M., Kogan, J., Bullock, R. and Van der Laan, P. (2004b) 'ISSP: an experiment in multi-systemic responses to persistent young offenders known to children's services', *British Journal of Criminology* 44 (2), 225–240.

Millham, S. (1993) *An embarrassment of riches or a rich embarrassment? Four decades of social policy research*, Inaugural Lecture, May 1992, University of Bristol, Dartington Social Research Unit.

Millham, S., Bullock, R. and Cherrett, P. (1975) *After Grace – Teeth: a comparative study of the residential experience of boys in approved schools*, Brighton, Human Context Books.

Millham, S., Bullock, R. and Hosie, K. (1978) *Locking Up Children*, Farnborough, Saxon House.

Millham, S., Bullock, R., Hosie, K. and Haak, M. (1986) *Lost in Care: the problems of maintaining links between children in care and their families*, Aldershot, Gower.

Monck, E., Sharland, E., Bentovim A., Goodall G., Hyde C. and Lewin, R. (1996) *Child Sexual Abuse: a descriptive and treatment study*, London, The Stationery Office.

Morpeth, L. (2004) *Organisation and Outcomes in Children's Services*, Unpublished PhD. Thesis, University of Exeter.

Newman, J. (2002) 'Putting the "policy" back into social policy', *Social Policy and Society* 1 (4), 347–354.

Nutley, S.M., Davies, H.T.O. and Walter, I. (2003) *Conceptual Synthesis 2: learning from knowledge management*, St Andrews, Research Unit for Research Utilisation.

Randall, J. (2002) 'The practice–research relationship: a case of ambivalent attachment?', *Journal of Social Work* 2 (1), 105–122.

Rossi, P., Freeman, H. and Lipsey, M. (1999) *Evaluation: a systematic approach*, 6th Edition, Thousand Oaks, Sage.

Rutter, M. (1989) 'Pathways from childhood to adulthood', *Journal of Child Psychology and Psychiatry* 30, 23–51.

Rutter, M. (1999) 'Psychosocial adversity and child psychopathology', *British Journal of Psychiatry* 174, 480–493.

Sinclair, R. and Little, M. (2002) 'Developing a taxonomy for children in need', in Ward, H. and Rose, W. (eds) *Approaches to Needs Assessment in Children's Services*, London, Jessica Kingsley Publishers.

Smith, M., Bee, P., Heverin, A. and Nobes, G. (1995) *Parental Control with the Family: the nature and extent of parental violence to children*, London, Thomas Coram Research Unit.

Taylor, C. and White, S. (2000) *Practising Reflexivity in Health and Welfare*, Buckingham, Open University Press.

Thistlethwaite, P. (2000) *Evidence and Ethical Practice: an evaluation of the DATAR project for Devon Social Services*, Dartington, Dartington Social Research Unit.

Tizard, B. (2003) *The Thomas Coram Research Unit, 1973–1990: a memoir*, London, TCRU/Institute of Education.

Walker, S., Shemmings, D. and Cleaver, H. (2003) *Write Enough: effective recording in children's services*. www.writeenough.org.uk (accessed 18 July 2003).

Weyts, A. (2002) *The Provision of Welfare for Children in Substitute Care: a comparative study of four European countries with special attention to the education of these children*, Unpublished PhD Thesis, University of Exeter.

Weyts, A., Morpeth, L. and Bullock, R. (2000) 'Department of Health research overviews – past, present and future: an evaluation of the dissemination of the Blue Book, "Child Protection: messages from research"', *Child and Family Social Work* 5 (3), 215–223.

15

MESSAGES FOR RESEARCH, POLICY AND PRACTICE IN CHILDREN'S SERVICES

Nick Axford, Vashti Berry, Michael Little,
Jill Madge and Louise Morpeth

INTRODUCTION

This book has looked at research, policy and practice in different areas of children's services in the UK over the last 40 years, and identified key trends and challenges. This chapter seeks to draw together some of the main themes, highlighting important challenges for research, policy and practice in the next decade or so. It finishes by considering Roger's legacy to the field and how it might be developed.

MESSAGES FOR RESEARCH

It is no longer possible – paraphrasing Roy Parker's observation of the 1960s – to read three books and know more or less what there is to know about the field covered by this book. There is a lot of research, so much so that small industries have evolved to ensure its effective dissemination and application to policy and practice. Much of this research and development is of an extremely high standard, as the chapters in this book testify. The emerging portfolio is hugely impressive when compared with the situation when Roger Bullock started his career. But what of another Roger Bullock starting his or her career in 2005? Should he or she continue to do more of the same? In certain respects the answer is 'yes'. It is not the place at the end of a festschrift to speak again of the strengths of the approaches used by authors in this book. Suffice to say that if the research question is 'Does voluntary reception increase the rate of return of children in care?' or 'What happens to children placed in secure accommodation?' or 'What lessons can be drawn from reviews of death or serious injury of children known to social services departments?' – all questions that studies in which Roger Bullock has been involved have sought to answer – then the methods applied by the authors of chapters in this book will be adequate.

Forty Years of Research, Policy and Practice in Children's Services.
Edited by N. Axford, V. Berry, M. Little and L. Morpeth.
© 2005 John Wiley & Sons, Ltd. ISBN 0-470-01219-6.

But there are other questions that remain unanswered by 40 years of research and other methods that remain relatively underused. We do not intend, in closing this book, to provide an exhaustive description of what the next Roger Bullock might do. The following six observations, however, might suggest some opportunities.

Topics

The first area requiring reflection is the choice of research topics. At a general level this involves asking timeless questions about major, broad-sweeping and critical issues that contribute to theory development rather than short-term policy-specific questions (Parker). As in the arts, social research endures or is forgotten, depending on how far it says something eternal rather than temporal; research that is too closely tied to specific policies emanating from government is likely to have a shelf-life only as long as the initiative in question (Bullock). Examples of perennial issues are the effect of separation from parents on children's development and why some children with a particular constellation of needs succeed while other similar children struggle. Of course, shifting the focus here depends as much on policy-makers as it does on researchers, since they influence which topics are studied.

In addition, the chapters in this volume have all highlighted specific areas about which relatively little is known. Some of these concern how problems develop and desist in children's lives. For example: adolescents who murder, sadistic and violent young people and juvenile sex offenders – in particular, how their psychosocial difficulties develop and what interventions are effective in tackling them (Bailey); institutional abuse and the comorbidity of child abuse with domestic violence and poverty (Berridge); 'turning-points' in children's lives, which is why and how maladaptive life trajectories sometimes take quite dramatic turns for the better and produce lasting change (Sinclair); and why a significant minority of children whose parents divorce experience detrimental outcomes while others do not (Murch and Hooper).

Other specific areas for further research identified by the contributors relate more to the effect of interventions. For instance: the strengths and weaknesses of custodial versus community-based sentences and how the early onset of offending may be addressed (Giller); the efficacy of civil interventions for young people displaying low-level antisocial behaviour (Van der Laan and Smit); the significance of the size of home for child outcomes (Clough); the issues that help birth relatives to deal with adoption (Thoburn); the effectiveness of 'thin' family support services routinely offered by many social services departments and the impact on child outcomes of involving children in discussions about service provision (Little and Sinclair); and how the school curriculum affects children's personal and social development (Anderson).

A broader development barely discussed in the chapters concerns advances in behavioural genetics (both quantitative genetics and molecular genetic studies). These require social research to consider the influence of both environmental *and* biological factors when examining childhood problems such as conduct disorder or mental health difficulties. The focus tends to be on the former – that is, on how particular experiences or environments (that deviate from the norm) affect children. While studies in child psychology and psychiatry have sought to look more at genetic risk and vulnerability (e.g. Lahey *et al.* 1999; Caspi *et al.* 2002), greater clarification is needed about the kinds of environments that trigger or interact with genetic risk to produce poor outcomes. This task fits into the social care research agenda and will require greater collaboration between psychologists, geneticists and sociologists.

Methods

Second, it is incumbent on applied social researchers in children's services to use methodologies that are more rigorous scientifically and to resist the fad for phenomenology, which struggles to generate reliable evidence upon which to build general policy and practice (Parker). The majority of the studies discussed in the preceding chapters concern processes and user perspectives. For example, there are studies of flows of cases through the residential care and child protection systems and of how children and families experience the procedures operating in foster care and family justice. Less emphasis has been given to the epidemiology of child development problems, to child outcomes measured in terms of children's well-being, or to the effectiveness of interventions. There are exceptions. For instance, there are good epidemiological studies in the mental health field (Bailey) and some research on the outcomes of adoption (Thoburn). Various youth justice and family support programmes have been subjected to rigorous evaluation involving control groups (Giller; Little and Sinclair). But the general pattern holds.

Advances might be achieved in part by tracing the interaction of risk and protective factors in children's developmental trajectories over time and testing the logic models that underpin services to discover how specified effects are produced (Axford and Morpeth). The latter will help with understanding how to put into practice the factors that are conducive to good outcomes (Clough). More specifically, there is a requirement for the replication of studies to test findings and develop new hypotheses and for prospective longitudinal designs, with particular attention to long-term outcomes. As Bailey notes in relation to the mental health of young offenders, a positive situation at age 18 does not necessarily mean 'a life happy thereafter'. Little is known about what happens to young people with disorders in the period 18–30 years, especially whether protective factors continue to operate and if the effects of treatment persist. Exploration of such questions will also indicate the stage at which extra 'top up' services might be beneficial and how a better transition can be made between children and adult services.

The opportunities created by access to longitudinal data are well documented. (They are also well understood by the research community that produced this book; the reluctance of consumers of research to fund such studies, however, has perpetuated the reliance on cross-sectional data.) Most important are advances in methods to understand within individual change over time, to supplement well-tried techniques for studying population change. The context in which research takes place should continue to produce opportunities. As this book goes to press, new legislation is requiring English local authorities to become more focused on outcomes for children. Some local authorities have recognised that the body of administrative data collected by the agencies that currently make up children's services – hidebound by particular organisational needs and dominated by output measures for service populations – will not be sufficient for future requirements. In this context, not only might researchers begin to use broad samples to understand service use and impact but so too might local authorities. Since the interest in these data is child outcomes, it follows that the same information might be collected year on year. As well as creating better and more reliable information for local authority planners and managers it would also produce chances to better understand secular changes in children's development, for example in behaviour, mental health and intelligence.

Another recognised lacuna in the current repertoire of children's services research is high-quality evaluation. There are well-reasoned arguments in favour of a broad portfolio of evaluation techniques and those that suggest that random allocation is the *only* way to do research are plainly wrong. It is equally unhelpful, however, to suggest that evaluation by random allocation has no place in children's services research. The approach is reasonably accepted in health and youth justice but traditionally lacking elsewhere in children's services (Macdonald 1996). Anderson, for example, highlights the dearth of trials of initiatives and proposals in education, arguably one reason why recent initiatives in that area owe more to ideology than to evidence. Similarly, the limited conclusions that Sinclair can draw from comparing outcomes for children who remain in foster care versus those who return home demonstrate a weakness that random allocation or even matched control studies could address.

Several opportunities for such studies exist, starting with natural experiments. Changes in administrative boundaries, for example, can result in children with similar backgrounds suddenly getting different services. Policies intended to produce fairness in the allocation of resources have a similar effect, for example the requirement by most US states for lotteries to decide who gets into so-called 'charter' schools. Another opportunity arises from using the techniques required by random allocation studies to help to establish and implement new interventions for children. For example, in a recent Dartington study, the need to (i) specify the target group, (ii) ensure that there were more applicants than places available, (iii) establish a theory of change that explained *why* the programme might lead to better outcomes for children, (iv) introduce sound ethical principles and (v) strengthen the consistency of service delivery not only meant that a service could be evaluated by random allocation but also improved the quality and consumer rating of the intervention.

A further opportunity for evaluation by random allocation is more hard-won. It involves doing the groundwork required to permit gold standard evaluations of major children's services interventions, such as accommodating children for short periods, taking children into care or introducing so-called 'openness' – the involvement of birth families – into adoption. Many would contend that random allocation in these contexts is impossible, but the nature of the intervention and the far-reaching potential impacts, negative and positive, on children's development almost *demand* the most rigorous study, and there are examples elsewhere in children's services, youth justice for example, of similarly difficult contexts being studied in this way. The groundwork is a mixture of the methodological – for example, applying the techniques mentioned in the previous paragraph – and ideological – demonstrating why evaluation of this kind should be an essential part of our understanding of these intensive interventions.

More provocatively, there may be a case for pooling some funds from evaluations whose methodological limitations make them unlikely to say anything new and channelling them instead into experimental studies. Such a strategy might be popular: 'Surely, if the general public and mass media could see the flaws in quick and dirty research, they would – as taxpayers – demand high-quality evaluations using the best possible methods, especially randomised experiments' (Farrington 2003, p. 225). And if this proves Utopian, even comparing actual trajectories with those predicted without intervention would help to account for extraneous factors and antecedents, so providing a more realistic appraisal of the effect of the intervention, for example residential care (Clough). Other ways of tightening up evaluation research include replicating programmes consistently, so that it is clear *what* is being effective, and targeting services precisely at the intended target group, so that it is clear *who* benefits (Little and Sinclair).

All the previously mentioned opportunities demand attention to questions of measurement. Much of the research described in this book has been based at least in part on researcher judgements. Since many of the studies have involved direct participation of the principal investigator in the fieldwork – a practice uncommon and largely impractical in other parts of the social sciences – the quality of judgement has probably been good. What may have been lost in terms of reliability and validity will, to some extent, have been compensated for by insights into children's circumstances, how services are received or how children and families respond to help that might have been missed by junior researchers completing instruments according to coda.

The critical point here is that the gains and losses will never be known since the essentially qualitative approach to measurement that has been taken in this field has never been evaluated. Would the results of *Lost in Care*, for example, have been different had Ian Sinclair and his colleagues applied the same methodology as Spencer Millham and the Dartington team? Among the dozens of studies referenced in this volume, only a relatively small proportion have used carefully assessed measures and few are based solely on this kind of methodology.

Much can be achieved by adopting existing validated measures, as routinely used by child development researchers for example. Another challenge is to find measures for other dimensions of research in this field, in particular concerning aspects of services. Whether or not a child is in care or getting family support or is the subject of a child protection enquiry would seem pretty obvious. Often it is not, at least from case files. Moreover, in understanding outcomes it is necessary to understand everything else that sits around these services, such as the visit to the speech therapist by the child in foster care or the respite with a grandmother for the recipient of family support or the availability of psychotherapy for the child protection case. At present, these interventions are counted in very different ways by researchers, leaving validity and reliability to be guessed at.

If the opportunities for improvements in the research mentioned here are taken up, it is hoped that time to think about, connect and apply the results will not be a casualty. One of the great skills of Roger Bullock and his contemporaries has been the ability to mix quantitative and qualitative methods in innovative ways, and also to bring to bear what might be called intelligent insight into the circumstances of the children and families who use services, the practitioners and managers who deliver them and the central government policy-makers responsible for their general administration and inspection. Improving the quality of research in our field continues to require, therefore, methods that capture the meaning attached by children and families to events in their lives. For example, case studies help to expose issues and highlight the narrowness of the research questions being asked (Parker), but they should be used to help to explain rather than simply to illustrate, and 'qualitative' questions should not be seen as an excuse for sloppiness (Bullock *et al.* 1992).

Strategy

A third set of messages emerging from the chapters concerns how researchers adapt to the commissioning and funding climate. Without doubt there is a pressing need to nurture new researchers in children's services and to develop career opportunities for them – an area in which there has been relatively little investment or thought until recently (Axford and Morpeth). One aspect of this task is addressing the poor employment conditions of most contract researchers (Bullock). Trends in the style of policy-making and the imminent and ongoing reforms to children's services in many western developed countries also mean that innovative and creative approaches are required to enable research to influence policy and practice. In particular, a more sophisticated understanding of and approach to dissemination is needed.

Too often, such activity is reduced to getting short, bullet-point summaries of studies into as many hands as possible. While this is progress on simply publishing monographs and academic journal articles – which few people read (Bullock *et al* 1998) – it is unclear whether it leads to changed thinking and practice and, ultimately, to improved outcomes for children (cf. Knott and Wildavsky 1981). Insights from other disciplines, notably communication design and cognitive psychology (e.g. Norman 1991; Tufte 1997), may assist with orienting dissemination activities towards the development of 'made' knowledge – worked through and understood implicitly – as opposed to more superficial 'used' knowledge (Taylor and White 2000).

Several contributors to this volume also advocate more far-reaching changes to the way that research is organised. The last 40 years has witnessed a move away from long-term research programmes based around established units and conducted by career researchers and towards a predilection for short-term problem-solving studies. Murch and Hooper argue that researchers must resist the pressure to conform by finding ways of building theory and knowledge in children's services more strategically. This might involve more cross-disciplinary working, for example bringing psychologists and educationalist together to study a particular subject such as the impact of children's mental health on school outcomes. Bullock encourages the use of a common conceptual framework, so that individual studies contribute in small ways to the development of theory. Beyond that, Parker contends that research administrators also have a responsibility, pointing to lessons from the past about how the research infrastructure affects the quality and influence of social research. More explicitly, developments have been enabled and progress constrained by the quantity, accessibility and quality of sources, by government decisions about administration and funding and by the nature of technology available.

Perspectives

A fourth theme elaborated by several contributors is the value of taking historical and sociological perspectives on research topics. The former provides some insight into 'what works'. Bailey, for example, notes that the last 200 years of youth justice in the UK have witnessed a pendulum swinging between punishment and retribution on the one hand and a concern with children's welfare and rehabilitation on the other. What were the effects of these shifts on young people's well-being and rates of recidivism? How might future policies avoid previous mistakes? She suggests that considering such questions might also help to resist knee-jerk reactions to demands from sections of the public and media for 'tough action' on persistent young offenders. The historical angle also helps with forecasting the policy areas that are likely to be relevant in the future and thus to demand research – in part because it highlights the perennial questions (see above).

Child welfare research is also often insufficiently theoretical or sociological in outlook (Berridge). Despite the importance of theory in enabling prediction and explanation, its role is jeopardised by those post-modernist accounts that delight in incomprehensibility or by short-term policy-specific studies (although clearly robust evaluations of specific initiatives are valuable). Further, it is easy within our disciplinary silos to forget that children's development is located in and shaped by a broader context – the environment and economy, class structures, social attitudes and so on. Child development research could easily become preoccupied with physical and psychological risk factors without considering their relation to questions of power and history; equally, sociologists are prone to make categorical statements about the impact on well-being of, say, discrimination, without spelling out how, logically, it 'gets into the body' (Haggerty 1994). Roger's work suggests that the understanding of child development and children's services will be furthered by concerted efforts to build theory and to bridge the micro–macro gap.

Childhood sociologists also point to the importance of the child's perspective, with a growing interest in recent years in the study of children as 'social actors' in their own right (e.g. Qvortrup et al. 1994). Yet despite considerable advances over the past decade or so, progress is still needed as regards eliciting information from children, using it to improve services and evaluating its impact in terms of child development outcomes (Sinclair and Little). These issues are beginning to be addressed, with various innovative approaches to gathering and interpreting children's views now in use (e.g. Thomas 2002). Other methodological questions concern the relationship between child and adult views and what ethical safeguards are appropriate, especially in research into child maltreatment (Amaya-Jackson et al. 2000). Equally challenging are the conceptual implications of childhood sociology, in particular whether certain phenomena, for example social exclusion, are qualitatively different for children and adults (e.g. Middleton and Adelman 2004).

Scope

A fifth challenge for the research community, evident in the preceding chapters, is the need to take into account all agencies (not just social services) and all children (not only service users). For example, Berridge notes that children who have been maltreated invariably have difficulties in other areas of their lives besides family and social relationships, and to some extent the call in the mid-1990s for a focus on 'the overall needs of children rather than a narrow concentration on the alleged incident' (DoH 1995, p. 55) has been heeded, aided in the UK by the ecological principles enshrined in official guidance on assessment (e.g. DoH 2001). However, much research in the children's services field is handicapped by its reliance on service populations, in particular children in care and those whose names are on the Child Protection Register. Both administrative groups have a relatively small place in the continuum of children's services and a negligible proportion of maltreated children are on the register.

More importantly, children in residential placements, in foster homes or supported at home by social services departments or subject to a child abuse investigation are heterogeneous in terms of their age, development, needs and many other characteristics. This means that while it is possible to study their common experience as a service recipient, it is almost impossible to say anything meaningful about other aspects of their lives, since these dimensions generally lack a commonality. Consequently, while there are many children with mental health problems, or with antisocial behaviour, or with disabilities in each of the studies described in this book, any observations on children's development are largely invalidated by the service focus of the research.

The opportunity is to follow the development of all children, or children with particular types of impairment, and then to look at service provision in this context. There are only a handful of studies of this nature in the world, and most of these have occurred as the result of a secondary interest by longitudinal researchers looking at what help children in their cohorts have sought and taken up. This perspective on services would contrast much with that afforded by work over the last 40 years.

Cross-National Research

The sixth message for research from the chapters is the value of a cross-national comparative perspective. This can shed light on what lies behind patterns of need among children and young people and illustrate the efficacy of different service responses to similar difficulties. For example, Berridge shows how this approach helps with interpreting statistical trends: the significant increase in child abuse and neglect referrals in recent years in several western industrial countries is arguably as much a product of policies and the process of social construction in the figures as it is a reflection of higher rates of maltreatment. Working in other contexts with researchers from other cultures also helps to explain childhood problems and their resolution in terms of wider social forces rather than local terms, and provide opportunities for the development of new ideas (Axford and Morpeth).

If this more international approach is to be developed further, however, thought will need to be given to the theoretical frameworks in which subjects are studied. Van der Laan and Smit, for instance, use the welfare, justice and restorative justice models of criminal justice systems to help to make sense of cross-national differences in juvenile justice. The use of such models is common in the analysis of European social policy generally – Esping-Anderson's (1990) threefold typology of welfare states inspired a decade of studies – but has been underused in children's services research, with a few exceptions (e.g. Cooper *et al.* 1995; Weyts 2002).

Changes may also be required to ways of working. In particular, there are many international meetings, but the idea of groups of researchers from around the world collaborating on single longitudinal datasets, which has become the bedrock of advances in medical research and in the field of developmental psychopathology, has not yet occurred in children's services research. Further, the need for a better infrastructure for gathering comparable data from European countries in relation to juvenile delinquency and juvenile justice policy (Van der Laan and Smit) applies equally in other subject areas.

MESSAGES FOR POLICY AND PRACTICE

The preceding chapters demonstrate that the extent to which policy and practice have been shaped by research varies widely. In some areas and on some occasions evidence has had a significant effect on both policy – notably the refocusing of child protection services in the 1990s (Little and Sinclair) – and practice; for example, the adoption of scientific assessment tools in mental health and youth justice (Bailey). The take-up of research varies according to several factors, with persuasive presentation (Sinclair) and an audience genuinely engaged in change (Murch and Hooper) particularly helpful. Factors that also shape policy and practice include: scandal, particularly in the arena of child protection (Berridge); legal requirements, including those from supranational bodies (Van der Laan and Smit); economic imperatives, which have driven recent educational reforms (Anderson); and moral and 'customer' views, for instance in relation to adoption (Thoburn). This section considers six key themes emerging from the preceding chapters concerning the place of evidence in improving children's services.

Service Development

First is the requirement to develop services that are more practical and sophisticated in order to meet children's needs. Bailey notes that for children with complex mental health problems, effective interventions are likely to be multi-modal, intensive, well structured and lengthy. She also argues that tighter, more focused interventions for young people are likely to emerge when service design is informed by the ideas and methods of developmental psychopathology. Requiring a degree of trial and error, these will help to indicate the required timing and order of discrete components – sometimes described as 'algorithms' (Harrington 2002). Little and Sinclair concur, noting the disconnection between the practical, focused and time-limited interventions that service users need and want and the services they often get. They also stress, however, that 'thick' services need to follow highly sensitive and specific risk assessments and become more mainstream.

The aspiration for more sophisticated services applies elsewhere. Sinclair highlights a need for varied models of foster care, with more creative patterns of contact and return. He notes that children favour various adaptations of the standard approach, such as return to the birth family *accompanied by* frequent contact with the foster family. In youth justice, Van der

Laan and Smit note how the application of 'What Works' principles is designed to assist with making services more evidence based; this highlights the value of developing logic models or 'theories of change' setting out how and why a service will break chains of risk in children's lives and so achieve specified desired and realistic outcomes (Little and Sinclair).

The objective of more effective services will be furthered if a more experimental approach is adopted, with greater innovation and creativity in service developments and the rigorous evaluation of pilot projects (prior to their being rolled out), using, where appropriate, randomised controlled trials (Parker). Indeed, government support for more rigorous research is 'necessary not only to achieve optimal outcomes but also to justify ever-increasing expenditure and to counter litigation' (Bullock). Especially where there is no proven 'off the shelf model', a greater willingness among practitioners to test out different options is warranted. In foster care, for example, where some children do better away from home and the children themselves desire various adaptations of the care/home model, different combinations of contact, care and return might be tried (Sinclair). Of course, conducting more robust evaluations is demanding and requires adequate buttressing. Van der Laan and Smit report how the Dutch pilot study of electronically monitored curfews was only implemented in one court district and then terminated prematurely owing to a lack of eligible candidates, highlighting the need for a more structured and supportive system for trialling new interventions.

In due course, attempts to explain the mechanisms whereby genes and experience combine to produce disordered behavioural development (Stevenson 2001) will also have profound effects on the diagnosis, prevention and treatment of children's development problems. While the clinical and social implications of this research are limited at present there is much that can be developed in this arena (Rutter 2002). For example, ensuring that assessments take full account of family history in evaluating risk and considering the interactions between genetic vulnerability and an individual's environment will contribute to a better matching of services to needs.

Responding to Evidence on Need

A second and related set of messages for policy and practice concerns the requirement to develop needs-led and evidence-based services for currently neglected groups – including those children and young people about whom little is known and those who fall into the gaps between administrative divisions. For example, various things can be done to improve the chances of successful return home for children in foster care, such as the provision of extra social work support for families when the child first returns home and therapeutic input – perhaps around positive identity or to address feelings of rejection by birth or foster families (Sinclair). In relation to adoption, Thoburn notes that it is rare for birth parents to find 'counselling to cope with loss' helpful in the early stages; professionals need to recognise that not everyone follows the same pathway over time and avoid the common reaction of regarding parents who refuse such support as 'unco-operative' and restricting their direct contact with their offspring. Recent research into the response of youth justice agencies and social services to under-age offenders demonstrates that such young people stand a real risk of falling between the perceived boundaries of agency responsibility (Giller), suggesting a need for greater collaboration and sharing of information between professionals.

Then there are children who are routinely failed or overlooked by services. For instance, continued efforts are required to improve the safety of young people in secure accommodation (Bailey). High levels of death, self-harm and suicide persist in such institutions, despite research evidence and practice experience being clear about strategies for preventing such tragedies. At a broader level, equity demands some refocusing of services away from expensive provision for a small minority of children in care and towards the much larger number of children in need who live at home (Sinclair). Practical methods for achieving this notoriously complex shift exist; for example, combining the rapid and efficient rehabilitation of looked-after children with investment in family support services (DSRU 2004). Even more generally, better management information about the volume and pattern of needs among the child population is a prerequisite to the efficient and appropriate use of resources (Little and Sinclair).

Connecting Research, Policy and Practice

A third and critical theme concerning provision for children that emanates from the preceding chapters is the value of improving the connections between research on the one hand and policy and practice on the other. This relationship is often haphazard, as indicated above, and not only because researchers tend to struggle to communicate findings beyond the ivory tower. Murch and Hooper trace the changing fortunes of research in the family justice arena, noting the effect of 'moral panics' and the personalities in power on its utilisation, and Parker identifies a trend in recent years of ideologically driven politicians who 'see little need for research to illuminate areas of uncertainty'. He argues that although dissemination is generally far higher up the agenda of most social researchers and funders than ever before, there is still considerable scope for improving the use of evidence by those in power. The question is: How this can be done?

Several avenues are laid out by the contributors. Clough argues that good residential care depends to a large extent on assertive planning using robust data, suggesting that local children's services agencies generally do not know enough about their services, either because they do not have the required data or because they are not exploiting adequately the data they do have. One might note that in the fields covered by this book there are too few clinically qualified researchers, and almost no movement of individuals between policy, research and practice contexts.

Bullock suggests that the traditional and rather dry format of reports often leaves managers and practitioners cold; by contrast, the arts demonstrate the power of stories, all interesting scenery, pithy quips and unexpected twists (see also Nutley 2004). Arguably there is room when communicating research messages for striking images as well as hard-headed arguments derived from rigorous analysis; as Sinclair puts it, 'myths may well be part of an effective process' and certainly the worlds of public relations and religion teach us that imaginative perspectives on topics and evocative phrases are part of the armoury of persuasion.

For Bullock, the dearth of public intellectuals in children's services is also a symptom of the environment that researchers inhabit. The pressure to churn out articles in learned journals, thereby scoring points in formal assessments of research output, absorbs much time and energy and stifles the creativity required to produce popular texts on topics that would normally leave most lay readers cold – recent examples include Lynne Truss's (2003) jaunty *Eats, Shoots and Leaves* on punctuation and Matt Ridley's (2003) elucidation of the science of genetics, *Nature Via Nurture*. Perhaps, as in art, there is some value in patronage – in being free within any bureaucratic post to pursue one's interests (Atkinson 2003). There is probably value, too, in educating the media in order to improve lay people's appreciation of research in children's services. The natural sciences have made good progress on this front, for example by creating posts and institutions – notably the British Association for the Advancement of Science – concerned with improving the public understanding of science, yet the social sciences lag behind.

Training

The fourth message for policy-makers to emerge strongly from the chapters is the need to ensure that the children's services professionals are properly equipped to deliver needs-led, evidence-based services. For example, among the reasons cited by Berridge for why children are disproportionately at risk of maltreatment in group settings are shortcomings in staff recruitment in residential care, inadequate line management, unsatisfactory placement policies and poor training. Fortunately, there are concerted efforts now in the UK to address these issues, notably the workforce reforms, a new and longer social work degree and consolidated post-qualifying training. But care is required to ensure that these advances are not undermined by other developments: one might query, for example, how appropriate it is that most street-level, outreach support workers in new agencies such as Sure Start and Connexions do not have social work training yet are discharging responsibilities held previously by social workers (cf. Jordan 2002).

Of course, part of the problem is the relative lack of reliable evidence on 'what works'. Even so, practical steps are possible. Training programmes should follow careful consideration of, in turn, children's needs, the services required to meet those needs and the kinds of staff who can deliver them. Where children have complex needs, access to multidisciplinary expertise is a prerequisite. Take, for example, work with young offenders who have mental health problems. Here, professional 'knowledge needs' might be met by expanding training in mental health awareness for youth justice workers and by providing youth justice and other professionals with easy access to advice from mental health specialists (Bailey). The interdisciplinary nature of family justice – and other professional areas – also demands more multi-agency training, perhaps with a core curriculum (Murch and Hooper). Of course, in some areas one might question the level of knowledge now expected of professionals. Anderson, for instance, points out that 'as parenting appears to have moved substantially from the home to the school a bewildering array of expertise appears to be required [of teachers]'. Generally, however, a case can be made for strengthening the research elements of training courses as well as the practice experience components (Clough). This should enable students to become more familiar with evidence on the development and tackling of psychosocial difficulties and also to develop 'research-mindedness' – an ability to think in terms of risk and protective mechanisms, to conduct one's own research (e.g. case and group evaluation) and to appraise critically and apply other people's evidence.

Values

A fifth recurring theme in the book that is of relevance to policy and practice concerns the benefits of reflecting on the values that underpin children's services. One aspect of this is the potential contradiction between needs-led and rights-based provision. Murch and Hooper, for example, contrast the preventative approach of family justice in the UK and its perhaps rather intrusive and paternalistic efforts to meet the needs of children whose parents divorce, with the Irish system and its emphasis on children as young citizens with rights to a range of community support services. Critically, it is unclear which is best for children – a conclusion that applies to reforms elsewhere that are driven by political beliefs. In child protection, for instance, services in the UK have increasingly focused on managing risk, been evaluated against performance indicators and reflected free market and 'tough love' principles, yet there is no evidence that such developments have contributed to better therapeutic services for abused children or violent adults or to improved outcomes (Berridge).

Ideological debates are particularly strong in education. Anderson suggests that the purpose of the school has been redefined from one where children were introduced to learning and prepared for life to a 'production line' for suitable outputs of use to work and industry. Connected to this is the perceived 'marketisation' of schools, leading to their being fully accountable and competitive in the same way as businesses. Whether this has been positive is widely debated, with some commentators arguing that treating children as 'products' is unacceptable and that education is about qualitative values that cannot always be measured. This focus on *instrumental* as opposed to *expressive* outcomes has also been apparent in residential care, although there are signs that a greater recognition of the latter is supporting efforts to enrich the quality of life for children in institutions (Clough). Consideration of the merits of various approaches to delivering children's services, independent of their ideological base, is critical to efforts to improve outcomes for children in need. Sinclair makes this point at another level, arguing that entrenched positions need to soften as ideology can be the enemy of good policy and practice; in foster care, for example, some children *do* perform better away from home, a finding that could easily be overlooked by fervent defenders of the sanctity of the family and parental rights.

Control

A sixth challenge for children's services professionals and policy-makers is achieving the right balance between central and local control in the delivery of services. A tension exists, for instance, between the use of inspection, performance indicators and approved systems for identifying vulnerable children on the one hand, and the desire for local flexibility on the other. Giller touches on these issues in relation to the youth justice sphere in the UK. Local managers must evaluate their team's activity against predetermined indicators and are expected to contribute to the national goal of reducing the proportion of children receiving custodial sentences. Yet the nature of programmes varies widely across the country – not necessarily a bad thing – and there is significant inconsistency in court culture regarding the use of custody. If nothing else, changes in the balance between central and local control can be unsettling. In education, for example, it has had major and varied impacts on budgets and curriculum over the years (Anderson). A critical task, then, is marrying the freedom to innovate – thereby encouraging local ownership and the development of new knowledge – with the requirements to heed expertise about 'what works' and to achieve consistency and equity of provision.

It is worth noting, too, that the issue extends beyond national borders. Although limited and ad hoc as yet, there are efforts at a supranational level to foster some convergence between countries in relation to services for children. Besides the UN *Convention on the Rights of the Child* (CRC), a prime example of this is recommendations by the Council of Europe regarding new ways of tackling youth crime (Van der Laan and Smit). These set out principles and guidance rather than mandates per se, and in that respect operate like UN policies (including the CRC): states must pursue the objectives set but they have flexibility over the methods of implementation. Although this approach appears weak, the pressure that it generates in more subtle ways (e.g. Atkinson 2003) means that national legislators need increasingly to take such supranational frameworks into account when planning children's services.

CONCLUSION

The first part of this chapter set out some of the moves apparent within the research community – as identified by authors in this volume – to maximise its contribution to developing improved services for children in need:

(1) exploring timeless questions that contribute to the development of theory and addressing neglected areas and groups of children;
(2) improving the scientific rigour of research, in particular through the use of longitudinal designs, experimental studies and standardised measures;
(3) adapting to the commissioning and funding climate by nurturing new research careers and developing programmes of linked studies;
(4) harnessing the sociological and historical perspectives in order to learn from the past and understand issues in their social, economic and political contexts;
(5) looking at children served by all agencies (not only social services) and at normative populations of children (not only those in contact with agencies);
(6) adopting a cross-national comparative perspective in order to help to explain phenomena in terms of wider political and cultural forces.

The second part of the chapter summarised some of the main challenges facing policy-makers and practitioners as they endeavour to provide effective services for vulnerable children:

(1) developing and testing more practical and sophisticated services that are tailored to children's needs and underpinned by a clear logic model;
(2) implementing needs-led, evidence-based services for groups of children that currently tend to be overlooked;

(3) strengthening the connection between research, policy and practice, including educating the media and public so that they can better interpret findings;
(4) equipping the workforce with the wherewithal to provide evidence-based services, for instance via a core curriculum and greater research-mindedness;
(5) reflecting on the ideology and values that underpin services and weighing the merits of different approaches as regards outcomes for children;
(6) balancing the central control necessary for consistency and equity of provision with the local flexibility conducive to practitioner innovation and ownership.

It is appropriate, however, to end with a few words about Roger Bullock, in whose honour this festschrift has been compiled. It is clear from the contributions in this volume that those who know Roger well, his colleagues, hold him in very high esteem for his work over the past 40 years to improve research, policy and practice in relation to vulnerable children. In particular, some of the perspectives he has brought to bear on various aspects of children's services continue to have their effect today: the broader welfare (or holistic) perspective of children, the concern for ensuring that new initiatives are based on evidence, the notion of a care career and the whole systems approach with its implications for multidisciplinary working and integrated care. Arguably it is because of this ability to think clearly and shed light on complex issues that so much of his work has endured and anticipated accurately future developments.

In other areas, too, Roger has been ahead of the field, most notably his investment in dissemination and communicating to various audiences (not just fellow academics), his efforts to nurture younger researchers and his interest in dissecting 'black-boxes' to uncover the often hidden mechanisms by which interventions effect change in children's lives. A more indirect, but nevertheless important, contribution has been to make Dartington a place for reflection for many children's services researchers and professionals over the years, with the seeds of several important policy initiatives sown there.

Most of the qualities that have enabled Roger to forge an illustrious career in social research remain more vital than ever, although of course some will need to be adapted to the changing context. In addition, researchers will need new sets of skills and experiences if they are to thrive and make a difference in the changing context. Careers in children's services research today are unlikely to resemble Roger's or to achieve so much, but if, collectively, researchers and professionals rise to some of the challenges identified above we should help to improve outcomes for many children in need.

REFERENCES

Amaya-Jackson, L., Socolar, R.S., Hunter, W., Runyan, D. and Colindres, R. (2000) 'Directly questioning children and adolescents about maltreatment: a review of survey measures', *Journal of Interpersonal Violence* 15 (7), 725–759.
Atkinson, A.B. (2003) 'Social Europe and social science', *Social Policy and Society* 2 (4), 261–272.
Bullock, R., Little, M. and Millham, S. (1992) 'The relationship between quantitative and qualitative approaches to social policy research', in Brannen, J. (ed.) *Mixing Methods: qualitative and quantitative research*, Aldershot, Avebury.
Bullock, R., Gooch, D., Little, M. and Mount, K. (1998) *Research in Practice: experiments in development and information design*, Aldershot, Ashgate.

Caspi, A., McClay, J., Moffitt, T.E., Mill, J., Martin, J., Craig, I.W., Taylor, A. and Poulton, R. (2002) 'Role of genotype in the cycle of violence in maltreated children', *Science* 297, 851–854.

Cooper, A., Hetherington, R., Baistow, K., Pitts, J. and Spriggs, A. (1995) *Positive Child Protection: the view from abroad*, Lyme Regis, Russell House.

DoH (Department of Health) (1995) *Child Protection: messages from research*, London, HMSO.

DoH (2001) *The Children Act Now: messages from research*, London, The Stationery Office.

DSRU (Dartington Social Research Unit) (2004) *Refocusing Children's Services Towards Prevention: lessons from the literature*, Research Report 510, Nottingham, DfES Publications.

Esping-Anderson, G. (1990) *The Three Worlds of Welfare Capitalism*, Cambridge, Polity Press.

Farrington, D.P. (2003) 'A short history of randomized experiments in criminology: a meager feast', *Evaluation Review* 27 (3), 218–227.

Haggerty, R. (1994) 'Stress and coping: a unifying theme', in Haggerty, R.J., Sherrod, L.R., Garmezy, N. and Rutter, R. (eds.) *Stress, Risk and Resilience in Children and Adolescents: processes, mechanisms, and intervention*, Cambridge, Cambridge University Press.

Harrington, R. (2002) 'Affective disorders', in Rutter, M. and Taylor, E. (eds.) *Child and Adolescent Psychiatry*, Fourth Edition, Oxford, Blackwell.

Jordan, B. (2002) *Widening Participation: equality, social work and social policy*, Inaugural Lecture, 4 December, Exeter University.

Knott, J. and Wildavsky, A. (1981) 'If dissemination is the solution, what is the problem?', in Rich, R. (ed.) *The Knowledge Cycle*, Beverly Hills, Sage.

Lahey, B.B., Waldman, I.D. and McBurnett, K. (1999) 'Annotation: the development of antisocial behaviour: an integrative causal model', *Journal of Child Psychology and Psychiatry* 40, 669–682.

Macdonald, G. (1996) 'Evaluating the effectiveness of social interventions', in Oakley, A. and Roberts, H. (eds.) *Evaluating Social Interventions*, Ilford, Barnardos.

Middleton, S. and Adelman, L. (2004) 'Social exclusion in childhood: more of the same or something different?', in Klöckner, C. and Paetzel, U. (eds) *Kindheitsforschung und kommunale Praxis: Praxisnahe Erkenntnisse aus der aktuellen Kindheitsforschung*, Wiesbaden, VS-Verlag.

Norman, D.A. (1991) 'Cognitive artefacts', in Carroll, J.M. (ed.) *Designing Interaction: psychology at the human-computer interface*, Cambridge, Cambridge University Press.

Nutley, S. (2004) 'Telling tales', *The Evaluator*, Spring, 8–9.

Qvortrup, J., Bardy, M., Sgritta, G. and Wintersberger, H. (1994) *Childhood Matters: social theory, practice and politics*, Aldershot, Avebury.

Ridley, M. (2003) *Nature Via Nurture: genes, experience and what makes us human*, London, Harper Perennial.

Rutter, M. (2002) 'Nature, nurture, and development: from evangelism through science toward policy and practice', *Child Development* 73, 1–21.

Stevenson, J. (2001) 'The significance of genetic variation for abnormal behavioural development', in Green, J. and Yule, W. (eds.) *Research and Innovation on the Road to Modern Child Psychiatry: Volume 1. Festschrift for Professor Sir Michael Rutter*, London, Gaskell.

Taylor, C. and White, S. (2000) *Practising Reflexivity in Health and Welfare*, Buckingham, Open University Press.

Thomas, N. (2002) *Children, Family and the State: decision-making and child participation*, Bristol, The Policy Press.

Truss, L. (2003) *Eats, Shoots and Leaves: the zero tolerance approach to punctuation*, London, Profile Books.

Tufte, E.R. (1997) *Visual Explanations: images and quantities, evidence and narrative*, Cheshire, CT, Graphics Press.

Weyts, A. (2002) *The Provision of Welfare for Children in Substitute Care: a comparative study of four European countries with special attention to the education of these children*, Unpublished PhD Thesis, University of Exeter.

Appendix A

ROGER BULLOCK – A BRIEF BIOGRAPHY

Roger Bullock studied sociology with Norbert Elias, Ilya Neustadt and Tony Giddens at Leicester (1961–1964) and took an MA at Essex (in pre-student unrest times, becoming the first graduate thereof) under Peter Townsend (1965). When Royston Lambert was asked to help to establish a research centre into boarding education at King's College, Cambridge, Roger became one of the assistants (also 1965), followed later by Spencer Millham. In that role he made contributions to *A Chance of a Lifetime?* and *A Manual to the Sociology of the School*, which became a model for current Dartington work directed towards a Common Language for Children in Need.

When Royston became headmaster of Dartington Hall School in 1968, Roger and Spencer moved with him to establish the Dartington Social Research Unit. Studies of reform schools for young offenders, known as approved schools, next led to *After Grace – Teeth*, which established the hallmarks of Dartington's work – a combination of quantitative and qualitative methods, a rich literary style and a firm connection to government policy-making.

When responsibility for young offenders moved from the Home Office to the newly created Department of Health and Social Security in 1973, Dartington became a designated centre for research. The compass of the studies Roger was involved in included: the training of residential social workers; secure accommodation for difficult and disordered young people; parental contact with children absent in state care; the return of children looked after by the state; specialised provision for the most difficult children in our society; and various aspects of family support and child protection.

In each of these areas, he worked as part of a team that became known for applying research to specific policy questions and for innovative methods of disseminating research and connecting findings to practice. Successive pieces of legislation, for example the *Children Act* 1989; government guidance, like that concerning access between children in care and their relatives; and policy decisions, such as the level of secure accommodation provided by local authorities, all show traces of Roger's research.

Forty Years of Research, Policy and Practice in Children's Services.
Edited by N. Axford, V. Berry, M. Little and L. Morpeth.
© 2005 John Wiley & Sons, Ltd. ISBN 0-470-01219-6.

The move to Dartington started a long association with the University of Bristol and with professors Roy Parker, Phyllida Parsloe and Peter Townsend. Roger was awarded a personal chair in the newly created School for Policy Studies in 1996 and became Professor Emeritus on his retirement. As director of the Research Unit, Roger worked to strengthen the connections between research and practice and was instrumental in helping to set up the dissemination organisation Research in Practice in 1996 and the Policy Research Bureau in 1997. During this period, Dartington also opened offices in Spain and the USA to support growing demand for applied work in those countries.

Roger is now a Fellow of the Centre for Social Policy: Warren House, an organisation for researchers, managers and professionals wishing to maintain their interests and facilitate their work during or immediately before their retirement. There are presently over 50 Centre Fellows who share dedicated office space on the Dartington Hall Estate. He is also Chair of Trustees of the Warren House Group at Dartington, the charity that shelters the five research, development, information design, dissemination and publishing activities that have emerged from the work of the Dartington Social Research Unit.

Roger still commutes between his childhood home in Birmingham and Totnes. He attends most home matches at West Bromwich Albion and is an accomplished pianist and cellist. In Birmingham, he regularly plays the organ in local churches and at weddings. He is an expert on music hall (opportunities to practise as a stand-up comedian have lately declined).

Roger continues to undertake research under the auspices of the Centre for Social Policy and development work for Dartington-i. A study in 2002 with Ruth Sinclair of Serious Case Reviews was widely cited and disseminated as local authorities sought to respond to the findings of the Laming Inquiry into the death of Victoria Climbié, and he has recently led a series of one-day seminars in London aimed at helping managers and professionals to implement the *Children Act* 2004. He serves on the editorial boards of several journals, is editor of *Adoption and Fostering* and is a mentor to PhD students working at Dartington. Roger's publications include some 16 books and numerous articles, book chapters and other contributions.

One of Roger's lesser-known pieces, 'Baggies They're Mine', is to be found in an anthology of essays by football fans published in 1992 by the campaigning charity Child Poverty Action Group. In this he applauds West Bromwich Albion in the choice company of the then Prime Minister John Major (a Chelsea supporter) and an upstart tabloid journalist called Alastair Campbell (subsequently press officer to Tony Blair and a Burnley fanatic). Press notices at the time were generally restrained, as was only to be expected, except in the Arsenal fanzine *The Gooner*, whose reviewer cheerfully described our man on the volley as a 'Stuck-up prick'. Thankfully, the contributors to this volume know him better.

Appendix B

ROGER BULLOCK'S MAIN PUBLICATIONS

BOOKS

Lambert, R., Millham, S., and Bullock, R. *A Manual to the Sociology of the School.* Weidenfeld & Nicolson, 1970.

Lambert, R., Millham, S. and Bullock, R. *The Chance of a Lifetime? A Survey of Boys' and Co-Educational Boarding Schools in England and Wales.* Weidenfeld & Nicolson, 1975.

Millham, S., Bullock, R. and Cherrett, P. *After Grace – Teeth: a comparative study of the residential experience of boys in approved schools.* Human Context Books, Chaucer Publishing Co., 1975.

Millham, S., Bullock, R. and Hosie, K. *Locking Up Children: secure provision within the child care system.* Saxon House, 1978.

Millham, S., Bullock, R. and Hosie, K. *Learning to Care: the training of staff for residential social work with young people.* Gower, 1980.

Millham, S., Bullock, R., Hosie, K. and Haak, M. *Issues of Control in Residential Child Care.* HMSO, 1981.

Millham, S., Bullock, R., Hosie, K. and Haak, M. *Lost in Care: the problems of maintaining links between children in care and their families.* Gower, 1986.

Millham, S., Bullock, R., Hosie, K., and Little, M. *Access Disputes in Child Care.* Gower, 1989.

Bullock, R., Little, M. and Millham, S. *Going Home: the return of children separated from their families.* Dartmouth, 1993.

Bullock, R., Little, M. and Millham, S. *Residential Care for Children: a review of the research.* HMSO, 1993.

Bullock, R., Little, M. and Mount, K. *Child Protection: messages from research.* HMSO, 1995.

Bullock, R., Little, M. and Mount, K. *Matching Needs and Services: the audit and planning of provision for children looked after by local authorities.* HMSO, 1995.

Bullock, R., Little, M. and Millham, S. *Secure Treatment Outcomes: the care careers of very difficult adolescents.* Ashgate, 1998.

Bullock, R., Gooch, D. and Little, M. *Children Going Home: the reunification of families.* Ashgate, 1998.

Brown, E., Bullock, R., Hobson, C. and Little, M. *Making Residential Care Work: structure and culture in children's homes.* Ashgate, 1998.

Bullock, R., Gooch, D., Little, M. and Mount, K. *Research in Practice: experiments in development and information design.* Ashgate, 1998.

Sinclair, R. and Bullock, R. *Learning from Past Experience: a review of serious case reviews.* Department of Health, 2002.

Forty Years of Research, Policy and Practice in Children's Services.
Edited by N. Axford, V. Berry, M. Little and L. Morpeth.
© 2005 John Wiley & Sons, Ltd. ISBN 0-470-01219-6.

Warren House Group Dartington Practice Tools 2001–2003

Paperwork: The clinical assessment of children in need.
Matching Needs and Services.
Aggregated Data: Better management information and planning in children's services.
Prediction: Perspectives on diagnosis, prognosis and interventions for children in need.
Structure, Culture and Outcome: How to improve residential care for children.
Going Home?: Findings and guidance to help professionals make good judgements about the reunification of families.
Threshold: Determining the extent of impairment to children's development.

CONTRIBUTIONS TO EDITED BOOKS

Lambert, R., Millham, S. and Bullock, R. 'The informal social system', in Brown, R.K. (ed.) *Knowledge, Education and Cultural Change: papers in the sociology of education*, pp. 297–316. Tavistock, 1973.

Millham, S., Bullock, R. and Cherrett, P. 'A conceptual scheme for the comparative analysis of residential institutions' and 'Socialisation in residential communities', in Tizard, J., Sinclair, I. and Clarke, R. (eds.) *Varieties of Residential Experience*, pp. 203–248. Routledge & Kegan Paul, 1975.

Millham, S., Bullock, R. and Hosie, K. 'On violence in community schools', in Tutt, N. (ed.) *Violence*, pp. 126–165. HMSO, 1976.

Millham, S., Bullock, R. and Hosie, K. 'Attents, besoins reels et participation des clients', in *Les Professions des Action Socio-Educatives dans les Interventions en Faveur des Enfants et Adolescents Handicapes et Defavorises*, pp. 553–577. UMOSEA, 1977.

Millham, S., Bullock, R. and Hosie, K. 'Another try: a new careers experiment for Borstal boys', in Tutt, N. (ed.) *Alternative Strategies for Coping with Crime*, pp. 137–163. Blackwell, 1978.

Bullock, R. 'Which staff?', in Bye, P. (ed.) *Securicare: a guide for staff working in secure units*, pp. 20–24. Derbyshire Social Services, 1979.

Millham, S. and Bullock, R. 'The strengths and weaknesses of residential institutions for young people', in Adiel, S., Shalom, H. and Arieli, M. (eds) *Fostering Deprived Youth and Residential Education*, pp. 195–209. Youth Aliyah, 1980.

Millham, S., Bullock, R., Hosie, K. and Haak, M. 'The effects of juvenile unemployment', in Moorsom, R.S. (ed.) *The Crisis of Education and Adolescence*, pp. 4–11. Institute of Community Studies, 1982.

Bullock, R., Hosie, K. and Haak, M. 'Secure provision for juveniles: some research findings from England and Wales', in Kerner, H.J. (ed.) *Gefahrlich oder Gefahret*, pp. 194–203. University of Heidelberg Press, 1983.

Bullock, R., Hosie, K., Little, M. and Berridge, D. 'Coming into substitute care', 'Residential styles and approaches', 'Children and group living', 'Boundaries' and 'Case studies', in *Course P653, Caring for Children and Young People*. Open University, 1985.

Millham, S., Bullock, R., Hosie, K. and Haak, M. 'Children lost in care: the family contacts of children in care', in *Social Work Decisions in Child Care: recent research findings and their implications*, pp. 26–27. HMSO, 1985.

Bullock, R. 'Public schools', in Hartnett, A. and Naish, M. (eds) *Education and Society Today*, pp. 77–88. Falmer Press, 1986.

Millham, S. and Bullock, R. 'A holistic approach to the evaluation of residential institutions', in Eiskovits, Z. and Kashti, Y. (eds) *Qualitative Research and Evaluation in Group Care*, pp. 5–18. Haworth Press, 1987.

Bullock, R. 'A research overview of the decision-making process', in McHugh, J. (ed.) *Creative Social Work with Families*, pp. 20–29. British Association of Social Workers, 1987.

Millham, S., Bullock, R. and Little, M. 'Residential education in Britain: continuity and conflict', in Kashti, Y. and Arieli, M. (eds) *Residential Settings and the Community: congruence and conflict*, pp. 190–205. Freund, 1987.

Parker, R., Millham, S., Bullock, R., Hosie, R. and Little, M. 'Residential care for children', in *The Research Reviewed* (The Wagner Report), pp. 57–124. National Institute for Social Work/ HMSO, 1988.

Bullock, R. 'The rehabilitation of children in care', in Holman, R. (ed.) *Planning for Children*, pp. 105–112. Family Rights Group, 1988.

Millham, S., Bullock, R., Hosie, K. and Little, M. Memorandum in House of Commons Social Services Committee, *Children in Care*, pp. 30–32. HMSO, 1988.

Bullock, R. 'Secure provision ten years on', in Stafford, W. and Hardy, C. (eds) *Secure Units, the Way Ahead*, pp. 15–24. Orchard Lodge Regional Resource Centre, 1989.

Bullock, R. 'The provision of secure settings in the United Kingdom', in Roberts, R. (ed.) *Adolescents in Secure Settings*, pp. 9–13. Thistletown Foundation, Ontario, 1989.

Bullock, R. 'Social research', in Kahan, B. (ed.) *Child Care Research, Policy and Practice*, pp. 14–29. Hodder and Stoughton, 1989.

Bullock, R. and Little, M. 'Managing the family contacts of children in care, professional and legislative issues: the experience of England and Wales', in Hudson, J. and Galaway, B. (eds) *International Research Perspectives on Interventions with Young Persons*, pp. 83–92. Kluwer, 1989.

Bullock, R. 'Residential services in their political and social work context', in Clough, R. and Parsloe, P. (eds) *Squaring the Circle: being cared for after Firth, Griffiths and Wagner*, pp. 68–73. Bristol Papers, School of Applied Social Studies, University of Bristol, 1989.

Millham, S., Bullock, R., Hosie, K. and Haak, M. 'Are links important?', in Morgan, S. and Righton, P. (eds) *Child Care: concerns and conflicts*, pp. 112–128. Hodder and Stoughton, 1989.

Bullock, R. 'Specialist family care for very difficult young people', in Galaway, R., Maglajlic, D., Hudson, J., Harman, P. and McLagan, J. (eds) *International Perspectives on Specialist Foster Family Care*, pp. 63–70. Human Service Associates, St Paul, MN 1990.

Milliham, S. and Little, M. 'Specialised residential treatment for difficult adolescents: some recent findings', in Hellinckx, W., Broekaert, E., Vanden Berge, A. and Colton, M. (eds) *Innovations in Residential Care*, pp. 237–246. Acco, 1991.

Bullock, R. 'Residential care for children: issues and developments', in Hellinckx, W., Broekaert, E., Vanden Berge, A. and Colton, M. (eds) *Innovations in Residential Care*, pp. 9–14. Acco, 1991.

Bullock, R., Little, M. and Millham, S. 'Applying restitutive justice to young offenders: observations from the United Kingdom', in Messmer, H. and Otto, H. (eds) *Restorative Justice on Trial*, pp. 367–378. Kluwer, 1992.

Bullock, R., Little, M. and Millham, S. 'The relationship between quantitative and qualitative approaches in social policy research', in Brannen, J. (ed.) *Mixing Methods: qualitative and quantitative research*, pp. 81–100. Avebury, 1992.

Bullock, R. 'Stepfamilies today' and 'Agenda for future action', in De'Ath, E. (ed.) *Stepfamilies: What do we know? What we need to know*, pp. 1–4, 85–88. Significant Publications, 1992.

Bullock, R., Little, M. and Millham, S. 'Establishing a family support group for parents with children in care or accommodation', in Marsh, P. and Triseliotis, J. (eds) *Prevention and Reunification in Child Care*, pp. 106–119. Batsford, 1993.

Bullock, R. 'The United Kingdom', in Colton, M.J. and Hellinckx, W. (eds) *Child Care in the EC: a country-specific guide to foster and residential care*, pp. 212–231. Arena, 1993.

Bullock, R. 'Residential care – what we know and don't know', in Kahan, B. (ed.) *Residential Care for Children*, pp. 5–18. Department of Health/HMSO, 1993.

Bullock, R., Little, M. and Millham, S. 'Going home: The return of children separated from their families', in Ambramczyk, L. (ed.) *International Reunification Seminar*, pp. 46–51. University of South Carolina Press, 1993.

Millham, S., Bullock, R. and Little, M. 'The care careers of extremely difficult and disturbed young people', in Broekaert, E. and Van Hore, G. (eds) *Orthopedagogische Recks Gent*, pp. 61–70. Universiteit Gent, 1993.

Bullock, R. 'What research can and cannot tell us about child care', in Grinde, T. (ed.) *Child Care Perspectives: English and Norwegian Views*, pp. 71–78. Barnevernets Utviklingssenter, 1993.

Bullock, R. 'Royaume Uni', in Corbillon, M., Hellinckx, W. and Colton, M. (eds) *Suppléance familiale en Europe: l'éducation en internat, les familles d'accueil et les alternatives en placement dans les pays de l'Union Européenne*, pp. 213–231. Vigneux: Matrice, 1993.

Bullock, R. 'Reino Unido', in Colton, M. and Hellinckx, W. (eds) *La Attencion a la Infancia en la Unión Europea: guia par praíses sobre acogimiento familiar y attención residecial*, pp. 241–264. Ministro de Asuntos Socales, 1993.

Bullock, R. 'Specijalisticka hraniteljska briga za vrlo teske slucajeve', in Maglajlic, D. and Selak-Zivkovic, A. (eds) *Specjalizirani Smjestajx drugu Obitelj kao Alternativa Insitucionalnom Smjestaju*, pp. 151–157. Socijalina Zastita, 1994.

Little, M. and Bullock, R. 'Research on partnerships', in Jackson, S. and Morris, K. (eds) *Looking at Partnership Teaching in Social Work Qualifying Programmes*, pp. 25–35. CCETSW, 1994.

Bullock, R. 'Return home as experienced by children in state care and their families', in Hudson, J. and Galaway, B. (eds) *Child Welfare in Canada: research and policy implications*, pp. 298–307. Thomson Educational, Toronto, 1995.

Bullock, R. and Little, M. 'Linking research and development: return home as experienced by separated children', in Colton, M., Hellinckx, W., Ghesquière, P. and Williams, M. (eds) *The Art and Science of Child Care*, pp. 19–32. Arena, 1995.

Bullock, R. 'Children's circumstances', in Little, M. (ed.) *A Life without Problems? The Achievements of a Therapeutic Community*, pp. 47–86. Arena, 1995.

Bullock, R., Gooch, D. and Little, M. 'Life after Caldecott', in Little, M. (ed.) *A Life without Problems? The Achievements of a Therapeutic Community*, pp. 151–188. Arena, 1995.

Bullock, R. 'Change in organisations: likely problems in implementing looking after children', in Ward, H. (ed.) *Looking After Children: research into practice*, pp. 91–108. HMSO, 1995.

Bullock, R. 'Dieci stadi di una ricera sull'infanazia a rischio', in Vecchiato, T. (ed.) *La Valutazione dei servizi sociali e sanitari*, pp. 240–244. Fondazione Emanuela Zancan, 1995.

Bullock, R. 'Ten stages in a study of vulnerable children', in Vecchiato, T. (ed.) *The Evaluation of Social and Health Services*, pp. 186–189. Fondazione Emanuela Zancan, 1995.

Bullock, R. 'Difficult adolescents – the experience in England and Wales', in Tisdall, E. (ed.) *Child Welfare: reviewing the framework*, pp. 43–50. HMSO, 1996.

Bullock, R. 'The Children Act 1948: residential care', in Stevenson, O. (ed.) *Child Welfare in the UK: 1948–1998*, pp. 156–174. Blackwell, 1998.

Bullock, R. 'Secure accommodation for adolescents in England and Wales: research messages for policy and practice', in Curran, D. and McCarney, W. (eds) *Psychological Perspectives on Serious Criminal Risk*, pp. 25–41. British Psychological Society, 1999.

Bullock, R. 'The implications of recent child care research findings for foster care', in Hill, M. (ed.) *Signposts in Fostering: policy, practice and research issues*, pp. 353–359. British Agencies for Adoption and Fostering, 1999.

Bullock, R., Cleaver, H., Freeman, P., Haak, M., Hosie, K., Little, M. and Millham, S. Seven chapters in *Handbuch Heimerzichung und Pflegekinderwesen in Europa* [Handbook Residential and Foster Care in Europe]. Kriftel, 1999.

Bullock, R., Little, M. and Millham, S. Children's return from state care to school', in Jackson, S. (ed.) *Nobody Ever Told Us School Mattered: raising the educational attainments of children in care*, pp. 95–110. BAAF, 2000.

Bullock, R. 'Treatment in residential settings', in Hollin, C. (ed.) *Offender Assessment and Treatment*, pp. 537–550. John Wiley & Sons, 2000.

Bullock, R. 'Work with children in residential care', in Hill, M. (ed.) *Effective Ways of Working with Children and Their Families: research highlights no. 35*, pp. 256–269. Jessica Kingsley, 2000.

Bullock, R. and Little, M. 'The contribution of children's services to the protection of children', in Browne, K., Hanks, H., Stratton, P. and Hamilton, C. (eds) *Early Prediction and Prevention of Child Abuse: a handbook*, pp. 267–278. John Wiley & Sons, 2002.

Bullock, R., Axford, N., Little, M. and Morpeth, L. 'Predicting the likelihood of family reunification in the foster care system', in *Diskurs 2/2003 – Riskio-einschatzung: Emprisch-quantitative Verhafen in der Sozialen Arbeit*, pp. 26–33. Deutches Jugend Institut, 2003.

Little, M. and Bullock, R. 'Administrative frameworks and services for very difficult adolescents in England', in Bailey, S. and Dolan, M. (eds) *Forensic Adolescent Psychiatry*, pp. 334–342. Hodder Arnold, 2004.

PUBLISHED RESEARCH MONOGRAPHS

Boarding Schools Association *Different Approaches to Boarding*. Research Centre, King's College, Cambridge, 1966.

Ames, W., Millham, S., Bullock, R. and Cherrett, P. *A Survey of Short-Term Residential Centres and Other Out of School Facilities in the County of Devon*. Devon County Council, 1971.

Millham, S., Bullock, R. and Hosie, K. *'Springboard': a study of CSV's job creation project in Sunderland*. Community Service Volunteers, 1978.

Bullock, R. *Secure Provision for Children*. Justice for Children, 1979.

Millham, S., Bullock, R., Hosie, K., Haak, M. and Mitchell, L. *Give and Take: a study of CSV's project for children in care*. Community Service Volunteers, 1980.

Millham, S., Bullock, R., Hosie, K., Haak, M. and Mitchell, L. *A Comparative Analysis of Volunteers on CSV's Current Child in Care Schemes and the Delinquent Volunteer*. Community Service Volunteers, 1982.

Dartington Social Research Unit *The Dissemination of Research Findings in Social Work*. Dartington Social Research Unit, University of Bristol, 1983.

Millham, S., Bullock, R. and Hosie, K. *Social Services for Adolescents in Croydon*. Barnardo's/Croydon Social Services, 1984.

Millham, S., Berridge, D., Bullock, R., Hosie, K. and Little, M. *Services for the Adolescent Offender in Somerset: the contribution of the CSV/Somerset local partnership scheme*. Community Service Volunteers, 1985.

Millham, S., Bullock, R., Hosie, K. and Little, M. *The Orbit Intermediate Treatment Project: research findings and suggestions for future developments*. National Children's Home, 1986.

Millham, S., Bullock, R., Hosie, K. and Little, M. *Adolescents in Rural Areas: the contribution of KITE and CITW (Cornwall) intermediate treatment projects*. National Children's Home, 1987.

Berridge, D., Bowyer, J., Bullock, R., Cleaver, H., Hosie, K., Little, M. and Millham, S. *Research into Four Barnardo's London Divisional Schools*. Dartington Social Research Unit /National Children's Bureau, 1987.

Bowyer, J., Bullock, R., Hosie, K., Little, M. and Millham, S. *Community Service Volunteers Independent Living Scheme*. Bristol Papers, School of Applied Social Studies, University of Bristol, 1989.

Bullock, R., Hosie, K., Little, M. and Millham, S. *Access to Children in Care: practitioners' views*. Bristol Papers, School of Applied Social Studies, University of Bristol, 1990.

Bullock, R. and Little, M. *Secure Accommodation for Children: Research Highlight No. 103*. National Children's Bureau, 1991.

Bullock, R., Kahan, B. and Little, M. *An Introduction to Social Services for Children and Families*. Open University, 1992.

Bullock, R. *Residential Care for Children: what we know and don't know*. National Children's Home, 1992.

Bullock, R. (ed.) *Problem Adolescents: an international view*. Whiting and Birch, 1992.

Bullock, R. (ed.) *The Effects on Residential Child Care Staff of Investigations of Abuse*. Department of Health, Social Services Inspectorate, 1994.

Little, M., Bullock, R. and Mount, K. *Area Child Protection Committees: a research study*. Mid and South Glamorgan ACPC, 1995.

Bullock, R., Randall, J. and Weyts, A. *The Contribution of Social Workers to Interventions with Children in Need and their Families*. Dartington Social Research Unit 2001.

ARTICLES IN REFEREED JOURNALS

Millham, S., Bullock, R. and Cherrett, P. 'Social control in organisations', *British Journal of Sociology*, 23, 406–421, 1972.

Millham, S., Bullock, R. and Hosie, K. 'Juvenile unemployment: a concept due for re-cycling', *Journal of Adolescence*, 1, 11–24, 1978.

Bullock, R., Hosie, K., Little, M. and Millham, S. 'The problems of managing the family contacts of children in residential care', *British Journal of Social Work* 20, 591–610, 1990.

Bullock, R., Hosie, K., Little, M. and Millham, S. 'Secure accommodation for very difficult adolescents: some recent research findings', *Journal of Adolescence* 13, 205–215, 1990.

Bullock, R., Hosie, K., Little, M. and Millham, S. 'The characteristics of young people in Youth Treatment Centres: a study based on leavers from St. Charles and Glenthorne between 1982 and 1985', *Journal of Forensic Psychiatry* 1, 329–350, 1990.

Bullock, R., Hosie, K., Little, M., Millham, S. 'The research background to the law on parental access to children in care', *Journal of Social Welfare and Family Law* 2, 85–93, 1991.

Colton, M., Hellinckx, W., Bullock, R. and Van Den Bruel, B. 'Caring for troubled children in Flanders, The Netherlands, and the United Kingdom', *British Journal of Social Work* 21, 381–392, 1991.

Little, M. and Bullock, R. 'Legislating for parental access to children in care', *Family and Conciliation Courts Review* 29 (4), 375–384, 1991.

Bullock, R., Little, M. and Millham, S. 'Children's return from state care to school', *Oxford Review of Education* 20, 307–316, 1994.

Bullock, R., Little, M. and Millham, S. 'Assessing the quality of life for children in local authority care or accommodation', *Journal of Adolescence* 17, 29–40, 1994.

Bullock, R., Little, M. and Millham, S. 'Il ritorno a casa', *Il Bambino in Compiuto* (Rome), 3, 83–92, 1994.

Bullock, R., Leitch, H. and Little, M. 'The care careers of long-stay children: the contribution of new theoretical approaches', *Child and Youth Services Review* 17, 661–675, 1995.

Little, M. and Bullock, R. 'Il processo di reunificazione familiare nell'esperienza della Dartington Social Research Unit', *Politiche Sociali* 4, 80–94, 1998.

Bullock, R. and Little, M. 'The interface between social and health services for children and adolescent persons', *Current Opinion in Psychiatry* 12, 421–4, 1999.

Weyts, A., Morpeth, L. and Bullock, R. 'Department of Health research overviews – past, present and future: the dissemination of the Blue Book, "Child Protection: messages from research"', *Child and Family Social Work* 5, 215–23, 2000.

Chipenda-Dansokho, S. and the Centre for Social Policy 'The determinants and influence of size on residential settings for children', *International Journal of Child and Family Welfare* 6, 66–76, 2003.

Little, M., Kogan, J., Bullock, R. and van der Laan, P. 'ISSP: an experiment in multi-systems responses to persistent young offenders known to social services', *British Journal of Criminology* 44, 225–240, 2004.

ARTICLES IN PROFESSIONAL JOURNALS

Bullock, R. 'The co-educational boarding schools', *Where?* No. 33, 1967.

Millham, S. and Bullock, R. 'When a child goes to school', *Where?* (January), 1969.

Millham, S. and Bullock, R. 'Research in approved schools', *Approved Schools Gazette* (June), 123–127, 1969.

Millham, S. and Bullock, R. 'Styles of co-educational boarding' and 'Co-education in approved schools', *Child in Care* 2, 18–28, 20–32, 1971.

Millham, S., Bullock, R. and Cherrett, P. 'Some findings of the first stage of research into approved schools', *Community Schools Gazette* (December), 502–517, 1971.

Bullock, R. 'Some effects of boarding education', *Proceedings of the Annual Conference*, Boarding Schools Association, 1974.

Bullock, R. 'After Grace – Teeth', *Proceedings of National Conference*, List D Schools, 1975.

Millham, S. and Bullock, R. 'New residential approaches', *Proceedings of 1976 Conference*, Association for the Psychiatric Study of Adolescents, 1976.

Millham, S., Bullock, R., Hosie, K. and Frankenberg, R. 'Absconding', *Community Home Schools Gazette* 71, 280–291, 325–337, 1977.

Bullock, R. 'Planning and management of secure units', *Community Home Schools Gazette* 73, 112–116, 1979.

Bullock, R. 'The magistrates and juvenile justice', *Christian Action* (Winter), 4–6, 1980.

Millham, S., Bullock, R., Hosie, K. and Little, M. 'Children in care: the problems of maintaining family links', *Adoption and Fostering* 9, 12–16, 1985.

Millham, S., Bullock, R., Hosie, K. and Little, M. 'Absent but not forgotten', *Community Care* 608 (April), 14–15, 1986.

Millham, S. and Bullock, R. 'A holistic approach to the evaluation of residential institutions', *Child and Youth Services* 8, 5–18, 1987.

Millham, S., Bullock. R, Hosie, K. and Little, M. 'Strategies emerge and policies drift: the evaluation of outcomes in social work', *Insight* 2 (15), 19–21, 1987.

Bullock, R. 'Children's homes: some recent research findings', *Maladjustment and Therapeutic Education* 5, 12–17, 1987.

Millham, S., Bullock, R., Hosie, K. and Little, M. 'Coming to terms with failure', *Insight* 4 (33), 26–28, 1989.

Bullock, R. 'The implications of recent child-care research findings for foster care', *Adoption and Fostering* 14 (3), 43–45, 1990.

Bullock, R. 'Doing justice to the system', *Community Care* 865 (May), 1991.

Bullock, R., Little, M. and Millham, S. 'Young offenders, grave crimes, and Section 53', *The Magistrate* 47 (7), 143–150, 1991.

Bullock, R. 'Research review: residential care', *Children and Society* 6, 382–384, 1993.

Bullock, R., Little, M. and Millham, S. 'The care careers of young people in Youth Treatment Centres', *Social Services Research*, 2, 28–33, 1994.

Bullock, R., Little, M. and Taylor, K. 'The balance of power: working for protection with children and families', *Community Care* 27 (July), 1995.

Bullock, R. and Little, M. 'Rights and needs in child protection', *Childright* (Autumn) 1995.

Bullock, R. and Little, M. 'Child protection', *Young Minds* (24 January), 17–19, 1996.

Little, M., Bullock, R., Madge, J. and Arruabarrena, I. 'How to develop needs-led, evidence-based services', *MCC – Building Knowledge for Integrated Care* 10, 28–32, 2002.

Sinclair, R. and Bullock, R. 'Serious case reviews', *Community Care* (July), 2002.

Bullock, R. 'Residential child care', *Research Matters: a digest of research in the social services, community care, bi-annually from April, 1996 to present time.*

Bullock, R. 'Child protection post-Laming: the wider agenda', *Journal of Integrated Care* 11, 13–17, 2003.

CONTRIBUTIONS TO DEPARTMENT OF HEALTH PUBLICATIONS

Millham, S. and Bullock, R. 'The boys at Risley Hall,' *Approved School to Community Home*, Report of a seminar at Risley Hall Community Home, DHSS and Nottinghamshire Social Services Department, 1974.

Bullock, R. 'A research overview on the decision-making process', *Social Work Decisions in Child Care*, SSI, East Midlands, North West/South-West/Welsh Office/London Region/ NCVCCO.

Millham, S., Bullock, R., Hosie, K. and Little, M. 'The care careers of young people in Youth Treatment Centres', in *Department of Health Yearbook of Research and Development, 1989*, pp. 44–45. HMSO, 1989.

Millham, S., Bullock, R., Hosie, K. and Little, M. 'The dissemination of research findings in social work', in *Department of Health Yearbook of Research and Development, 1990*, pp. 61–63. HMSO, 1990.

See also contributions and material presented in:

DHSS and Kent C.C. 'Residential child-care policy in Kent with particular reference to the community home, North Downs'. 1975.

DHSS and Isle of Wight C.C. *Decisions and Resources*. HMSO, 1976.

UNPUBLISHED RESEARCH REPORTS

Millham, S., Bullock, R. and Cherrett, P. *The effects of approved school training.* 1974.

Millham, S. and Bullock, R. *Towards community homes; a study of Risley Hall School.* 1974.

Millham, S., Bullock, R. and Hosie, K. *Turner's Court: boys' perspectives on their residential experience.* 1974.

Millham, S., Bullock, R. and Hosie, K. *The future of Reedham's School.* 1975.

Millham, S., Bullock, R. and Hosie, K. *Research at North Downs: some findings to inform discussion.* 1975.

Millham, S., Bullock, R., Hosie, K. and Tutt, N. *Legislation and institutions for juvenile delinquents in England and Wales and a review of research into residential institutions for juvenile delinquents in England and Wales*. 1978.

Millham, S., Bullock, R., Hosie, K. and Haak, M. *A study of children in care with particular reference to their family characteristics*. 1979.

Millham, S., Bullock, R., Hosie, K., Mitchell, L. and Haak, M. *Children remanded to care*. 1983.

Millham, S., Bullock, R. and Hosie, K. *Predicting children's length of stay in care and the relevance of family links*. 1983.

Millham, S., Bullock, R., Hosie, K. and Berridge, D. *Evidence to the House of Commons Social Services Committee*. 1983.

Millham, S., Bullock, R. and Hosie, K. *New residential projects: some issues for consideration*. 1984.

Millham, S., Bullock, R., Hosie, K. and Little, M. *Delinquents in care*. 1985.

Millham, S., Bullock, R., Hosie, K., Little, M. and Berridge, D. *The education of children in care*. 1985.

Millham, S., Bullock, R., Hosie, K. and Little, M. *The characteristics of young people in Youth Treatment Centres*. 1988.

Millham, S., Bullock, R., Hosie, K. and Little, M. *The problems of maintaining links between children in care and their families – Developmental phase*. 1988.

Millham, S., Bullock, R., Hosie, K. and Little, M. *Personal social services for adolescents in Wirral*. 1988.

Millham, S., Bullock, R., Hosie, K. and Little, M. *Alternative care careers: the experience of very difficult adolescents outside Youth Treatment Centre provision*. 1989.

Millham, S., Bullock, R., Hosie, K. and Little, M. *The experiences and careers of young people leaving the Youth Treatment Centres*. 1989.

Millham, S., Bullock, R. and Little, M. *The experience of YTC look-alikes sheltered in other secure settings*. 1991.

Bullock, R., Little, M. and Millham, S. *The part played by career, individual circumstance and treatment interventions for leavers from the Youth Treatment Centres*. 1994.

INDEX

abuse
  future research 113–14
  going home from foster care 100–1
  protection from 9, 83, 107–17
    family support 120, 121, 122–3, 129–30
  in residential care 49, 112–13
academic journals 17, 175, 176, 198, 204
Acts of Parliament *see* legislation
Adoption and Children Act (2002) 90–1, 140
adoption for children in care 8, 81–91
  birth family contact 81, 82, 86, 87–8, 89, 90
  children's characteristics 82–4, 86
  children's wishes 86, 87, 88–9, 90–1, 98
  legislation 82, 90–1
  numbers placed for 48
  outcome research 82–3, 85–90
    adoptive family variables 86
    birth family contact 86, 87–8, 89
    birth family variables 86
    child variables 86
    long-term fostering 88–9
    matching decisions 87
    measures of 'success' 85–6
    social worker's role 87, 89–90
    work with birth parents 89–90
  placement processes 84–5, 87
  sibling groups 84, 87, 89, 90
After Grace – Teeth 40–1, 43–4
antisocial behaviour
  routes to 124
  youth justice 159, 162
approved schools 40
  Dartington research 40, 43–4, 71–2
  history of 70
architecture 169, 170, 178
artistic creativity *see* creative arts

behavioural genetics 194–5, 202
Blue Book 9, 110–12
boarding school research 38–41, 43–4
  see also residential care
boot camp style programmes 161–2
Bullock, Roger, biography 209–10
bullying 113

CAFCASS 140, 142
campaigning groups 17–18
care proceedings, children's voice 139–40
central government
  child protection 109, 110, 114–15
  Dartington research and 186
  education 31–2, 34–6
    research changes and 16, 19, 20, 25, 145
  family justice system 136–7, 144–5
  family support 120–1, 125
  social research changes 15–16, 19, 20–3, 25–6, 145, 186
  youth justice 58–9
  see also policy implications of research
The Chance of a Lifetime? 39–41
child abuse *see* abuse
child and adolescent mental health services (CAMHS) 67–9, 72, 75–8
child protection 9, 107–17
  adoption for children in care 83
  assessment of developments 110–12
  Dartington research 110, 115–16
  family support 120, 121, 122–3, 129
  future research 113–14
  history of 108–9
  institutional abuse 112–13
  policy–research relation 114–15, 129–30
  system dynamics 122–3
Children Act (1948) 70
Children Act (1975) 82, 139
Children Act (1989)
  adoption 90
  family justice system 136, 138, 139, 142
  family support 120
Children Act (2004) 62, 121
Children and Family Court Advisory and Support Service (CAFCASS) 140, 142
children in need
  family support 120, 121, 122–3, 129
  identifying 182, 199–200
  responding to evidence on 202–3
  values underpinning services for 205
Children and Young Persons Act (1963) 3, 70
Children and Young Persons Act (1969) 57, 70